It's another quality book from CGP...

Grade 9-1 GCSE Religious Studies is no picnic, but help is at hand —
this fantastic CGP book has everything you need for the Edexcel B course!

It's packed with crystal-clear study notes covering Christianity, Catholic Christianity, Islam
and Judaism, plus plenty of exam-style questions to make sure you're ready for the real thing.

How to access your free Online Edition

This book includes a free Online Edition to read on your PC, Mac or tablet.
To access it, just go to **cgpbooks.co.uk/extras** and enter this code...

4449 3995 7164 6346

By the way, this code only works for one person. If somebody else has used
this book before you, they might have already claimed the Online Edition.

CGP — still the best! ☺

Our sole aim here at CGP is to produce the highest quality books —
carefully written, immaculately presented and dangerously close to being funny.

Then we work our socks off to get them out to you
— at the cheapest possible prices.

Contents

These sections are for Areas of Study 1, 2 and 3:

Christian Beliefs and Living the Christian Life — This section also covers Catholic Christianity.

Introduction to Christianity 1
The Trinity 2
Creation 3
Jesus Christ and Salvation 4
The Afterlife 6
Evil and Suffering 7
Different Forms of Worship 8
The Sacraments 9
Prayer and Pilgrimage 11
Christmas and Easter 12
The Work of the Church 13
Revision Summary 15

Muslim Beliefs and Living the Muslim Life

Introduction to Islam 16
Key Beliefs in Islam 17
Life after Death 20
Worship and Duties 21
Festivals 24
Revision Summary 25

Jewish Beliefs and Living the Jewish Life

Introduction to Judaism 26
Key Beliefs in Judaism 27
Worship 30
Family Life 32
Festivals 34
Revision Summary 36

These sections are for Area of Study 1:

Marriage and the Family

Sexuality and Sexual Relationships 37
Contraception 38
Marriage and Divorce 39
Families 42
Families & Gender Equality 44
Gender Equality 45
Revision Summary 46

Matters of Life and Death

The Origins of the Universe 47
The Environment and Stewardship 48
Animal Rights 50
Abortion and Euthanasia 51
The Afterlife 54
Revision Summary 55

These sections are for Area of Study 2:

Crime and Punishment

Justice, Good and Evil 56

Crime 57

Forgiveness 59

Punishment & Treatment of Criminals 60

The Death Penalty 62

Revision Summary 63

Peace and Conflict

Peace and Conflict 64

Weapons of Mass Destruction 69

Peacemaking 70

Revision Summary 72

These sections are for Area of Study 3:

Philosophy of Religion

Design and Causation 73

Miracles 75

Revelation 76

Arguments Against the Existence of God 79

Revision Summary 80

Equality

Attitudes to Equality 81

Human Rights 84

Freedom of Belief 85

Social Justice 86

Wealth and Poverty 87

Revision Summary 90

Do Well in Your Exam and SPaG 91

Glossary 96

Index 99

You have to cover <u>two Areas of Study</u> for the Edexcel B course. For each Area of Study, you'll need to learn about the topics in the context of <u>one religion</u>. It has to be a <u>different religion</u> for each Area of Study.

The green religion tags on the pages of each section tell you whether the page covers:

| **Christianity** | ...information about a specific religion... | **All religions** | ...information about all religions... | **General** | ...or general information. |

These tags will tell you which pages you need to read for the religion you're studying. Sometimes more than one religion is covered on a page — if so, the section headings will tell you which bits of the page are relevant to each religion. If a heading doesn't mention a religion, you should read it whichever religion you're studying.

Published by CGP

Editors: Chloe Anderson, Cathy Lear, Ruth Wilbourne

Contributors: Jill Hudson, Duncan Raynor, Paul Smith, Philip West

Proofreading: Stephen Darlington, Karen Wells

ISBN: 978 1 78294 6 427

With thanks to Ana Pungartnik for the copyright research.

Sacred Text References

References from the Bible always go in the order: Book Chapter:Verse(s). So whenever you see something like: Genesis 1:14, it means it's from the book of Genesis, Chapter 1, verse 14.

Similarly, references from the Qur'an are shown with the Surah (Chapter) followed by the Ayah (Verse).

For all collections of hadith, we've used the English referencing system.
This gives the book number followed by the hadith number, e.g. Sahih al-Bukhari 1:3.

Exam-style questions are based on the style of Edexcel.

Scripture quotations [marked NIV] taken from the Holy Bible,
New International Version Anglicised
Copyright © 1979, 1984, 2011 Biblica, Used by permission of Hodder & Stoughton Ltd, an Hachette UK company
All rights reserved
'NIV' is a registered trademark of Biblica
UK trademark number 1448790.

Holy Qur'an quotations taken from the Holy Qur'an, Sahih International Version. https://quran.com/

Quotations from the Catechism of the Catholic Church © Libreria Editrice Vaticana
Quotations from Lumen gentium on page 10, Gaudium et spes on page 13, Evangelii Gaudium on pages 13 and 14,
Humanae Vitae on pages 38 and 51, Familiaris Consortio on pages 42, 43 and 45, and a speech by Pope Francis on page 47
© Libreria Editrice Vaticana

Quotes on pages 2, 4, 6, 9, 39, 47 and 81 from The Church of England, https://www.churchofengland.org.
© The Archbishops' Council.

Image on page 24 © REUTERS / Alamy Stock Photo

Quotes on pages 26 and 70 from Chabad.org

Image on page 51 © Isabelle Plasschaert / Alamy Stock Photo

Sahih Muslim 16:4152 quote on page 62 from https://muflihun.com

Image on page 71 © iStock.com / sadikgulec

Source of statistic on belief in evolution on page 73: Theos

Quote on page 74 from The Guide of the Perplexed, Volume 1 by Moses Maimonides, translated by Shlomo Pines.
Published by The University of Chicago Press, 1963.

Quote on page 83 from Islam and the West: A Rational Perspective by Mohammed Jabar,
published by Mereo Books, an imprint of Memoirs Publishing, 2014.

Quotation on page 84 © www.cbcew.org.uk

Data about wealth inequality on page 87 contains public sector information licensed under the Open Government Licence v3.0.
http://www.nationalarchives.gov.uk/doc/open-government-licence/version/3/

Every effort has been made to locate copyright holders and obtain permission to reproduce sources. For those sources where it has been difficult to trace the originator of the work, we would be grateful for information. If any copyright holder would like us to make an amendment to the acknowledgements, please notify us and we will gladly update the book at the next reprint. Thank you.

Printed by Elanders Ltd, Newcastle upon Tyne
Clipart from Corel®

Based on the classic CGP style created by Richard Parsons.

Introduction to Christianity

Christianity is based on the belief in <u>Jesus Christ</u> being the <u>Son of God</u>. It is the <u>main</u> religion in Britain.

The Bible is the Christian Sacred Text

The Bible is divided into two main parts — the <u>Old</u> and <u>New Testaments</u>:

1) Depending on the version, the <u>Old Testament</u> has at least 39 books, which include the <u>Creation</u> story (see p.3) and the <u>Ten Commandments</u>. These 39 books are the <u>Jewish scriptures</u> — they are also considered <u>sacred</u> by Jews.

2) The <u>New Testament</u> is the <u>specifically Christian</u> part of the Bible. Its 27 books include the <u>4 Gospels</u> (Matthew, Mark, Luke and John), which are accounts of <u>Jesus's life</u>. The <u>Acts of the Apostles</u> and the <u>letters of St Paul</u> describe the <u>early years</u> of Christianity.

Christianity is Divided into Different Traditions

The different branches of Christianity are called <u>denominations</u>. They share key beliefs, but interpret some points of the faith differently and worship in different ways (see p.8).

1) <u>Roman Catholics</u> respect the authority of the <u>Bible</u> and <u>Church tradition</u>, plus the authority of the <u>Pope</u> and his teachings. The <u>seven sacraments</u> (which include the Eucharist — see p.10) are an important part of their faith.

> The <u>Church of England</u> has both Roman Catholic and Protestant features. Its beliefs are set out in the <u>39 Articles</u>. <u>Anglicanism</u> is the worldwide 'communion' of Churches in fellowship with the parent Church of England.

2) <u>Protestants</u> base their beliefs and practices on the <u>Bible</u>, rather than Church tradition or the teachings of the Pope. In England and Wales, Protestant denominations that are not part of the 'Anglican Communion' are often called '<u>Nonconformists</u>'. These include Methodists, Baptists, Pentecostals, The Society of Friends (Quakers) and the Salvation Army.

3) <u>Orthodox Christians</u> are found mainly in Eastern Europe, Russia and Greece. They also have <u>7 sacraments</u>, and honour (but don't worship) <u>icons</u> — pictures of Saints.

There are Many Beliefs About the Nature of God

Christianity is a <u>monotheistic</u> (one god) religion. The Ten Commandments say "you shall have no other gods" (Exodus 20:3 NIV). Christians believe God has the following <u>characteristics</u>, though they <u>differ</u> in the <u>emphasis</u> placed on each, e.g. some focus more on God's loving nature than his role as judge.

1) **OMNIPOTENT** — God is <u>all-powerful</u>, although he still allows each person <u>free will</u>.

2) **BENEVOLENT** — God is <u>loving</u> and <u>caring</u>: "For God so loved the world that he gave his one and only Son" (John 3:16 NIV). Christians try to <u>follow</u> his example in their actions.

3) **JUST JUDGE** — God <u>judges</u> people's actions fairly. Those who reject him and live sinful lives will be <u>punished</u>, as shown in the story of the sheep and goats in Matthew 25:31-46 (see p.14). But God <u>forgives</u> people who are sorry for what they've done and become faithful to him — the story of the <u>prodigal son</u> (Luke 15:11-32) shows God will forgive anyone who returns to his ways.

4) **OMNISCIENT** — God <u>knows</u> everything — in the past, present and future.

5) **ETERNAL** — God has always existed, and he will continue to exist forever.

6) **TRANSCENDENT** — God is <u>beyond</u> this world — he doesn't depend on it to exist.

7) **IMMANENT** — But God is <u>present</u> in the human world, and takes an <u>active role</u> in humanity.

8) **PERSONAL** — God is a '<u>person</u>', albeit an almighty and <u>divine person</u>. If God is personal, then a relationship is possible through <u>prayer</u> — which can be a '<u>conversation</u>' with God.

Omnipotent or omniscient? Get them the right way round...

Cover this page and see how many characteristics of God you can write down. No peeking now...

REVISION TASK

The Trinity

Although Christians believe in <u>one God</u>, they also believe that God has <u>three parts</u>.

Christians Believe in God as the Trinity

The <u>Trinity</u> is the idea that God exists in three '<u>persons</u>' — the Father, the Son (Jesus) and the Holy Spirit.
The <u>importance</u> of all three is shown in the Bible:

Matthew 3:16-17 describes how at Jesus's baptism, Jesus "...saw the Spirit of God descending like a dove and alighting on him. And a voice from heaven said, 'This is my Son, whom I love; with him I am well pleased.' " (NIV)

In Philippians 2:6, St Paul described Jesus as having "equality with God" (NIV).

The Trinity is Explained in the Nicene Creed

1) In 325 AD, Church leaders from around the world gathered at the <u>Council of Nicaea</u>.
They produced a <u>creed</u> — a statement of beliefs. This was further developed at the <u>Council of Constantinople</u> in 381 AD, and is known as the <u>Nicene Creed</u>. It describes how Christians see God:

"We believe in one God, the Father, the Almighty, maker of heaven and earth... We believe in one Lord, Jesus Christ, the only Son of God... of one Being with the Father... was made man... he suffered death and... he rose again... We believe in the Holy Spirit... the giver of life, who proceeds from the Father and the Son... who has spoken through the prophets."

2) Before this, not everyone had <u>agreed</u> that the Son of God (Jesus) was <u>one with God</u>, rather than having been <u>made by God</u>. Now they agreed that he was <u>equally</u> important.

3) The <u>importance</u> the <u>early Church</u> placed on the <u>Trinity</u> in the Nicene Creed means it is a <u>key belief</u> for most Christians — it is usually recited during the <u>Eucharist</u> service (see p.8). But some groups, such as <u>Christadelphians</u>, don't believe in the Trinity.

4) Christians see the three parts of the Trinity as having <u>different characteristics</u> and <u>roles</u>:

The Father

- For many Christians, <u>God the Father</u> is the God of the <u>Old Testament</u>. He <u>created</u> Heaven and Earth and <u>sustains</u> them. <u>God the Father</u> might be described as the <u>transcendent part</u> of God.
- The title 'Father' is a mark of <u>respect</u> for God, e.g. the <u>Lord's Prayer</u> starts with 'Our Father' (see p.11).

The Son

- Christians believe <u>Jesus</u> (see p.4-5) is the <u>incarnation</u> of God in human form. He is seen as both divine and human — the <u>immanent</u> and <u>personal</u> part of God, who understands human suffering.
- Christians believe that Jesus provides a <u>model</u> for Christian behaviour in <u>obedience</u> to God the Father. The <u>Gospels</u> contain a record of his life and teachings, and are an important source of <u>guidance</u> for Christians on how they should live their lives.

The Holy Spirit

- Christians believe that the <u>Holy Spirit</u> is the <u>presence</u> of God in the world. Before his death, Jesus promised his disciples: "I will ask the Father, and he will give you another advocate to help you and be with you for ever — the Spirit of truth" (John 14:16-17 NIV).
- The Holy Spirit is seen as the <u>immanent yet impersonal</u> part of God — it continues to <u>guide</u> the <u>Church</u>.
- Some Christians feel that the Holy Spirit also guides them <u>personally</u> in being good Christians. The Catechism of the Catholic Church 736 says "By this power of the Spirit, God's children can bear much fruit."

Three into one doesn't go in maths — but this is RS...

For the 5 mark exam questions, you have to refer to sacred texts or religious teachings to get full marks.
You can write quotes or describe what is said — you'll need to say where the information comes from.

Creation

The story of creation can be understood in different ways. Some take it <u>literally</u>, for others it's a <u>metaphor</u>.

The Bible Describes how God Created the Universe

1) <u>Genesis</u> chapter 1 says that <u>God</u> created everything.
The process took <u>six days</u>, and on the seventh day God <u>rested</u>.

2) On day one, <u>light</u> and <u>darkness</u> were made, and on day two the <u>sky</u>. On the third day <u>oceans</u>, <u>land</u> and <u>plants</u> on the land were created, and on the fourth day the <u>sun</u>, <u>moon</u> and <u>stars</u>. On the fifth day it was the creatures of the water and sky (e.g. <u>fish</u> and <u>birds</u>) and on the sixth day, <u>land animals</u> and <u>people</u>.

3) Christians see God the Father as the <u>creator</u>, but the Bible also describes how the other <u>beings</u> of the Trinity were involved. God created the world by acting <u>through</u> the Holy Spirit.

> "...the Spirit of God was hovering over the waters. And God said, 'Let there be light,' and there was light." Genesis 1:2-3 NIV

4) The role of the <u>Son of God</u> is described in the Gospel of John. He uses the phrase '<u>the Word</u>', but it is clear he is referring to <u>Jesus</u> as he later says "The Word became flesh and made his dwelling among us" (John 1:14 NIV). John makes it clear that Jesus was <u>vital for creation</u>.

> "In the beginning was the Word, and the Word was with God, and the Word was God. He was with God in the beginning. Through him all things were made; without him nothing was made that has been made." John 1:1-3 NIV

It Explains how Human Beings were Created

1) The creation of human beings is described in <u>Genesis</u> chapters <u>1</u> and <u>2</u>.
The first two humans were <u>Adam and Eve</u>, and they lived in the <u>Garden of Eden</u>.

2) <u>Genesis</u> chapter 1 says "So God created mankind in his own image, in the image of God he created them; male and female he created them" (Genesis 1:27 NIV).

3) Genesis chapter 2 says "the Lord God formed a man from the dust of the ground" (Genesis 2:7 NIV) and "made a woman from the rib he had taken out of the man" (Genesis 2:22 NIV).

4) The fact that God created humans in <u>his image</u> is important. Because of this, Christians believe that humans are <u>special</u>. They think humans should <u>behave</u> like God by being <u>loving</u> and <u>fair</u> (see p.1). It also shows that humans are <u>important to God</u>, and so <u>everyone</u> should be treated with <u>respect</u>.

5) In Genesis 1:28, God told Adam and Eve to "Rule over the fish in the sea and the birds in the sky and over every living creature that moves on the ground" (NIV). Some Christians believe God gave humans '<u>dominion</u>' (power) over his creation and they can <u>use</u> it as they like. However, Genesis 2:15 says "The Lord God took the man and put him in the Garden of Eden to work it and take care of it" (NIV). Many Christians interpret this as humans having '<u>stewardship</u>' of the Earth — God expects them to <u>care</u> for it.

There are Different Ways to Interpret the Creation Story

1) Some Christians take the creation story <u>literally</u> — they are known as <u>creationists</u>. They believe that the process took six days, and humans are descended from Adam and Eve.

2) Other Christians are more <u>liberal</u> in their understanding of the Bible's events. They view Genesis as more of a <u>parable</u>, or a <u>symbolic</u> description — they acknowledge God as the creator, but are open to <u>other theories</u>, such as the <u>Big Bang theory</u> and <u>evolution</u>. These theories can offer more <u>information</u> to Christians about how <u>God</u> made the universe. The Roman Catholic Church has <u>accepted</u> both theories.

3) The creation story can help Christians further understand <u>God's nature</u>. God is <u>eternal</u> as he made time, and was present 'prior' to it. He is <u>omnipotent</u> as he created the universe through words. God's <u>benevolence</u> can be seen through creation too as he brought humankind to life and gave them the world.

And you thought revision was tiring...

Grab a pen and paper and see if you can quickly summarise what Genesis chapters 1 and 2 say about the story of creation. Once you've done that, try jotting down some different interpretations of creation.

Jesus Christ and Salvation

Christians believe that Jesus Christ, the second Person of the Trinity, is the <u>Son of God</u>.

God Became Human at the Incarnation

1) The <u>incarnation</u> was the act by which <u>God</u> became a <u>human being</u> as Jesus Christ. John's Gospel describes Jesus as the <u>Word of God</u>, made human.

> "The Word became flesh and made his dwelling among us. We have seen his glory, the glory of the one and only Son, who came from the Father, full of grace and truth." John 1:14 NIV

2) An <u>angel</u> told a woman called <u>Mary</u> in Nazareth that she would have a <u>son</u> — and that "the holy one to be born will be called the Son of God" (Luke 1:35 NIV).

3) This belief is stated in the <u>Nicene Creed</u>: "he... was incarnate from the Holy Spirit and the Virgin Mary and was made man".

4) Christians don't believe that Jesus was 'half God and half man' — he was <u>fully both</u>. The Bible describes how God "appeared in the flesh" (1 Timothy 3:16 NIV).

5) Jesus is referred to as '<u>Christ</u>' or '<u>Messiah</u>' — the '<u>Anointed One of God</u>'.

6) Christians see Jesus's time on Earth as God's way of showing how much he <u>loves</u> the world. They study the <u>Gospels</u> to find out about <u>Jesus's life</u>, and to see how they should live their own.

> After being baptised by John the Baptist, Jesus began <u>teaching</u>. He had many followers, including <u>12 chosen disciples</u>. Some of his key teachings are in the <u>Sermon on the Mount</u> (Matthew 5-7) — he taught how the poor and meek are <u>highly valued</u> by God, and how <u>peacemakers</u> are blessed. He also taught the importance of <u>kindness</u>, such as in the story of the <u>Good Samaritan</u> (Luke 10:30-37). He performed miracles such as <u>healing</u> the sick, showing that he was the <u>Son of God</u> and demonstrating God's <u>love</u>.

Jesus was Crucified and Resurrected

The Last Supper, Jesus's Arrest and Trial

1) Shortly before his death, Jesus and his disciples ate their <u>Passover</u> meal in Jerusalem. It was their <u>final meal</u> together and became known as the <u>Last Supper</u>.

2) At the meal, Jesus gave the disciples <u>bread</u> saying "this is my body" and <u>wine</u> saying "this is my blood" (Mark 14:22-24 NIV). Luke's Gospel tells us he said "do this in remembrance of me" (Luke 22:19 NIV). These words are important to many Christians today who remember Jesus with bread and wine through the <u>Eucharist</u> (see p.9).

3) At the Last Supper, Jesus also <u>washed</u> his disciples' <u>feet</u>, which teaches Christians about how important it is to <u>serve</u> others.

4) Next, Jesus went to pray in the <u>Garden of Gethsemane</u>, where he was <u>arrested</u> after Judas <u>betrayed</u> him. The authorities felt <u>threatened</u> by Jesus — earlier that week, crowds had called him the '<u>King of Israel</u>'.

5) He was put on <u>trial</u> before the Jewish <u>high priest</u> and found guilty of <u>blasphemy</u>. Then Jesus was tried before the Roman governor, <u>Pilate</u> — he offered to release Jesus, but the crowd said "<u>Crucify him!</u>" (Mark 15:13 NIV). He was <u>flogged</u>, before being sent to die.

Crucifixion

1) Jesus was <u>crucified</u> at a place called <u>Golgotha</u>, next to two robbers. A sign was fixed to Jesus's cross that read 'The King of the Jews', to record the <u>charge</u> against him. Passers-by threw <u>insults</u> at Jesus, saying that he could <u>save others</u>, but couldn't <u>save himself</u>.

2) In his suffering, Jesus cried out, "My God, my God, why have you forsaken me?" (Mark 15:34 NIV). This shows that Jesus understands how people can feel abandoned in their <u>suffering</u>.

3) Christians also believe the crucifixion helped to <u>repair</u> the <u>relationship</u> between God and mankind — the <u>atonement</u> (see next page).

Resurrection

1) After the crucifixion, Jesus's body was put in a tomb. But he was <u>resurrected</u> (brought back to life), and his tomb was found <u>empty</u>.

2) Jesus talked to two women and told them "Go and tell my brothers to go to Galilee; there they will see me" (Matthew 28:10 NIV).

3) The resurrection is important to Christians as it shows them that there is <u>life after death</u> — <u>death</u> becomes <u>less frightening</u>.

4) It shows them just how <u>powerful</u> God is. This power that raised Jesus from the dead gives people the <u>strength</u> to live Christian lives.

5) Christians also see the resurrection as further <u>proof</u> that Jesus is the <u>Son of God</u> as he was "...appointed the Son of God in power by his resurrection from the dead..." (Romans 1:4 NIV). This strengthens people's <u>faith</u>.

> "...Why do you look for the living among the dead? He is not here; he has risen!" Luke 24:5-6 NIV

> Roman Catholics refer to the crucifixion, resurrection and ascension of Jesus as 'The Paschal Mystery'.

Areas of Study 1, 2 & 3 — Christian Beliefs and Living the Christian Life

Jesus Christ and Salvation

Christianity & Catholic Christianity

Salvation is needed before Christians can go to Heaven, and Jesus's actions made it possible.

Jesus Going to Heaven is Called the Ascension

1) Over the 40 days after the resurrection, many of Jesus's disciples said they had met him alive in various places around Jerusalem.

2) Then, Jesus 'ascended into Heaven' to be with God the Father once again. He had done what he was sent to Earth to do, and it was time for him to go back to God.

"While he was blessing them, he left them and was taken up into heaven." Luke 24:51 NIV

3) In John 14:2, Jesus tells his disciples he will "prepare a place" (NIV) for them in heaven. 1 John 2:1 says that, in Jesus, Christians have an 'advocate' with God (someone who will look out for them).

4) Pope Benedict XVI said that since Jesus was human and went to be with God, the ascension shows there's a place for all human beings with God.

5) The ascension shows Jesus's power — he is now "at the right hand of the mighty God" (Luke 22:69 NIV).

Jesus Died to Save Humanity

1) 'Original sin' (see p.7) means that everyone is born capable of sin. Many Christians believe that Jesus's suffering and death won forgiveness for everyone and ensured their redemption (freeing them from sin).

2) They believe that Jesus was perfect (without sin), but God placed all the sins of the world on him at his crucifixion. Romans 3:21-26 teaches that his sacrifice paid for their sins, so long as they have faith in him.

"For God so loved the world that he gave his one and only Son, that whoever believes in him shall not perish but have eternal life. For God did not send his Son into the world to condemn the world, but to save the world through him." John 3:16-17 NIV

3) Jesus's actions brought about the reconciliation between God and humanity — known as the atonement.

4) His power and goodness were so great that after he was crucified, death couldn't keep hold of him.

5) However, not all Christians believe that Jesus had to die to pay for people's sins:

- 1 Corinthians 13:5 says that love "keeps no record of wrongs" (NIV). Many Christians think that Jesus's death wasn't required for a loving and merciful God to be able to forgive people's sins.
- Some people argue that it was Jesus's ministry that showed people how to be free from sin — he showed them how to live their lives in a Godly way.
- Some say Jesus's death shows God's love for humankind through his willingness to suffer and die as humans do. His resurrection showed how God could triumph over sin and death, so people don't have to fear evil.

Christians Must Seek Salvation to Get to Heaven

1) Salvation means the soul being saved from death and sin, allowing it to reach heaven. For this to happen, Christians believe they must have faith in Jesus: "Salvation is found in no one else..." (Acts 4:12 NIV).

2) Salvation is only possible through God's grace — God showing favour to those who haven't earned it: "For it is by grace you have been saved, through faith... it is the gift of God" (Ephesians 2:8 NIV).

3) But people can't just say they believe — if they're a true believer they'll try to live a Christian life. The Bible contains many laws, such as the Ten Commandments (see p.28), which provide Christians with guidance on how they should behave. Everyone will sin, but the laws mean they'll "become conscious of ... sin" (Romans 3:20 NIV) and "turn to God in repentance" (Acts 20:21 NIV).

4) The Holy Spirit helps Christians to follow the teachings of God and his laws and keep their faith, helping them to find salvation.

Revision can save you from exam failure...

Explain two Christian teachings about salvation.
Your answer should include an example from a source of wisdom and authority. [5]

Areas of Study 1, 2 & 3 — Christian Beliefs and Living the Christian Life

The Afterlife

What people believe will happen to them after __death__ can influence the way they __live__ their lives.

Christians Believe in Heaven and Hell

1) __Life after death__ is the idea that, although your __body__ may die and decay, your __soul__ can live on.

2) Christianity teaches that the __soul__ lives on after death (__immortality__ of the soul), and that the body will be __resurrected__ (brought back to life) for Judgement Day, just as Jesus was resurrected after his crucifixion.

3) Christians believe that God will judge you, and you'll go to either __heaven__ or __hell__:

> Heaven is often portrayed as a place of great beauty and serenity, a __paradise__ where you'll spend eternity with God — as long as you believe in __Jesus__ and have followed his __teachings__, you can be saved by __God's grace__ (see p.5). The __soul__ can go to heaven even though the body ('earthly tent') is gone.

> "I am the resurrection and the life. The one who believes in me will live, even though they die..." John 11:25 NIV

> "For we know that if the earthly tent we live in is destroyed, we have a building from God, an eternal house in heaven, not built by human hands." 2 Corinthians 5:1 NIV

Freshly-washed bedding was Arnie's idea of heaven.

> Hell, on the other hand, is often portrayed as a place of __torment__ and __pain__ — the final destination of __nonbelievers__ and those who have led __bad__ lives.

> "Then they will go away to eternal punishment, but the righteous to eternal life." Matthew 25:46 NIV

4) However, not all Christians believe that heaven and hell are __real__ places — many Christians see heaven and hell as __states of mind__. In heaven you'll be __happy__, and know God — in hell you'll be __unable__ to know God's love. Pope John Paul II said that hell was a __metaphor__ for how people who've __rejected__ God will __feel__.

5) Some Christians, for example Roman Catholics, believe that going to hell means that any __connection__ they have to God will be __severed__ forever: "This state of definitive self-exclusion from communion with God... is called 'hell'" (Catechism of the Catholic Church 1033).

6) Some believe God __wouldn't__ punish people for __eternity__. A few believe that those who God finds __unacceptable__ will be __annihilated__. In a report called 'The Mystery of Salvation', senior members of the __Church of England__ said that for those people "the only end is __total non-being__".

7) Some believe that a loving God __wouldn't__ allow anyone to go to hell.

Purgatory

Roman Catholics believe in a place, or state of existence, called __Purgatory__. Here __sins__ are punished and the person must "undergo purification" (Catechism of the Catholic Church, 1030) before the soul can move on to heaven. Protestants believe this isn't in the Bible, so they __reject__ it.

Christians Believe Resurrection Happens at the Last Judgement

1) Many Christians believe that Jesus will return to Earth in the __Second Coming__ (__Parousia__), and everyone who has died will be __resurrected__: "in Christ all will be made alive" (1 Corinthians 15:22 NIV).

> "Christ... ascended into Heaven, and there sitteth, until he return to judge all Men at the last day." 39 Articles IV

2) Some believe that all of humanity will then be judged at the __Last Judgement__. Those that God finds __acceptable__ will enter __heaven__ — the rest will go to hell, as in the story of the sheep and the goats (Matthew 25:31-46).

> "For we must all appear before the judgment seat of Christ, so that each of us may receive what is due to us for the things done while in the body, whether good or bad." 2 Corinthians 5:10 NIV

3) Some Christians, e.g. __Roman Catholics__, believe in a __personal__ day of __judgement__ straight after a person __dies__ — their actions will be judged and they'll go to heaven or hell __straight away__. Some think they'll be __judged again__ at the Last Judgement, and will __re-enter__ heaven or hell in their __resurrected forms__.

4) Others don't believe in a personal judgement — the soul must __wait__ to be judged at the __Last Judgement__.

You need to be able to compare beliefs about the afterlife...

For Catholic Christianity, you need to compare Catholic views with other Christian views.
For Christianity, you need to compare Christian views with those of another religion (see p.20 and p.29).

EXAM TIP

Evil and Suffering

Evil comes in <u>different forms</u>, and can have an <u>impact</u> on a person's relationship with their faith.

Free Will Led to Evil Entering the World

1) <u>Christianity</u> teaches that evil <u>entered</u> the world as a result of <u>Adam and Eve</u> giving in to <u>temptation</u> in the Garden of Eden — they <u>disobeyed</u> God by eating the <u>fruit</u> of the tree of knowledge. This switch from a perfect world to one containing evil is known as '<u>The Fall</u>'.

> "When the woman saw... the fruit of the tree... she took some and ate it. She also gave some to her husband... and he ate it." Genesis 3:6 NIV

2) After the Fall, every human being was born with a <u>flawed</u> nature, capable of causing suffering — this is the idea of <u>original sin</u>.

3) Christians believe God created humans with <u>free will</u> — it's up to them to <u>choose</u> whether they perform evil deeds or not, just as it was up to <u>Adam and Eve</u> whether to give in to temptation or not. <u>Good</u> is the opposite of <u>evil</u>, and since God is good, Christians try to follow his <u>example</u>.

Suffering can be Human-Made or Natural

Suffering can be divided into <u>two types</u>:

Moral (human-made) Suffering	Natural Suffering
1) This is when suffering is brought about by the <u>cruel</u> actions of <u>people</u>. 2) This includes things like murder, war, rape and torture. 3) The person causing the suffering is able to make a <u>choice</u> about what is morally <u>right or wrong</u>.	1) This kind of suffering is <u>caused by the world</u> in which we live, and is <u>no one's 'fault'</u>. 2) This includes things like disease, floods, earthquakes and hurricanes. 3) However, many <u>recent natural disasters</u> may have been caused by <u>human interference</u> in the natural world, raising the question of whether that makes those events human-made.

Evil can Lead People to Question their Faith

1) <u>Evil</u> and <u>suffering</u> may lead some people to <u>question</u> their belief in God — or even to <u>reject</u> their faith.

2) Some might say that since suffering exists, God <u>can't</u> be <u>both</u> benevolent and omnipotent — a loving and all-powerful God wouldn't <u>allow</u> it to happen. They might argue that he <u>doesn't exist</u>, or that he can't have the <u>characteristics</u> that believers say he has.

> "the Lord is compassionate and gracious, slow to anger, abounding in love... he does not treat us as our sins deserve..." Psalm 103:8-10 NIV

3) But others would say that although God has these characteristics, he gave people <u>free will</u> and so doesn't <u>interfere</u>. Or some may say that he <u>wants</u> to <u>help</u>, but isn't <u>powerful</u> enough.

4) Christians <u>react</u> to evil and suffering in various ways. <u>Suffering</u> is often seen as a <u>test of faith</u> — <u>God</u> has his <u>reasons</u> (even if we <u>don't know</u> what they are). Many believe that God is <u>with</u> people in their suffering, and that it can bring people <u>closer</u> to him.

> "I know, Lord, that your laws are righteous, and that in faithfulness you have afflicted me. May your unfailing love be my comfort..." Psalm 119:75-76 NIV

5) Others say life on Earth <u>isn't</u> meant to be perfect — the focus should be on reaching <u>heaven</u>.

6) Some believe in the '<u>vale of soul-making</u>' — responding to suffering in both themselves and others <u>develops</u> the human <u>soul</u>, improving people's character so they live as God wants them to.

7) The <u>Book of Job</u> tells of the <u>suffering</u> Job endures and how he <u>questions</u> God. He concludes that God is <u>all-powerful</u> and knows what he's doing, and that suffering must be <u>accepted</u> because people can't really <u>understand</u> the world or <u>God's plan</u>: "Though he slay me, yet will I hope in him..." (Job 13:15 NIV).

8) Christians try to <u>help</u> people who are suffering — <u>practically</u> (charity) and by <u>praying</u>. Jesus said: "whatever you did for one of... these brothers and sisters of mine, you did for me" (Matthew 25:40 NIV).

Not the cheeriest of topics...

Christians explain and respond to evil and suffering in a variety of different ways.
Cover this page, see how many you can think of and write them all down.

REVISION TASK

Different Forms of Worship

Christian Denominations have Different Forms of Worship

For Christians, Sunday is the 'Lord's Day', when they celebrate the Sabbath (the holy day of rest). Most churches have their main service on a Sunday morning. Worship often includes prayers, readings from the Bible, a sermon and the Eucharist (see p.9) — the different denominations place varying amounts of importance on each, creating differences in worship.

Some Worship is Liturgical...

'Liturgical' means that services follow a set pattern written out by the Church.

1) Anglican Sunday morning services usually include the Eucharist, and Catholic Sunday morning services always do (Catholics call the Eucharist 'Mass'). For Catholics, the 'Roman Missal' sets out the contents of the service. Anglican worship is guided by the 'Common Worship' book, based on the Book of Common Prayer from 1662. The main Orthodox Sunday service is the 'Divine Liturgy', which centres on the Eucharist — it's usually based on the liturgy of St John Chrysostom.

Anglican and Catholic Eucharist services share many similarities:
- A confession of sin and a request for God's mercy is said by everyone (called the 'penitential rite' by Catholics).
- There are readings (including one gospel reading) and a sermon — this part is known as the 'liturgy of the Word'. The Nicene or Apostle's Creed is then recited.
- The priest says prayers over bread and wine — this is called the 'liturgy of the Eucharist'.
- Then the congregation says the Lord's Prayer (see p.11) and 'shares the peace' by shaking hands. They receive the bread and wine. Catholics call this the 'rite of Communion'.

- Orthodox services contain similar elements to Anglican and Catholic ones: a sermon, Bible readings, the Nicene Creed and blessing of bread and wine.
- They include the 'Litany', where the priest says prayers and the congregation responds with 'Lord have mercy'. Worshippers sing or chant for most of the service.
- Services are often longer than most Anglican and Catholic services, and people stand for the majority of the time.

2) For many, public worship helps them to feel involved in a wider Christian community. It can also help them feel closer to Jesus as they believe he is there in the church with them: "For where two or three gather in my name, there am I with them" (Matthew 18:20 NIV). Following traditions also helps Christians to feel connected to other worshippers throughout history.

...and Other Worship is Non-Liturgical

The worship of the Society of Friends (Quakers) is non-liturgical, and it is usually unstructured. Worshippers sit together in silence, but they are free to pray or speak out loud.

Methodist services don't have to follow a set structure, but there is a 'Methodist Worship Book' with suggested liturgy for parts of worship, e.g. the Eucharist. Services feature hymns, readings, a sermon and prayers. The Eucharist also takes place, but not every week.

Worship in Evangelical Churches (e.g. Pentecostals) is often spontaneous. Worshippers believe they're inspired by the Spirit — this is called 'charismatic' worship. It might inspire them to pray, clap, dance or shout. Sometimes they 'speak in tongues' — praying in an unrecognisable language.

Some Christians prefer the freedom of worshipping God in a less-structured way. Others view non-liturgical worship as unsuitable for the level of respect that religious services require.

Some Christians also Engage in Private Worship

You don't need this section if you're studying Catholic Christianity.

1) Many Christians worship informally at home (not just on Sundays). This can be anything from saying grace before a meal to singing worship songs with family, to reading the Bible or praying (see p.11).

2) Lots of Christians worship both publicly and privately — private worship can help them keep God in mind throughout their everyday lives. Some also find greater freedom in private worship — they decide how they worship God and so feel a better connection with God.

Who's singing out of tune? Hymn...

For Catholic Christianity, you need to be able to compare Catholic worship with other denominations. For Christianity, you should compare with the worship of another religion — see p.21-22 and 30-31.

The Sacraments

Sacraments play a key role in worship and belief for many Christians.

Different Denominations Believe in Different Sacraments

1) A sacrament is a ceremony (usually carried out by a minister or priest) through which Christians believe they receive God's grace. It's a sign of God's grace working within them.

2) Roman Catholic and Orthodox Churches believe in seven sacraments (see p.10), but most Protestants accept only baptism and the Eucharist as sacraments — they believe only these two were prescribed by Jesus in the Gospels. Many believe that the sacraments bring people closer to God.

3) Baptists use the word 'ordinance' instead of 'sacrament' — they see them more as symbols. Quakers and the Salvation Army don't have any sacraments — they think they're unnecessary.

Baptism is an Important Sacrament for Many Christians

1) Baptism is seen as a sacrament because Jesus was baptised. After his resurrection, he told his disciples to go out and baptise people: "...go and make disciples of all nations, baptising them in the name of the Father and of the Son and of the Holy Spirit" (Matthew 28:19 NIV).

2) Jesus also said "no one can enter the kingdom of God unless they are born of water and the Spirit" (John 3:5 NIV).

3) Baptism makes someone a member of God's family and welcomes them to the Church. Some Christians believe that baptising cleanses people from the original sin that everyone is born with.

4) Babies are baptised in many denominations, e.g. Anglican, Catholic and Methodist. (They will also baptise adults if they weren't baptised as children and want to join the Church.)

5) A sign of the cross is made on the baby, and in many Churches holy water is poured three times over the forehead (in the name of the Father, Son and Holy Spirit). Orthodox Christians baptise babies by total immersion.

6) Denominations that baptise babies also usually have confirmation — a person 'confirms' their faith when they reach an age that they can declare it themselves.

7) But some denominations — for example Baptists and Pentecostals — believe you shouldn't be baptised until you're old enough to accept Christianity for yourself. They hold believers' baptisms, when adults who wish to join the Church are baptised by total immersion.

There are Many Different Understandings of the Eucharist

The Eucharist is where Christians remember the Last Supper (see p.4) with bread and wine. Many denominations see it as a sacrament, but have different beliefs about the bread and wine:

- Roman Catholics believe in transubstantiation (i.e. the bread and wine used at Mass become the flesh and blood of Christ), and every Mass is a re-enactment of Christ's sacrifice (see p.4). They believe that they receive the saving power of Jesus into themselves through the bread and wine.

- Lutherans, Methodists and most Anglicans believe Holy Communion is more than just an 'intellectual' commemoration of the Last Supper — it's a re-enactment. They believe that there is a 'real presence' of Christ in the bread and wine, but they don't believe that transubstantiation occurs.

"Transubstantiation... in the Supper of the Lord, cannot be proved by holy Writ..." 39 Articles XXVIII

- Baptists view the bread and wine as symbols, but believe that God is present through the act of Christians coming together to share Communion. The bread and non-alcoholic wine are set out on a simple table. The bread is later offered from person to person, and the wine drunk from small individual cups.

- Denominations which place more meaning on the bread and wine (e.g. Catholicism and Orthodox) hold Eucharists more often — they believe it's essential for sustaining their relationship with God. They tend to use a more ornate table (an altar), and have more ritual surrounding the Eucharist (e.g. using incense). Catholics will be given bread by the priest and drink wine from a shared cup. Orthodox Christians are given the bread and wine together on a special spoon.

Immerse yourself and learn all about baptism...

Close the book and jot down the beliefs of the different denominations about baptism and the Eucharist.

REVISION TASK

Catholic Christianity

The Sacraments

Catholics believe there are <u>seven</u> specific sacraments through which God can communicate his <u>grace</u> directly. Some see the <u>whole world</u> as <u>sacramental</u> — they can experience <u>God's grace</u> through his creation.

The Seven Sacraments — God Shows His Grace

1 Baptism This marks a person's official <u>entry</u> into the Church (see p.9).

2 Confirmation In this ceremony, a Christian (often a teenager) <u>renews</u> the vows made on their behalf at baptism. <u>Confirmation</u> is believed to <u>strengthen the ties</u> of the confirmed to the Church and to God. In Catholic confirmations, the bishop anoints the believer's forehead with holy oil called <u>chrism</u>.

3 Reconciliation This involves <u>confession</u> of a sin, following by <u>contrition</u>, <u>penance</u> and <u>absolution</u>. This is how Catholics seek to obtain <u>forgiveness</u> for the sins they commit. They must <u>tell</u> a priest about any <u>sinful</u> things that they've done. The priest will give a <u>penance</u> (a certain number of prayers to be said, or an action to be done) and will then pronounce <u>absolution</u> (God's forgiveness).

4 Anointing the sick A priest or bishop anoints a <u>seriously unwell person</u> with the <u>oil of the sick</u>. Catholics believe that, through this, the <u>Holy Spirit</u> renews the person's <u>faith</u> and <u>strength</u> to <u>cope</u> with their illness and <u>accept</u> their suffering. The anointing is also believed to <u>link</u> the person's suffering to <u>Christ's</u> suffering, allow their <u>sins</u> to be forgiven and to <u>heal</u> them, if that is <u>God's will</u>.

5 Matrimony Catholics believe Jesus performed his <u>first miracle</u> at a <u>wedding</u>. They believe that God is <u>present</u> at the ceremony and <u>promises</u> are made before him — couples joined in <u>Holy Matrimony</u> should be together for <u>life</u>. As it's a sacrament, the union is a way that God <u>blesses</u> the couple, and he also blesses them <u>through</u> one another.

6 Holy orders This is the process by which men are ordained as <u>deacons</u>, <u>priests</u> or <u>bishops</u>. Like matrimony, it is a <u>commitment</u> for life.

7 Eucharist The Eucharist (Mass) is seen as "the source and summit of the Christian life" (Catechism of the Catholic Church 1324). Receiving the <u>body</u> and <u>blood</u> of Christ (see p.9) <u>joins</u> people together in their faith and gives them the <u>strength</u> to live Christian lives and face any <u>problems</u> they may encounter.

Some of the bread and wine that is <u>blessed</u> but <u>not consumed</u> is kept in the church — people believe <u>Jesus</u> is still <u>present</u> in it, and <u>focus</u> on it as they pray and express their love for Jesus. This is known as '<u>eucharistic adoration</u>'.

"The seven sacraments touch all the stages and all the important moments of Christian life..." Catechism of the Catholic Church, 1210

"...in the breaking of the Eucharistic bread, we are taken up into communion with Him and with one another." Lumen gentium Chapter 1 Paragraph 7:53

Catholic Funerals have Three Parts

The funeral rite isn't a sacrament, but it's important.

1) The <u>Vigil of Prayer</u> takes place the day before the funeral and is sometimes held at home. Readings and prayers form the service, which aims to <u>help</u> family and friends prepare to say <u>goodbye</u>.

2) Attending a funeral allows Catholics to join together in <u>praying</u> to God to <u>take care</u> of the person. Funerals remind people of the hope of <u>eternal life</u> — one day the bereaved will be <u>reunited</u> with the <u>deceased</u>.

3) The <u>Funeral Liturgy</u> often includes Holy Communion (the '<u>Requiem Mass</u>'). Its purpose is to pray for the soul of the dead person. The coffin is sprinkled with <u>holy water</u> and the priest says, "In the waters of baptism [name] died with Christ, and rose with him to new life. May s/he now share with him in eternal glory." The coffin is later sprinkled again and perfumed with <u>incense</u>. The <u>Paschal candle</u> sits beside it.

4) The <u>Committal</u> is a short ceremony that happens at the <u>cemetery</u> (or the <u>crematorium</u> if the person wished to be cremated). The priest says "ashes to ashes, dust to dust" as the body goes back to the <u>earth</u>.

Big Cats Rarely Ask Me 'Ham Or Egg?'...

...is a handy way to remember the first letters of the sacraments. Now try out this exam question:
Explain two ways that the sacraments communicate God's grace. [4]

Areas of Study 1, 2 & 3 — Christian Beliefs and Living the Christian Life

Prayer and Pilgrimage

Prayer and pilgrimage are both ways in which Christians might strengthen their relationship with God.

Prayer Puts People In Touch with their God

1) Prayer is when believers mentally or vocally communicate with God — it should be part of daily life. The Catechism of the Catholic Church (2559) says that "Prayer is the raising of one's mind and heart to God". During prayer people might thank God (thanksgiving), worship God (adoration) or admit sins (confession). They might ask God for something (supplication) or to help other people (intercession).

2) Believers draw comfort from the fact that God is listening to them. They also listen for what he is saying to them — many believe prayer helps them to find out what God wants them to do in life.

3) Most denominations have set (formulaic) prayers that are Church tradition — they can be said during acts of worship in church, and also in private.

4) The Lord's Prayer is very important. It's based on the words Jesus used when he told his disciples how to pray. It covers key themes — e.g. the idea that God is 'Our Father' and he provides for people's physical needs.

5) Informal prayers are where the individual talks to God in their own words. They're sometimes called 'extempore' prayers, and can be used in worship and privately. Informal prayers are more personal and show the individual's connection with God — many Christians prefer them to set prayers.

> "This, then, is how you should pray: 'Our Father in heaven, hallowed be your name, your kingdom come, your will be done, on earth as it is in heaven. Give us today our daily bread. And forgive us our debts, as we also have forgiven our debtors. And lead us not into temptation, but deliver us from the evil one.' "
> Matthew 6:9-13 NIV

Catholic Forms of Popular Piety ← This box is only for people studying Catholic Christianity.

1) Catholics use the Rosary (a string with a cross and beads) when praying. The cross is held when reciting the Apostles' Creed, and prayers are said as the beads are moved through the fingers, e.g. Ave Maria (Hail Mary). The beads represent the key events in Christianity (known as mysteries), such as the birth, death and resurrection of Jesus — the Rosary helps people think about these while praying.

2) The 'Stations of the Cross' are pictures in church of Jesus's suffering — Catholics use them as a focus for contemplation on these events. The Catechism of the Catholic Church recognises the use of different forms of piety, but says that they "...extend the liturgical life of the Church, but do not replace it" (1675).

3) Some disagree with these forms of 'popular piety'. Some Protestants think the Rosary encourages prayers to be repeated without giving thought to the words themselves. Many Protestants wouldn't say the Hail Mary prayer, as most don't believe in praying to Mary. Some people might argue that praying while focusing on the Stations of the Cross creates a danger of worshipping idols.

Pilgrimages can help Believers feel Nearer to God

1) Pilgrimages aren't compulsory in Christianity, but many see them as important. The Catechism of the Catholic Church (2691) says that "Pilgrimages evoke our earthly journey toward heaven...". Luke 2:41-43 tells the story of the pilgrimage Jesus and his parents made to Jerusalem.

2) Christians make pilgrimages to seek healing or forgiveness, to connect to God or to deepen their faith. Pilgrimages also provide the chance to escape normal life and to concentrate more on religion. Pilgrims can learn from each other. The journey reflects the path they're trying to follow towards God.

3) People may visit places that are significant in Christianity — such as Jerusalem, where they can visit key places in Jesus's life and death. Roman Catholics often visit Rome, the home of the Pope.

4) Some Christians, especially Catholics, make pilgrimages to shrines where Mary has appeared. These include Walsingham (which is popular with some Anglicans as well as Catholics) and Lourdes. The water in Lourdes is said to have healing properties which can cure ill health, and lots of people believe miracles take place there. Catholics also visit shrines to saints.

5) Protestants are more likely to visit places they can find peace to study the Bible and pray — e.g. the quiet island of Iona (which has a long history of Christianity), or Taizé where they can join worship at the monastery. Some Christians see shrines such as Lourdes as being too commercialised, with too many people. Some regard pilgrimage as unnecessary — the journey inside is what matters.

I make a daily pilgrimage to the biscuit tin...

Make sure you know why people go on pilgrimages and the differences between the most famous sites.

EXAM TIP

Areas of Study 1, 2 & 3 — Christian Beliefs and Living the Christian Life

Christianity	Christmas and Easter

Christmas and Easter are the two most important <u>celebrations</u> in the Christian calendar.

Christmas is a Celebration of Jesus's Birth

1) Christmas is celebrated by most Christians on <u>25th December</u> (for <u>Orthodox</u> Christians it's <u>7th January</u>). It celebrates how Jesus was born in <u>Bethlehem</u> — there he was worshipped by <u>shepherds</u> after an <u>angel</u> told them that "a Saviour has been born to you; he is the Messiah, the Lord" (Luke 2:11 NIV).

2) Christmas comes after a period called <u>Advent</u>, which begins four Sundays before Christmas. Advent is significant for many Christians as it's time they spend <u>getting ready</u> to celebrate <u>Jesus's birth</u> — a time for <u>prayer</u> and <u>reflection</u>. <u>Advent candles</u> are lit in homes and churches, and children may use <u>Advent calendars</u> to count off the days until Christmas.

3) Lots of Roman Catholic, Orthodox and Anglican churches have a '<u>Midnight Mass</u>' to welcome Christmas Day, and most Christians go to church on <u>Christmas morning</u> to <u>celebrate</u>.

4) Many churches hold services in the days <u>after Christmas</u>, carrying on to <u>Epiphany</u> (6th January) — the day that the <u>Magi</u> (wise men) went to see Jesus in Bethlehem.

5) Customs <u>vary</u> around the world. <u>Gifts</u> are exchanged to symbolise the fact that Jesus was <u>God's gift</u> to the world, and to remember how the <u>Magi</u> "presented him with gifts of gold, frankincense and myrrh" (Matthew 2:11 NIV).

6) Some Christians dislike modern Christmas <u>traditions</u> and <u>customs</u>, e.g. <u>Santa Claus</u> (Father Christmas), giving <u>expensive presents</u>, and <u>excessive eating</u> and <u>drinking</u>. They believe that some of these modern traditions <u>devalue</u> the <u>true meaning</u> of Christmas. Others feel that it has retained too much <u>pagan</u> influence, such as Christmas trees.

Easter celebrates Jesus's Resurrection

1) Easter is the most <u>important</u> festival for Christians, since it celebrates <u>Jesus's victory</u> over death, when God raised him <u>back to life</u> after his crucifixion (see p.4). This reminds people that God <u>loves</u> them so much that he was <u>willing</u> to suffer death on the cross and gives them hope of <u>eternal life</u>.

> 1 Corinthians 15:14 outlines how important the Resurrection is for Christians and their beliefs: "And if Christ has not been raised, our preaching is useless and so is your faith" (NIV).

2) <u>Lent</u> is the <u>40 days</u> before Easter. On <u>Ash Wednesday</u> (the first day of Lent), ash is put on believers' <u>foreheads</u> to show they're sorry for their <u>sins</u>. Some Christians <u>fast</u> (<u>eat less</u> and have only <u>simple food</u>) during Lent to mark when Jesus fasted for 40 days in the desert. They <u>stop fasting</u> on <u>Easter Sunday</u>.

3) The lead-up to <u>Easter Day</u>, the day of resurrection, is marked by a number of important events:

- <u>Palm Sunday</u> is the Sunday before Easter, when Christians remember Jesus's <u>triumphant entry</u> into Jerusalem. This marks the beginning of <u>Holy Week</u> — Jesus's final week before his <u>crucifixion</u>.
- <u>Maundy Thursday</u> commemorates the <u>Last Supper</u> held on the night before Jesus died.
- <u>Good Friday</u> recalls Jesus's <u>crucifixion</u> — special services are held, particularly on Friday afternoon. Some services last <u>three hours</u> to mark Jesus's final three hours on the <u>cross</u>, when the sky became <u>dark</u>.

4) <u>Easter Day</u> is a <u>joyous</u> occasion when Jesus's resurrection is celebrated.

- Some churches hold services on the Saturday night, and most have <u>special services</u> on the Sunday morning.
- The <u>Paschal candle</u> is lit during services in Anglican and Catholic churches. Worshippers light their own candle from its flame, which represents Jesus as the <u>Light of the World</u>.
- Some churches hold <u>sunrise services</u> to remember how Mary Magdalene discovered at daybreak that Jesus's tomb was empty. The rising of the <u>sun</u> is symbolic of <u>God's Son</u> rising from the dead.
- <u>Eggs</u> are associated with Easter as a symbol of <u>new life</u>. Some view chocolate Easter eggs as <u>commercialisation</u> of the festival.

Learning about Easter is an eggcellent way to gain marks...

Working from Lent to Easter Sunday, draw a timeline of Christian Easter celebrations. Next to each day, scribble down what happens and then check your answers against this page.

Areas of Study 1, 2 & 3 — Christian Beliefs and Living the Christian Life

The Work of the Church

Churches aren't just about holding services. They're active in the local community too.

Churches are Important in the Local Community

You don't need this first section if you're studying Catholic Christianity.

Most communities in the UK have access to at least one church. The role of the local church is to put the Christian faith into action — this includes caring for the community, as seen in lots of Christian teaching:

In 1 Peter 5:2-3, the leaders of the church are asked to set an example for the congregation through their actions: "...be shepherds of God's flock that is under your care, watching over them... being examples to the flock" (NIV).	In Mark 12:31, Jesus said that the second most important commandment is "Love your neighbour as yourself" (NIV).	Paragraph 26 of Gaudium et spes, a key document of the Second Vatican Council, states: "Every social group must take account of the needs and legitimate aspirations of other groups, and even of the general welfare of the entire human family."

Churches put this into practice in many different ways:

1) By providing regular services and a place for quiet reflection — most churches hold a Sunday service and may also have other acts of worship throughout the week.

2) By providing rites of passage such as baptisms, confirmations, weddings and funerals (see p.9-10).

3) By running youth groups and Sunday Schools to engage young people in the local community.

4) By offering support and advice to people in need — e.g. visiting and praying for people in hospital.

5) Some churchgoers work as Street Pastors — they volunteer in towns and cities on Friday and Saturday nights to support anyone in need of help. This demonstrates Christian love.

6) Some foodbanks in the UK are run by churches. People donate food which the foodbank then distributes to those who need it the most.

Different denominations might work together, e.g. through community projects or joint services. This is called 'ecumenism'.

7) Many churches also raise money for charity.

Evangelism Tells People about Christianity

1) Evangelism means spreading the Christian message with the aim of converting people. As church attendance falls, evangelism is increasingly important.

"As the Father has sent me, I am sending you." John 20:21 NIV

2) In Mark 16:15, Jesus told his disciples to "Go into all the world and preach the gospel to all creation" (NIV). Many Christians believe that they should be prepared to do the same.

3) They believe that by evangelising they can help people discover their real purpose in life and find salvation. They feel excited to tell other people about Jesus's love — Pope Francis said "The primary reason for evangelizing is the love of Jesus which we have received..." (Evangelii Gaudium 264).

4) For some, evangelism is about telling people directly about God. This can cause problems — people may feel offended. Others try to demonstrate God's love through their actions, to bring people closer to God. Churches might ask the congregation to bring along a friend who wouldn't normally go to church.

5) Missionaries spread the Christian message abroad. In the past they went where Christianity was unknown, with the aim of converting people. Now many missionaries use their skills to help disadvantaged people, e.g. a doctor working in a poor country. These people show what Christianity is through their actions.

Other examples of evangelism You don't need to read this box if you're studying Catholic Christianity.

- The Church of England and Church in Wales are finding ways to interest new people in churches that don't follow the traditional model — for example worshipping in alternative venues like cafés, or creating a café atmosphere in church. Through initiatives called 'Fresh Expressions' and 'Pioneer Ministry', they offer a new approach for modern society.
- Gideons distribute copies of the Bible in places like hotels and care homes.
- The Salvation Army helps people by providing hot meals and beds for homeless people. They also attend emergencies, such as floods.

It's my mission to get you to learn this page...

Outline three ways that Christians might try to evangelise others. [3]

Areas of Study 1, 2 & 3 — Christian Beliefs and Living the Christian Life

The Work of the Church

Reconciliation works Towards Peace and Unity

1) Christians believe in justice — all people are equal in God's eyes, so they should be treated fairly. Christian organisations help people being treated unfairly due to war, religious persecution or poverty.

2) In Matthew 5:9 Jesus said "Blessed are the peacemakers" (NIV). Christians believe that reconciliation (coming together and making peace) is needed between people who have been in conflict with one another — just as Jesus brought God and humankind together through the atonement (p.5).

3) These are two examples of organisations that work for reconciliation:

> The Corrymeela Community in Northern Ireland was founded to help heal the country's political and religious divisions. It works with people in areas where there is tension and strives to help people understand each other and reconcile through group activities and discussions.

> Pax Christi is an international Catholic organisation working for human rights, disarmament and peace. They believe violence should be avoided, and they work to create a world where people can live in harmony.

Organisations and Churches help Persecuted Christians

Skip these 3 points if you're doing Catholic Christianity.

1) Millions around the world suffer for being Christians — some endure prison sentences or even death.

2) Organisations give support by providing Bibles so people can continue worshipping in secret. They offer training to church members and support people who have lost their homes.

3) Churches pray for the persecuted and may send money. Christians might petition for government help.

Christian Charities help Those in Need

1) In the story of the sheep and goats (Matthew 25:31-46), Jesus explains that people who have been good (the sheep) and have helped others will be looked after by God. People who haven't (the goats) will suffer. The story tells Christians that they are helping Jesus when they help others.

2) Because of this, charity is very important to many Christians. But it's not all about giving money — it must be done with love. In 1 Corinthians 13:3, St Paul said "If I give all I possess to the poor... but do not have love, I gain nothing" (NIV).

3) Christians can follow these teachings in various ways. They might carry the teachings out directly — e.g. by donating food or working for a charity. Or they might choose to support a charity that's working to help people escape poverty, and to give them better education and healthcare.

4) There are many Christian charities that help people in need. Lots believe in development — 'helping people to help themselves', whatever their faith.

You don't need to learn about this charity for Catholic Christianity.

> Christian Aid works globally to relieve poverty. They set up projects in the developing world, drawing on the skills of local people. The organisation also aims to change government policy to help reduce the suffering of the world's poor, e.g. through debt relief, and fair-trade products.

There are many Catholic Charities ◄— This section is only for people studying Catholic Christianity.

Evangelii Gaudium (187) says that Catholics should strive to help the poor "to be fully a part of society". CAFOD is a Roman Catholic organisation, and there are many others that help those in need:

> CAFOD (Catholic Agency for Overseas Development) works to fight poverty and injustice around the world. They work through churches, helping in emergencies, but also giving people the skills to help themselves.

Sheep — good, goats — baaaad...

EXAM TIP

In the exam, the 4 mark questions will ask you to either 'Explain' or 'Describe'. The 'explain' question will ask you to make two points — you need to develop them to get the full 4 marks.

Revision Summary

That was a lot to take in there, so now see how you get on with these exam-style questions. Answer 1-13 if you're studying Christianity. If you're studying Catholic Christianity, answer them all except 3, 4 and 8.

If there's anything you can't answer, go back through the section and have another go when you've re-read it. For some questions — you'll be told which ones — there are extra marks for spelling, punctuation, grammar and specialist terminology, so check your writing carefully.

Christianity and Catholic Christianity

Let's get cracking — have a go at these 3 mark questions. Write three short points to get the marks.

1) Outline three beliefs about purgatory.
2) Outline three Christian teachings about the Trinity.
3) Outline three Christian beliefs about suffering. ◄——— Only answer these questions if you're studying Christianity.
4) Outline three ways that Christians celebrate Easter. ◄———

You've found your feet now, so let's jump up to 4 marks. You need to give two points and develop them.

5) Explain two reasons why liturgical worship is important for some Christians.
6) Explain two Christian beliefs about creation.
7) Explain two ways in which Christians interpret the Eucharist.
8) Describe two differences in types of worship between Christianity and another religious tradition in the UK. ◄——— Only answer this question if you're studying Christianity. You might need to come back to it after you've revised your other religion.

Up to 5 marks now. Explain your points and include an example from a source of wisdom and authority.

9) Explain two reasons why evangelism is important to Christians.
10) Explain two reasons why Jesus's resurrection is important.
11) Explain two reasons why prayer is important to Christians.
12) Explain two Christian teachings on baptism.

Organise your points and write concisely in the 4 and 5 mark questions — make your points crystal clear to the marker.

It's the one you've been looking forward to — the 15 mark question (3 marks are for SPaG and specialist terminology). You'll get a list of things that you've got to have in your answer, which is handy for creating a plan. You'll be asked to give arguments for and against a statement, so be sure to include plenty of detail.

13) 'Pilgrimage is the best way for a Christian to develop their relationship with God.'
    Evaluate this statement.
    Give arguments that support the statement and arguments that disagree with the statement.
    You must include:
    • examples from Christian teachings
    • different Christian opinions
    • a conclusion.

Turn to the 'Do Well in Your Exam' section for tips on writing essays.

Catholic Christianity

14) Outline three features of a Catholic funeral.   [3]
15) Explain two Christian attitudes to the Rosary.   [4]
16) Describe two differences in beliefs on life after death between Catholic Christianity and other denominations of the main religious tradition in the UK.   [4]
17) Explain two reasons why Catholics believe it's important to 'love your neighbour'.
    You should include an example from a source of wisdom and authority in your answer.   [5]
18) 'The sacraments are the most important part of a Catholic's faith.'
    Evaluate this statement.
    Give arguments that support the statement and arguments that disagree with the statement.
    You must include:
    • examples from Catholic teachings
    • different Christian opinions
    • a conclusion. [15]

3 marks are for SPaG and specialist terminology.

Areas of Study 1, 2 & 3 — Christian Beliefs and Living the Christian Life

Islam	# Introduction to Islam

Islam was founded in the 7th century. It shares some ideas with Judaism and Christianity. Muslims believe in one god, Allah. The Qur'an is the Muslim holy book — Muslims also follow the prophet Muhammad's teaching.

Islam is Divided into Two Main Traditions — Sunni and Shi'a

1) About 85-90% of Muslims are Sunni Muslims — most of the rest are Shi'a Muslims.

2) Muhammad was the founder of Islam — Allah revealed the Qur'an to him. After Muhammad died, Muslims had to choose a new leader (caliph). The next four caliphs were Abu Bakr, Umar, Uthman and Ali.

3) However, some Muslims had wanted Ali to be the first caliph, and thought the first three caliphs shouldn't have been given the role. Others said Ali shouldn't be the caliph at all.

4) After Ali died, two groups formed — the Sunnis and the Shi'as. Each group followed a different line of caliphs. The Sunnis accepted the next caliph after Ali, but the Shi'as (Shi'at Ali or Party of Ali) followed Ali's descendants. Sunnis and Shi'as have been separate groups ever since.

Sunnis and Shi'as have Many Similar Beliefs

Sunnis and Shi'as share many beliefs, but have some different ideas. Their basic beliefs — articles of faith — are slightly different, but they share beliefs in Allah, the holy books, prophets and a day of judgement. These, along with a belief in angels, are mentioned in the Qur'an (4:136) and other teachings, e.g. Sahih Muslim 1:4.

There are six articles of faith in Sunni Islam:	There are five articles of faith in Shi'a Islam. They're known as the 'Usul ad-Din — foundations of faith:
1) belief that Allah is the one and only god (Tawhid)	1) belief that Allah is the one and only god (Tawhid)
2) belief in angels (Malaikah)	2) belief in divine justice ('Adl)
3) belief in the holy books	3) belief in prophethood (Nubuwwah)
4) belief in Allah's prophets (Nubuwwah)	4) belief in the authority of imams (Imamah)
5) belief in the Day of Judgement	5) belief in the Day of Resurrection (Mi'ad)
6) belief that Allah knows and decides everything that's going to happen (predestination — al-Qadr)	

Key Sunni Beliefs

1) No one after Muhammad received knowledge from Allah. Muslims should focus on Muhammad and his way of life (sunnah — see p.19) rather than paying too much attention to Ali and his sons.

2) Muslims should be guided by the consensus (majority view) of the community.

Key Shi'a Beliefs

1) Ali was the first true caliph. Allah gave him knowledge to ensure his teaching and actions were right.

2) There are many branches of Shi'a Islam. They share a common belief in a line of imams after Ali, who all had the same knowledge from Allah as Ali. Shi'a imams are leaders and figureheads of the religion. They're all descendants of Muhammad. In Sunni Islam, the word 'imam' simply means 'prayer leader'.

3) The different branches of Shi'a Islam split off from each other after disagreements about the line of imams. The Twelvers are the largest branch, but there are many others.

4) Twelver Shi'as believe in a line of 12 imams, the last of whom is in hiding and will eventually return. The Twelvers are led by religious scholars while they wait for the last imam's return.

5) Isma'ili Shi'as (often called 'Seveners') thought the seventh imam should be Isma'il, the elder brother of the one chosen by the Twelvers. The biggest group of Isma'ilis today, the Nizaris, think each imam can select the next and are still led by an imam now, known as the Aga Khan.

Seveners, Twelvers — sounds like maths, not RS...

As a quick task to keep you on your toes — shut this book, grab a piece of paper and see if you can write down the articles of faith for Sunni and Shi'a Islam.

Key Beliefs in Islam | Islam

Islam is a <u>monotheistic</u> religion — Muslims believe in only <u>one god</u>, <u>Allah</u>. They believe in many <u>prophets</u>.

Tawhid is Central to Islam

"Say, 'He is Allah, [who is] One.' " Qur'an 112:1

1) The word <u>Allah</u> is from the Arabic <u>al-ilah</u>, meaning '<u>the god</u>', i.e. the <u>only</u> god. Several of the <u>ninety-nine</u> <u>names</u> of Allah (see below) make this clear, including <u>al-Ahad</u> (the one and only) and <u>al-Wahid</u> (the one).

2) Saying Allah is the <u>only god</u> is the first part of the <u>shahadah</u>, the Muslim <u>declaration of faith</u> (see p.21).

3) <u>Shirk</u> — believing in <u>other gods</u> as well as Allah, or that anyone or thing could share in Allah's <u>oneness</u> — is seen as the <u>worst sin</u>. Muslims therefore disagree with the <u>Christian</u> idea of the <u>Holy Trinity</u> (see p.2) and with <u>polytheism</u> (believing in <u>multiple gods</u>). <u>Images</u> of Muhammad aren't allowed, in case of <u>shirk</u>.

"Allah does not forgive association with Him, but He forgives what is less than that..." Qur'an 4:116.
'Association with Him' is worshipping other gods as well as Allah.

"let the first thing to which you will invite them, be the Tauhid [Tawhid] of Allah." Sahih al-Bukhari 93:469

4) According to a <u>hadith</u> (see p.19), <u>Muhammad</u> said that when telling <u>non-Muslims</u> about Islam, the <u>first thing</u> Muslims should mention is <u>Tawhid</u>.

Allah has Many Characteristics

"In the name of Allah, the Entirely Merciful, the Especially Merciful" (Qur'an 1:1) is the phrase known as the <u>bismillah</u>.

1) **MERCIFUL** — Muslims believe Allah shows <u>mercy</u> and <u>compassion</u>. <u>All but one</u> of the Qur'an's chapters <u>begin</u> by saying this — it's known as the <u>bismillah</u>. They believe Allah is <u>kind</u> and <u>forgives</u> people's <u>sins</u>.

2) **OMNIPOTENT** — Allah is <u>all-powerful</u>. He <u>created</u> the <u>universe</u> and is in <u>control</u> of everything. He has <u>predetermined</u> people's lives (decided <u>what will happen</u>), though people do have <u>free will</u> (see p.20).

3) **BENEVOLENT** — Allah is <u>all-good</u> — he can do no evil. He <u>cares</u> for his people — this is seen in his <u>intervention</u> in the world, e.g. his <u>revelations</u> to the prophets were to show people how to live a <u>good life</u>.

4) **JUST** — Muslims believe Allah will <u>judge</u> people's behaviour in a <u>fair way</u>. This concept is particularly <u>important</u> to <u>Shi'a</u> Muslims — known as <u>'Adl</u>, it's one of the <u>'Usul ad-Din</u> (see p.16).

5) **IMMANENT** — Allah is <u>present</u> and <u>involved</u> in the world. He's <u>close</u> to every human and <u>knows</u> them.

6) **TRANSCENDENT** — Allah's also <u>above everything</u> — he can't be thought of in <u>human</u> terms. He has <u>no equal</u>.

"And We have already created man and know what his soul whispers to him, and We are closer to him than [his] jugular vein." Qur'an 50:16

There are <u>ninety-nine names</u> for Allah listed in the Qur'an. Each refers to one of his <u>characteristics</u>. Points <u>1-4</u> above are <u>each</u> English translations of one of these names (originally in <u>Arabic</u>). Muslims recite them in <u>daily prayers</u>.

Adam and Ibrahim were Prophets...

Belief in the prophets is an article of faith for both Sunnis and Shi'as (p.16).

1) Allah's <u>compassion</u> means he can't leave people to <u>sin</u> without <u>helping</u> them. So he sends <u>messages</u> about how to live a <u>good</u> life. He almost always does this via <u>angels</u>, who pass on his words to human <u>prophets</u> (rasuls). <u>Risalah</u> is the concept of <u>messengership</u> — the way Allah <u>communicates</u> with <u>humans</u>.

2) Allah <u>chose</u> many people as <u>prophets</u>. <u>25</u> prophets are mentioned in the <u>Qur'an</u>, although some believe there have been <u>124 000</u>. Some prophets were given <u>holy books</u> to pass on to humankind.

3) Muslims believe the prophets taught the <u>same basic ideas</u>, most importantly belief in <u>one god</u>. They see all the prophets as <u>equal</u> to each other — "We make no distinction between any of them" (Qur'an 2:136).

4) Muslims believe the <u>prophets</u> performed <u>miracles</u> — they did so to <u>prove</u> they were really prophets.

5) The first prophet was <u>Adam</u>, who was also the <u>first man</u>, created by Allah in his image. Others were <u>Ibrahim</u> (Abraham), <u>Isma'il</u> (Ishmael), <u>Musa</u> (Moses), <u>Dawud</u> (David), <u>Isa</u> (Jesus) and <u>Muhammad</u>.

6) <u>Adam</u> was sent to <u>Earth</u> after eating fruit <u>forbidden</u> to him by Allah. Allah <u>forgave</u> him his sin though. Adam is considered to have been the first <u>Muslim</u>. Some believe he first built the <u>Ka'aba</u> (p.23).

7) <u>Ibrahim rejected</u> the idea of <u>many different</u> gods. Muslims can learn from his <u>devotion</u> to Allah — he proved his <u>faith</u> by being willing to <u>sacrifice</u> his own son, <u>Isma'il</u> (see p.24). Ibrahim is thought to have rebuilt the <u>Ka'aba</u> and he and his family's story plays an <u>important role</u> in the <u>hajj</u> rituals (see p.23).

Key Beliefs in Islam

...Isma'il, Musa, Dawud, Isa and Muhammad were Prophets too

1) Ibrahim's son Isma'il was also a prophet and helped him build the Ka'aba. It's believed many Arabs, including Muhammad, are descended from Isma'il — he's known as Abul Arab, the father of the Arabs.

2) Musa is the only prophet that Allah spoke to directly, rather than through the angel Jibril (Gabriel). He's important as he kept trying to guide people to believing in one god, even when they worshipped others.

3) Dawud is known for killing Jalut (Goliath) during a battle between Jalut's large army and Talut's (Saul's) smaller one. Dawud later succeeded Talut as king. As well as his bravery, Muslims can learn from his wisdom and his loyalty to Allah — he would pray for a third of each night.

4) Allah sent Isa when he thought people had strayed from Musa's teachings. Muslims believe Isa wasn't crucified (Allah wouldn't let that happen) but after 3 years' teaching Allah brought him up into heaven.

5) Muslims believe all these prophets paved the way for Muhammad:

> **Muhammad**
>
> - Muhammad was born about 570 CE in Makkah (Mecca). One day, while Muhammad was meditating, Allah sent the angel Jibril to him with a message.
> - Muhammad was scared at first, but as Jibril gradually revealed more and more of the message from Allah, Muhammad began preaching this message to others.
> - The early messages said people should worship one god, Allah, and that people would be judged on their behaviour. Later on, the revelations gave more detail on how Muslims should live their lives.
> - Eventually, this message from Allah was written down as the Qur'an. The Qur'an is seen by Muslims as a miracle — the final revelation from Allah.
> - Muhammad is often called the 'seal of the prophets' — most Muslims believe he was the last prophet that there will be. He is believed to have been a wise leader, who settled disputes and brought different communities together. He performed several miracles.
> - As Muhammad was Allah's last prophet, Muslims pay particular attention to his words and actions. They use them to work out how to live their lives (p.19), as they see him as a role model.

The Qur'an is the Word of Allah

Qur'an is sometimes spelt 'Koran' in English.

1) Muslims think the Qur'an is the most important holy book. They believe it's a complete and accurate record of Allah's exact words to Muhammad, as Qur'an 53:10-11 describes: "he revealed to His Servant what he revealed. The heart did not lie [about] what it saw." The Qur'an allows humans to know Allah.

2) In the Qur'an, Allah tells Muslims what they need to know and how to lead their lives to please him. Muslims try to live according to its guidance. This helps them be rewarded by Allah and get to Paradise.

3) Many Muslims learn the Qur'an by heart. The Qur'an was revealed in Arabic — if it's written in another language the meaning might change, so Muslims learn Arabic to ensure they're reading the true Qur'an.

4) There's often dispute over how to interpret the Qur'an though, e.g. in relation to jihad (p.23). It can be difficult to apply its teachings to modern life, because so much has changed since it was revealed.

The Qur'an is Divided into 114 Surahs

1) The Qur'an is organised into 114 surahs (chapters), each made up of ayahs (verses). The surahs are in order of length — longest first, shortest last (except surah 1, a short statement of Muslims' basic beliefs).

2) Because the Qur'an is so important, Muslims treat it with great respect. The Qur'an is often ornately decorated, inside and out. Many Muslims:

> 1. keep their Qur'an wrapped up to keep it clean
> 2. wash their hands before touching it
> 3. keep it on a higher shelf than all other books
> 4. place it on a special stand when they read it

3) The Qur'an is read during private and public prayers, so Muslims get to know it well.

Key Beliefs in Islam

Allah revealed <u>holy books</u> to <u>other prophets</u> as well. Angels were <u>messengers</u> for Allah.

There are Other Holy Books in Islam

As well as the <u>Qur'an</u>, Muslims see the <u>Sahifah</u>, the <u>Tawrat</u>, the <u>Zabur</u> and the <u>Injil</u> as <u>holy books</u>. But they believe they've been <u>changed</u> over time through <u>editing</u>, and <u>only the Qur'an</u> exists in its <u>original form</u>.

1) The first <u>holy book</u> is thought to have been given to <u>Ibrahim</u>. Known as the <u>Sahifah</u> (scrolls), it is now <u>lost</u>. The Qur'an <u>mentions</u> it several times, for example in Qur'an 87:18-19.

2) The <u>Tawrat</u> (Torah) is the book given to <u>Musa</u>. It's the main <u>Jewish</u> holy book. The Qur'an says it contains the "judgement of Allah" (Qur'an 5:43) so it's <u>valued</u> by Muslims. It includes the <u>Ten Commandments</u>, basic rules for a <u>religious life</u>.

> "We sent down the Torah, in which was guidance and light." Qur'an 5:44

3) The <u>Zabur</u> (Psalms) was given to <u>Dawud</u>. It's thought to be linked to the <u>Psalms</u> of <u>David</u> in the Christian <u>Bible</u> and the Jewish <u>Tenakh</u>, but many Muslims believe the <u>original</u> has been corrupted, perhaps beyond recognition.

> "...to David We gave the book [of Psalms]." Qur'an 4:163

4) Muslims believe Allah gave the <u>Injil</u> to <u>Isa</u> — Qur'an 57:27 says "We sent ... Our messengers and followed [them] with Jesus ... and gave him the Gospel". They think the Injil <u>prophesies</u> the coming of <u>Muhammad</u>. Many Muslims believe the Christian <u>New Testament</u> contains the <u>same ideas</u> as those given to Isa, but not his exact words. Others think the <u>Injil</u> was <u>another book</u> entirely.

5) Muslims also pay a lot of attention to the <u>guidance</u> and <u>example</u> they get from the following:

Hadith	**Sunnah**
The <u>hadith</u> are <u>reports</u> of <u>Muhammad's</u> words and actions, recorded by his <u>followers</u>. They're <u>not</u> in the <u>Qur'an</u> — they weren't revealed by <u>Allah</u>. Each one's been assessed as to how <u>authentic</u> it is. There are different <u>collections</u> of them, e.g. Sahih al-Bukhari, Sahih Muslim and Sunan Abi Dawud.	The <u>sunnah</u> sets out <u>Muhammad's way of life</u>, as recorded in the <u>hadith</u>.

6) The <u>hadith</u> and the <u>sunnah</u> give <u>valuable advice</u> in <u>addition</u> to the Qur'an, especially on issues concerning <u>daily life</u> — but some Muslims believe it's <u>best</u> just to use the <u>Qur'an</u>, as the hadith might be <u>unreliable</u>.

7) <u>Shi'a</u> Muslims also follow the <u>hadith</u> (sayings) of the <u>imams</u>, especially those of <u>Ali</u>.

Angels are Allah's Messengers

> "They exalt [Him] night and day [and] do not slacken." Qur'an 21:20

1) The <u>purpose</u> of angels is to <u>follow</u> Allah's <u>orders</u> and <u>communicate</u> with humans, often via the <u>prophets</u>. In heaven, they <u>praise</u> him and <u>guard</u> his throne. They <u>welcome</u> humans into <u>paradise</u>.

2) They're thought to be <u>genderless</u>, made of <u>light</u> and to have <u>wings</u>. They're <u>immortal</u> and don't have <u>free will</u>, as their role is to obey Allah — they're therefore <u>incapable</u> of <u>sin</u>. Allah created them <u>before</u> humans.

3) Some angels <u>record</u> people's <u>good</u> and <u>bad deeds</u> for the <u>Day of Judgement</u> — Qur'an 43:80 says "Our messengers are with them recording". <u>Guardian</u> angels <u>protect</u> people from <u>danger</u> and <u>evil</u>. Some think they're the same thing and <u>recording</u> angels act as <u>guardians</u> too.

4) Belief in angels is an <u>article of faith</u> for <u>Sunnis</u>, so it's <u>important</u>. The thought of a guardian angel can be <u>comforting</u> for Muslims. Having an angel recording their deeds can <u>influence</u> Muslims to do <u>good things</u>.

5) <u>Jibril</u> (who you might know as <u>Gabriel</u>) is an <u>important angel</u>. He revealed Allah's words (the <u>Qur'an</u>) to <u>Muhammad</u>. He also revealed messages to <u>other prophets</u>, so he's known as the <u>angel of revelation</u>. He told <u>Maryam</u> (Mary) she was pregnant with <u>Isa</u> (Jesus) — see Qur'an 19:16-22.

> "Gabriel ... has brought the Qur'an down upon your heart, [O Muhammad], by permission of Allah." Qur'an 2:97

6) <u>Mika'il</u> (Michael) is <u>important</u> too — he's named in Qur'an 2:98. He asks <u>Allah</u> to <u>forgive</u> people's <u>sins</u>.

7) <u>Izra'il</u> (Azrael) is the <u>angel of death</u> (Qur'an 32:11). He takes <u>souls</u> from people's <u>bodies</u> when they die.

8) It's believed that <u>Israfil</u> (Raphael) will blow the trumpet on the <u>Day of Judgement</u>.

Tawrat, Zabur, Injil, Jibril, Izra'il...

...there are lots of names on this page. Without looking at the book, see if you can write down all the names of the holy books and of the angels, as well as a sentence about each one.

Islam	Life after Death

You have to be able to compare <u>Muslim</u> beliefs about the <u>afterlife</u> with <u>Christian</u> ones — have a look at p.6.

Al-Qadr means Predestination

1) <u>Al-Qadr</u> is the idea that Allah has decided <u>everything</u> that will <u>happen</u>. This idea appears in teachings such as Sahih al-Bukhari 78:685, in which Muhammad said <u>vowing</u> to do something "does not bring about ... anything [Allah] has not decreed" — humans <u>can't</u> choose to do something Allah hasn't <u>chosen</u> for them.

2) This might seem to be <u>contradicted</u> by the idea of the <u>Day of Judgement</u> (see below) when Allah will judge people on the basis of their <u>actions</u>. That suggests people have <u>free will</u> and can <u>choose</u> how they <u>act</u> — there'd be <u>no point</u> judging them on their actions if what they did had <u>already</u> been <u>decided</u> by Allah.

3) However, many Muslims believe in a <u>mix</u> of these two ideas:

<u>Sunnis</u> tend to believe Allah knows everything that's going to happen — he's <u>above</u> normal laws of <u>time</u>, so knows what humans will choose <u>before</u> they've chosen it. It's believed humans <u>choose</u> their actions, but Allah has made it <u>impossible</u> that they'll choose anything <u>other</u> than what he's <u>decided</u>. Some think once someone's <u>chosen to act</u>, the act becomes 'theirs' so they can be <u>judged</u> for it.

<u>Shi'as</u> focus a bit more on <u>free will</u>. They often believe Allah has <u>ultimate control</u> and the <u>power</u> to <u>change</u> things in the world if he <u>wants</u>, but that people's lives are usually <u>determined</u> by their <u>choices</u>. Like Sunnis, they tend to believe Allah <u>knows</u> what's going to happen as he is <u>outside</u> 'human' <u>time</u> — but for Shi'as, what happens is what people <u>choose</u> for themselves.

4) To some Muslims, the idea of al-Qadr is <u>comforting</u> — if something <u>bad</u> has happened, it's <u>reassuring</u> to feel it's part of Allah's <u>plan</u>. Some people like to feel that they're <u>guided</u> to do Allah's <u>will</u> by al-Qadr.

Yawm ad-Din is the Day of Judgement

1) On Yawm ad-Din, Allah <u>decides</u> how people will spend the <u>afterlife</u>, based on their <u>behaviour</u> during their lives. It's then <u>too late</u> to <u>beg forgiveness</u> for any <u>wrongdoing</u>.

2) Allah will judge <u>everyone</u> — not just Muslims. On Yawm ad-Din, the dead will be <u>resurrected</u>. Everyone will receive a <u>record</u> of their <u>good</u> and <u>bad</u> deeds, on which they'll be <u>judged</u>.

"We will call forth every people with their record [of deeds]." Qur'an 17:71

3) The idea of judgement is <u>important</u> as it encourages Muslims to live their lives in a <u>good way</u>. It can be comforting to think <u>bad</u> people will be <u>punished</u>. Other Muslims think it's best to concentrate on <u>this life</u> — they think people should do <u>good</u> things anyway, not just because they're focusing on their <u>afterlife</u>.

4) <u>Intentions</u> are also important — <u>intending</u> to do something <u>good</u> counts, but intending to do something <u>bad</u> but <u>not doing</u> it <u>doesn't</u> count <u>against</u> you (Sahih Muslim 1:233).

It was paradise for everyone except the gardeners...

Al-Akhirah Means the Afterlife

1) Belief in the afterlife — <u>al-Akhirah</u> — is a key part of Islam. The <u>afterlife</u> is where people <u>go</u> after the <u>Day of Judgement</u>.

2) The <u>reward</u> for good people will be entry into <u>jannah</u> (<u>paradise</u>) — this is a place of <u>peace</u>, <u>happiness</u> and <u>beauty</u>. The <u>Qur'an</u> refers to Paradise as "Gardens of Pleasure" (Qur'an 31:8).

"...for one whose scales are heavy [with good deeds], He will be in a pleasant life. ...for one whose scales are light, His refuge will be an abyss." Qur'an 101:6-9

3) For those who have done bad deeds, the punishment is <u>jahannam</u> (<u>hell</u>). The Qur'an describes jahannam as a place of <u>scorching fire</u> and <u>boiling water</u>. Here, those who have <u>ignored</u> Allah's teaching and failed to act <u>righteously</u> will be punished. Allah is <u>merciful</u> though, so they may eventually be sent to <u>paradise</u>.

4) The <u>Qur'an</u> sometimes mentions a 'barrier' between this world and the next called <u>barzakh</u>, where people's <u>souls</u> stay from the time they <u>die</u> until <u>Yawm ad-Din</u>. Many Muslims focus more on <u>jannah</u> and <u>jahannam</u> than <u>barzakh</u>.

"...behind them is a barrier, until the Day they are resurrected." Qur'an 23:100

The Day of Judgement — yeah, when is the exam exactly?

To help you when the day arrives, try out this exam-style question.

Describe two differences between Muslim and Christian teachings about the afterlife. [4]

EXAM QUESTION

Worship and Duties

To be faithful Muslims, <u>Sunni</u> Muslims need to follow the <u>Five Pillars</u>, and <u>Shi'as</u> the <u>Ten Obligatory Acts</u>.

Sunni Muslims are Required to Follow the Five Pillars of Islam

1. Shahadah — declaration of faith

"There is no god but Allah, and Muhammad is his messenger." Muslims should say this <u>several times</u> a day. It's said at <u>birth</u> and <u>death</u>, as well as in the <u>call to prayer</u> (adhan) and <u>prayers</u>. People can <u>convert</u> to Islam by saying it. The exact words aren't in the <u>Qur'an</u>, but come from <u>passages</u> such as Qur'an 3:18 — "Allah witnesses that there is no deity except Him". It's <u>essential</u> to <u>Shi'a</u> Muslims too, though it's <u>not</u> one of their <u>Ten Obligatory Acts</u> (see below). They add "Ali is the helper of Allah", as Ali is <u>significant</u> to their faith (see p.16).

2. Salah — prayer five times a day

The <u>second most important</u> duty in Islam. Muslims should pray <u>five times</u> a day — at <u>sunrise</u>, around <u>noon</u>, late <u>afternoon</u>, after <u>sunset</u>, and late <u>evening</u>. See below for more detail.

3. Zakah — charitable giving

Each person decides <u>where</u> to <u>donate</u> their money. Zakah encourages <u>generosity</u> and <u>compassion</u>. See p.22 for more detail.

4. Sawm — obligation to fast during Ramadan

<u>Ramadan</u> is the <u>ninth month</u> of the Muslim calendar. Muslims are obliged to fast during it. This teaches <u>self-discipline</u>, which brings Muslims <u>closer</u> to Allah. See p.22 for more detail.

5. Hajj — pilgrimage to Makkah

<u>Every</u> Muslim should do <u>hajj</u> at least once. It's only <u>obligatory</u> if you can <u>afford</u> it and you're <u>healthy</u> enough to do it. See p.23 for more.

Shi'a Muslims Follow the Ten Obligatory Acts

<u>Four</u> — <u>salah</u>, <u>sawm</u>, <u>zakah</u> and <u>hajj</u> — are the same as the <u>Five Pillars</u>. The rest are:

Sunnis may also see the <u>acts</u> in the <u>blue</u> boxes as <u>important</u>, but <u>don't follow</u> those in the <u>purple</u> boxes.

Khums — annual tax

<u>Khums</u> is a kind of <u>tax</u> Shi'as pay each year on any 'profit' (<u>excess money</u>) they <u>earn</u>, at a rate of <u>20%</u>. It goes towards supporting <u>Islamic education</u> and anyone <u>descended</u> from <u>Muhammad</u> who's in need.

Jihad — 'struggle'

The word means '<u>struggle</u>' or '<u>striving</u>'. There are <u>two types</u> of jihad — the '<u>greater</u>' jihad is Muslims' <u>personal</u> struggle to live a <u>good life</u>, and the '<u>lesser</u>' jihad is Muslims' struggle to <u>defend Islam</u> against its <u>critics</u>. See p.23 for more.

Amr-bil-Maroof and Nahi Anil Munkar

These come as a <u>pair</u>. The phrase means "enjoin what is right and forbid what is wrong" (Qur'an 9:71) — it asks Muslims to encourage <u>good</u> deeds and avoid <u>bad</u> ones.

Tawalla and Tabarra

These also come as a <u>pair</u>. They mean '<u>love</u>' and '<u>aloofness</u>' — Muslims should <u>love</u> those who <u>follow Allah</u> and they <u>shouldn't associate</u> themselves with anyone who's an 'enemy' of Allah or Muhammad.

<u>Twelver</u> Shi'as follow these ten acts. Other Shi'as follow <u>different</u> sets of acts.

Salah is Very Important

You need to be able to compare <u>salah</u> with <u>Christian worship</u> — see p.8 and p.11. There's more on <u>salah</u> on the next page.

1) <u>Salah</u>, the five daily prayers, should ideally take place in a <u>mosque</u>, but they can be done anywhere. Sunnis only <u>combine</u> the prayers if they have a very <u>good reason</u> that <u>prevents</u> them praying at five separate times, e.g. if they're <u>travelling</u>. Shi'as <u>combine</u> some prayers, so they tend to pray <u>three</u> times a day rather than <u>five</u> — but they still say <u>all</u> the <u>same</u> prayers.

2) Each <u>prayer cycle</u> (<u>rak'ah</u>, see p.22) includes saying '<u>Allahu akbar</u>' ('<u>God is great</u>') multiple times, as well as reciting the <u>first surah</u> of the Qur'an (known as the <u>Fatiha</u>) and <u>other verses</u> from the Qur'an.

3) Most men are obliged to go to <u>Friday</u> prayers (<u>Jummah</u>) at the mosque. Requirements <u>vary</u>, but a <u>certain number</u> of people should be present. The Friday prayers are <u>led</u> by an <u>imam</u>, who also gives two <u>sermons</u>.

4) Salah keeps Muslims in <u>close contact</u> with Allah and encourages moral and spiritual <u>discipline</u>. This keeps them from committing <u>shirk</u> (see p.17) and increases <u>taqwa</u> (reverence for Allah). It's an expression of <u>solidarity</u> — doing the same as other Muslims, which is a reminder that everyone's <u>equal</u>.

"...prayer prohibits immorality and wrongdoing, and the remembrance of Allah is greater." Qur'an 29:45

Worship and Duties

There are Rituals to Follow with Salah

You need to be able to compare salah to Christian worship (see p.8 and 11). There's more on salah on the previous page.

1) Wudu (washing before prayer) is important — Muslims must be pure and clean when approaching Allah, both physically and spiritually. Muslims wash their face, arms, feet and part of the hair before prayers. A prayer mat is often used when not praying in a mosque, in order to ensure cleanliness.

2) Muslims should face Makkah in Saudi Arabia when praying. The direction of Makkah is called the qiblah.

3) The rak'ah is a set prayer ritual. It may be repeated several times at each prayer session. Each rak'ah involves standing, then kneeling, then putting your forehead to the ground as a sign of submission to Allah. If several Muslims are praying in one place, then the rak'ah is done together at the same time.

4) Shi'a prayers are a bit different. Shi'as touch their foreheads to a clay or wooden tablet during the rak'ah — they believe putting their forehead on something natural is what Muhammad advised. The tablet is often made of clay from Karbala, where Husayn was killed (p.24), to remind Shi'as of his sacrifice.

5) When at the mosque, women and men pray separately — so people concentrate on Allah rather than on the opposite sex. This has changed in some mosques though, where mixed prayer is allowed.

6) Many Muslims perform salah in the home rather than at the mosque, particularly women. It's seen as an important way for children to learn about Islam. Some Muslim families may have a room just for salah.

Zakah is Charitable Giving

Some Shi'as pay khums (see p.21) in addition to zakah.

1) Zakah involves redistributing wealth. Muslims think wealth's given by Allah, so should be used to serve him.

2) The amount is usually 2.5% of a person's wealth each year. Muslims can decide how much to give and who they want to donate it to. It's often used to help Muslims who are less well off, or given to charities or mosques.

> "Zakah...[is] for bringing hearts together." Qur'an 9:60. This verse also lists who zakah is for, including the "poor and... needy".

3) Zakah is beneficial because it makes the distribution of wealth fairer and helps those in need. It encourages Muslims to think of others who may not be as well off as them. It's a sign of concern for others and encourages generosity.

Sawm is Fasting During Ramadan

> "O you who have believed, decreed upon you is fasting ... that you may become righteous..." Qur'an 2:183

1) Muslims must fast between sunrise and sunset during the month of Ramadan. The Muslim calendar is lunar (determined by the moon) so Ramadan isn't always at the same time of the solar (sun) year.

2) Muslims eat just before sunrise (suhur) and just after sunset (iftar). The fast is often broken slowly with dates, before a bigger meal later. Iftar is often eaten with family or friends, or sometimes at the mosque.

> There are exceptions to the obligation to fast — the Qur'an recognises it might not be possible or healthy for everyone to fast.
> 1. Children don't have to fast until they're about 12 years old. Old people (there's no specific age) don't have to fast either.
> 2. People can be excused for medical reasons. Women who are pregnant, breastfeeding or menstruating can also be excused. It's fine to take medicine which has to be regular, e.g. antibiotics. If you're on a journey, you can be excused too.
> 3. If you've missed a few days of the fast, Qur'an 2:184 says that you should make up for it, either by fasting for the same number of days later on, or by giving food to someone who might need it.

3) Sawm doesn't just involve not eating or drinking, but also abstaining from other things such as listening to music, sex and smoking. Muslims should also try particularly hard to avoid bad thoughts or actions.

4) Ramadan is a time of both physical and moral self-discipline, and a time of obedience to Allah. It's supposed to help Muslims understand hunger, and so makes them more willing to help others.

5) It's also a time to show publicly that Allah matters more than any physical needs.

> Laylat al-Qadr (the Night of Destiny or Power) falls during Ramadan. Muslims believe Muhammad received at least part of the Qur'an during this night. So Ramadan is also a time of thanksgiving for the Qur'an — during Ramadan it's read from beginning to end at the mosque. Laylat al-Qadr is the holiest night of the year — the Qur'an says it's "better than a thousand months" (Qur'an 97:3) and many Muslims spend the whole night at the mosque to celebrate it, praying and listening to readings of the Qur'an. It's important because many Muslims believe Allah will forgive their sins on this night.

Worship and Duties

The <u>hajj</u> is an important action for a Muslim to do. Around <u>2 million</u> Muslims go each year.

The Hajj is the Pilgrimage to Makkah

"...proclaim to the people the Hajj..." Qur'an 22:27

1) Muslims must make the pilgrimage at least <u>once</u> in their lifetime, as long as they can <u>afford</u> it and they're <u>healthy</u> enough to cope with the journey. It has to happen in the Muslim month of Dhu'l-Hijja to <u>count</u>.

2) <u>Adam</u>, <u>Ibrahim</u> and <u>Isma'il</u> are all associated with <u>Makkah</u> and <u>Muhammad</u> lived there, so it's a holy place.

3) <u>All pilgrims</u> wear simple white clothing (<u>ihram</u>) so they're <u>equal</u> before Allah.

4) The <u>Ka'aba</u> is in Makkah — it's a giant <u>stone cube</u> covered with <u>black cloth</u>. Some Muslims think <u>Ibrahim</u> and <u>Isma'il</u> built it as a place of worship — Qur'an 2:127 suggests they did. Others think <u>Adam</u> built it. It's the <u>holiest place</u> in Islam. Muslims must do <u>seven circuits</u> anticlockwise of the <u>Ka'aba</u>, touching the stone if possible — this ritual is called the <u>tawaf</u>.

5) Next, a pilgrim must make <u>seven journeys</u> between the hills of <u>Safa</u> and <u>Marwa</u> (where Hajar, Ibrahim's wife and servant, searched for water for their son <u>Isma'il</u>). This part of the pilgrimage is called the <u>sa'y</u>. Pilgrims then draw <u>water</u> from the <u>Zamzam Well</u>, which <u>Allah</u> made for Hajar.

6) Then pilgrims go to <u>Mount Arafat</u> to <u>stand</u> and <u>pray</u> for Allah's <u>forgiveness</u>. This is where Muslims believe <u>Adam</u> was <u>forgiven</u> after being <u>thrown out</u> of Eden and also where the <u>Day of Judgement</u> will take place.

7) The pilgrims spend the night at <u>Muzdalifa</u>, a valley between <u>Arafat</u> and <u>Mina</u>, where they collect <u>pebbles</u>.

8) The <u>pebbles</u> are then thrown at three <u>pillars</u> in <u>Mina</u>, to symbolise driving the <u>devil</u> away — Ibrahim is believed to have once thrown stones at <u>Shaytan</u> (the devil). This happens on <u>Id ul-Adha</u> (see p.24).

9) The title 'hajji' is given to those who <u>complete</u> the hajj. Many find the <u>hajj</u> helps their <u>faith</u> and increases <u>unity</u> between Muslims. Some <u>hadith</u> say it cleanses the hajji of <u>all sins</u>, e.g. Sahih al-Bukhari 26:596: "he will return (after Hajj free from all sins) as if he were born anew".

There are Two Kinds of Jihad

Jihad means '<u>striving</u>' or '<u>struggle</u>' and is often <u>misunderstood</u> by non-Muslims. It's one of the <u>Ten Obligatory Acts</u> for <u>Shi'as</u> (see p.21) but it's part of <u>Sunni</u> Islam too. Most Muslims believe there are <u>two kinds</u>:

The Greater Jihad

1) This is every Muslim's struggle to <u>obey</u> Allah, <u>follow</u> his teachings and become a <u>better</u> Muslim.
2) It's the <u>greater struggle</u> because it's <u>individual</u> and <u>personal</u>. Qur'an 35:18 says "no bearer of burdens will bear the burden of another" (burdens mean sins), so you and you alone will be held <u>responsible</u> for your <u>behaviour</u>. If you're not a good Muslim, it's <u>harder</u> to help make the world better (<u>lesser jihad</u>).

The Lesser Jihad

See p.67 for the <u>requirements</u> for declaring <u>military jihad</u>.

1) This is the <u>struggle</u> to make the world a <u>better place</u>. Part of this means struggling against wrongs such as <u>poverty</u> and <u>injustice</u>.
2) Part of it is the struggle to <u>defend Islam</u> against threats. It can be in <u>peaceful</u> ways, such as helping others be good Muslims.

> When Islam began, Muslims fought to survive as people of other religions persecuted them. The Qur'an reflects this struggle, which is why it refers to defending Islam against its enemies.

3) The <u>Qur'an</u> and Islamic law say that actual fighting should only be in <u>self-defence</u> and <u>not</u> against people who <u>aren't fighting</u> (<u>non-combatants</u>) — "Permission [to fight] has been given to those who are being fought" (Qur'an 22:39). Qur'an 4:75 says Muslims should fight on behalf of people being <u>oppressed</u>.
4) <u>Islamic terrorists</u> claim the Qur'an supports <u>violence</u> to <u>defend</u> Islam against <u>oppression</u>, e.g. Qur'an 2:193 says "...if they cease, then there is to be no aggression <u>except</u> against the <u>oppressors</u>". The <u>vast majority</u> of Muslims <u>condemn</u> this and think that Islamic terrorists aren't <u>true Muslims</u>.

And that's the last of the duties...

You might see some of the Arabic words spelt slightly differently, e.g. zakat rather than zakah or Eid al-Adha rather than Id ul-Adha. Make sure you always stick to one spelling in the exam.

Areas of Study 1, 2 & 3 — Muslim Beliefs and Living the Muslim Life

Islam | **Festivals**

Id ul-Adha is Important to Sunnis and Shi'as

1) <u>Id ul-Adha</u> is a <u>festival</u> celebrating complete <u>obedience</u> to Allah, as it commemorates the time when <u>Ibrahim</u> nearly <u>sacrificed</u> his own <u>son</u>, <u>Isma'il</u>. It's a very <u>important</u> festival and it forms part of the <u>hajj</u>.

2) Ibrahim <u>dreamt</u> that Allah told him to sacrifice <u>Isma'il</u>. He told Isma'il about it and Isma'il <u>agreed</u> it had to be done. But at the last minute, Allah told Ibrahim to sacrifice a <u>ram</u> in place of <u>Isma'il</u>, so Isma'il <u>survived</u>. It was a test of Ibrahim's <u>loyalty</u> to Allah.

> " '...my son, indeed I have seen in a dream that I [must] sacrifice you ...' He said, 'O my father, do as you are commanded.' " Qur'an 37:102

3) Muslims should attend mosque on Id ul-Adha — the <u>service</u> includes communal <u>prayers</u> and a <u>sermon</u> focused on the importance of <u>obedience</u> to Allah and the <u>lessons</u> to be learnt from Ibrahim and Isma'il.

4) Id ul-Adha is a time of communal <u>joy</u> and <u>festivity</u> lasting up to <u>four</u> days. Muslims dress up in their <u>best clothes</u> and spend time with <u>family</u> and <u>friends</u>. <u>Presents</u> are often exchanged. An animal is often <u>sacrificed</u> — the <u>family</u> keeps a third, a third goes to <u>relatives</u> or <u>neighbours</u> and a third to the <u>poor</u>.

Id ul-Fitr Marks the End of Ramadan

<u>Id ul-Fitr</u> is important to Sunnis <u>and</u> Shi'as.

1) <u>Id ul-Fitr</u> is at the <u>end</u> of <u>Ramadan</u> (see p.22). It's a day of <u>thanksgiving</u> to <u>Allah</u> for giving Muslims the <u>strength</u> to <u>fast</u> for a month. It's a <u>joyful</u> festival which also celebrates the fact that Muslims have <u>completed</u> the <u>fourth pillar</u> of Islam by observing <u>sawm</u>, and therefore have become <u>closer</u> to Allah.

2) Muslims pay a special <u>zakah</u> for Id ul-Fitr. About £5, it <u>helps</u> Muslims who are <u>less well off</u> to celebrate.

3) The festival involves a <u>service</u> at the mosque or outdoors, and a meal to <u>break the fast</u>. It's a time of <u>celebration</u>, when <u>family</u> and <u>friends</u> meet up and <u>presents</u> are exchanged. <u>Thousands</u> attend <u>celebrations</u> of <u>Id ul-Adha</u> and <u>Id ul-Fitr</u> in the <u>UK</u> — many find it important for <u>community cohesion</u> between <u>Muslims</u> and with those of <u>other faiths</u>.

Id ul-Ghadeer is Important for Shi'a Muslims

<u>Sunnis</u> don't celebrate Id ul-Ghadeer.

1) <u>Id ul-Ghadeer</u> commemorates a speech, recorded in <u>hadith</u>, which <u>Muhammad</u> made after his <u>final hajj</u>. <u>Shi'as</u> believe he said <u>Ali</u> should be the <u>next Muslim leader</u> after his <u>death</u> — he used a word for '<u>master</u>'. <u>Sunnis</u> think Muhammad was just saying Ali should be <u>respected</u>, as the word also means '<u>trusted friend</u>'.

2) After the speech, it's believed Qur'an 5:3 was revealed: "This day I have perfected for you your religion".

3) <u>Shi'as</u> venerate Ali and <u>celebrate</u> the festival as the day he was <u>chosen</u> as <u>leader</u>. Shi'as <u>fast</u>, have a <u>ritual bath</u> and say prayers, including the <u>Du'a Nudba</u>. They reaffirm their <u>commitment</u> to Islam with a <u>vow</u>.

Ashura Commemorates the Death of Husayn

1) <u>Ashura</u> is mostly a <u>Shi'a</u> festival, but it was <u>originally</u> a <u>compulsory</u> day of <u>fasting</u> for all Muslims. When Muhammad said Muslims should observe <u>sawm</u> during <u>Ramadan</u>, fasting on <u>Ashura</u> became <u>voluntary</u>.

2) <u>Sunnis</u> now tend to think of it as a day of <u>atonement</u>. Many Sunnis <u>fast</u>, but it's <u>not</u> compulsory. It's believed that fasting may <u>absolve</u> people of their <u>minor sins</u> in the <u>previous year</u>.

3) It's significant for <u>Shi'as</u> as the day <u>Husayn</u>, Ali's son and Muhammad's grandson (see p.16), was <u>killed</u> in a battle. The <u>ten days</u> up to and including Ashura (Ashura is the <u>tenth</u> day) are a period of <u>mourning</u>.

4) On Ashura, Shi'as wear <u>black</u> as a sign of <u>mourning</u>. There are often public <u>processions</u> and '<u>passion plays</u>', in which the story of <u>Husayn</u> is <u>performed</u>. <u>Poems</u> or <u>stories</u> about Husayn are often read out.

5) Some Shi'as hurt themselves to <u>commemorate</u> Husayn's <u>suffering</u>. This is <u>banned</u> in some countries.

6) For Shi'as, Ashura is a reminder of the <u>suffering</u> the Shi'a <u>community</u> has experienced — Shi'as have been <u>persecuted</u> as a minority. The <u>processions</u> are sometimes used as <u>protests</u> against <u>injustice</u>.

Feeling festive? Celebrate with an exam-style question...

Explain two ways in which Muslims celebrate Id ul-Fitr.   [4]

EXAM QUESTION

Revision Summary

There was a lot in that section, so now it's your chance to find out how much you remember. These are exam-style questions, so you can get an idea of how long and detailed your answers have to be.

If you're stuck on anything, go back to the relevant page in the section and then try the question again. There are extra marks for spelling, punctuation, grammar and use of specialist terminology available in some questions, so make sure you check your writing and use technical jargon where appropriate.

These questions are worth 3 marks. You need to make three brief points in your answer.

1) Outline three of the Shi'a beliefs included in the 'Usul ad-Din.

2) Outline three characteristics of Allah.

3) Outline three of the Five Pillars followed by Sunni Muslims.

4) Outline three features of the rituals that are part of salah.

5) Outline three reasons someone might be exempt from the obligation to fast during Ramadan.

6) Outline three aspects of the hajj.

7) Outline three beliefs about jihad.

8) Outline three features of Id ul-Ghadeer.

These are 4 mark questions. To get full marks, you need to develop the points you make.

9) Explain two ways in which Muhammad is important for Muslims.

10) Explain two Muslim beliefs about angels.

11) Explain two ways of giving to charity in Islam.

12) Explain two reasons why Ashura is important for Shi'a Muslims.

Your points need to be nice and clear in the longer answer questions. This means you need to make sure your writing is well organised.

These questions are worth 5 marks, so you need to develop and explain your answer. You also need to include an example from Muslim teachings in your answer.

13) Explain two Muslim beliefs about the Qur'an.

14) Explain two Muslim teachings about judgement.

15) Explain two reasons why Laylat al-Qadr is important for Muslims.

16) Explain two reasons why performing hajj is important for Muslims.

And the big one — this is a 15 mark question (3 marks are for SPaG and specialist terminology). Use the bullet point list below to help you plan your answer — the list gives you the things you need to include. Remember, you'll need to make sure you've covered arguments for and against the statement.

17) 'The most important thing a Muslim can do is pray five times a day.'
Evaluate this statement. Give arguments that support the statement and arguments that disagree with the statement. You must include:
- examples from Islamic teachings
- different Muslim points of view
- a conclusion.

There's advice on writing essays in the 'Do Well in Your Exam' section.

Judaism   Introduction to Judaism

There are different branches of Judaism, but all Jews believe in one God and follow the Torah as a sacred text.

The Tenakh and the Talmud are the Jewish Sacred Texts

1) The **Tenakh** is the main sacred Jewish text. It's basically the same as the Christian Old Testament, except it's in a different order. The word 'TeNaKh' will help you remember what's in it.

T = Torah (Instructions / Law / Teachings)

The Torah is made up of Genesis, Exodus, Leviticus, Numbers and Deuteronomy.

The Torah is the first five books of the Old Testament. It's seen as the holiest part of the Tenakh — God gave it to Moses. It contains the mitzvot (commandments, see p.28) which Jews are meant to follow. 'Torah' can refer to all Jewish teachings, or to the whole Tenakh, as well as this first part of the Tenakh.

N = Nevi'im (Prophets)

The prophets are believed to have been inspired by God.

This is a collection of books, divided into two parts. The Former Prophets trace the history of the Israelites (ancestors of the Jews) after the death of Moses. The Latter Prophets contain the words of 15 prophets such as Isaiah, Jeremiah and Ezekiel. They encourage Jews to obey God and follow the Torah.

K = Ketuvim (Writings)

This part of the Tenakh is less authoritative than the others.

Among other things, this contains the 'three Ps': Psalms (hymns), Proverbs, and Philosophy.

2) The **Talmud** is a collection of teachings and a record of originally spoken discussions between Torah scholars. It's made up of two parts — the Mishnah, which explains how the mitzvot in the Torah should be applied, and the Gemara, which discusses the Mishnah. It stresses the importance of the Torah:

> "If you have learned much Torah, do not take credit ... — it is for this that you have been formed." Pirkei Avot 2:8

There are Different Branches of Judaism

Orthodox Judaism

1) Orthodox Jews believe that the Torah and Talmud are of divine origin (they come from God). They should be followed to the letter — their teachings should not be changed to adapt to life today.

2) They strictly observe Shabbat (day of rest, see p.31-32), and kashrut (dietary laws, see p.32).

Progressive Judaism

1) Progressive Jews believe the Torah and Talmud are people's interpretation of God's word. They see Judaism as a developing religion, so they apply the sacred texts to modern life in a more flexible way.

2) They tend to follow the mitzvot about morality (see p.28). However, they believe the ritual commandments, e.g. dietary laws, can be adapted or abandoned in response to changes in society.

3) There are two main movements of Progressive Jews:

Reform Judaism	Liberal Judaism
• This is a mix of new and old traditions, e.g. Reform Jews have a Shabbat service but at a different time to Orthodox Jews (p.31).	• Liberal Judaism formed from Reform Judaism — it's similar to but more radical than Reform. It has a similar emphasis on treating everyone equally.
• A key difference from Orthodox Judaism is that women and men are completely equal. Men and women sit together in services and there are male and female rabbis (religious leaders).	• It teaches that observing any of the mitzvot is a matter of carefully considered personal choice.

Masorti (Conservative) Jews follow Jewish law like Orthodox Jews, but with a more liberal interpretation.

Remember, the word 'Torah' can be used in different ways...

EXAM TIP

Make sure it's clear which way you're using it in the exam, so the examiner doesn't get confused.

Key Beliefs in Judaism

Jews have many names for God. One name is 'the Almighty', which is how the exam papers will refer to God.

Jews Believe God has Certain Characteristics

Some write 'G-d' to stop the word 'God' being accidentally erased or damaged.

Although there are different strands of Judaism (see p.26), nearly all Jews believe that God is...

1) **ONE** — Judaism is a monotheistic religion — Jews believe there's only one God. They believe God is one entity — they don't believe God has different parts, as most Christians do (p.2).

2) **ETERNAL** — Jews believe God has and always will exist.

3) **THE CREATOR** — He made everything in the universe. His role as creator is described in Genesis 1 and 2.

4) **OMNIPOTENT** — God is all-powerful — although he still allows each person free will.

5) **OMNISCIENT** — God knows everything, even people's thoughts.

6) **OMNIBENEVOLENT** — God is all-good — he can do no evil.

> "The Lord is good to all; he has compassion on all he has made." Psalm 145:9 NIV

7) **OMNIPRESENT** — God is everywhere at all times. He's beyond time and space.

8) **THE LAWGIVER** — Jews believe they should obey God's laws as part of the covenant (see below).

9) **THE JUDGE** — Jews believe their behaviour will be judged by God after they die (see p.29). However, they believe he is just and merciful. He will save his people from sin and suffering.

10) **TRANSCENDENT** — God is beyond this world. His existence doesn't rely on the universe.

11) **IMMANENT** — But God is present in the world and sustains it — see the concept of Shekhinah below.

Shekhinah is God's Presence on Earth

> "The glory of the Lord filled the temple." 2 Chronicles 7:1

1) The word Shekhinah is used to refer to God when he is present in a particular place on Earth.

2) The term is used to describe God's presence in the tabernacle (a portable place of worship used by Moses — p.28) and the Temple Jews built in Jerusalem. Many Jews pray at the remaining part of the Temple walls in Jerusalem (the Western Wall) as they believe that Shekhinah is still present there.

3) Some Jews believe that Shekhinah is present when they're praying together or discussing the Torah.

4) Shekhinah is often seen as feminine, and has 'feminine' characteristics, such as being caring.

5) The concept of Shekhinah helps Jews understand suffering, as it means God is there alongside them.

Jews Believe in a Covenant Between Them and God

A covenant is a formal agreement between two or more people. God made a covenant with the Jews which defines them as his chosen people.

1) The first covenant was between God and Abraham. Abraham was the first of the founders of Judaism. Jews call him Avraham Avinu ('our father Abraham').

2) God told Abraham to leave his home and go to Canaan (the 'Promised Land').

3) God promised to give Abraham and his wife Sarah a child, and to protect them and their descendants as his chosen people. In return, God asked Abraham and his descendants (known as the Israelites) to obey God and lead by example.

> "The whole land of Canaan ... I will give as an everlasting possession to you and your descendants ... and I will be their God." Genesis 17:8 NIV

4) He asked for all of their male descendants to be circumcised as a sign of this covenant (see p.32).

Israel, in the Middle East, is a state that was founded in 1948 in roughly the same area as Canaan had been. Many Jews see the state of Israel as the fulfilment of the promise of the Promised Land. However, some Orthodox Jews believe that Jews shouldn't have created the state themselves — they should have waited for God's action. Many Progressive Jews only became supportive of the formation of a Jewish state after the Holocaust, in which 6 million Jews were killed by the Nazis.

Make sure you learn how to spell the 'omni-' words correctly.

Shut this book and see if you can write down the characteristics of God listed above, as well as what they mean — you'll only be able to use them correctly in the exam if you understand them.

Key Beliefs in Judaism

God also made a Covenant with Moses

1) <u>Moses</u> was also a <u>founder</u> of Judaism. He led the Jews back to <u>freedom</u> in <u>Canaan</u> after they'd been <u>slaves</u> in Egypt for 400 years (they'd had to leave Canaan due to a famine). This was called the <u>Exodus</u>.

2) On the way back, God made a <u>covenant</u> with Moses at <u>Mount Sinai</u>, setting out in detail what the Israelites had to <u>do</u> in <u>return</u> for being God's <u>chosen people</u>.

3) God gave the <u>Torah</u> to Moses. This included the mitzvot — the <u>Ten Commandments</u> plus many other laws. The Ten Commandments (the <u>Decalogue</u>) were written separately on <u>stone tablets</u>. Moses was also given an <u>explanation</u> of the <u>Torah</u>, known as the <u>oral Torah</u>, which was eventually <u>written down</u> in the <u>Mishnah</u> (p.26).

4) The Israelites <u>promised</u> to "do everything the Lord has said" (Exodus 19:8 NIV).

5) <u>Orthodox</u> Jews believe the <u>Torah</u> came directly from God, but <u>Progressive</u> Jews believe the Torah is people's <u>interpretation</u> of God's word — they think it was written by <u>people</u> rather than <u>God</u>.

> "Now if you obey me fully and keep my covenant, then out of all nations you will be my treasured possession." Exodus 19:5 NIV

The Mitzvot are Jewish Laws

The singular form of mitzvot is <u>mitzvah</u>. It's sometimes translated as a '<u>good deed</u>'.

1) The <u>613 mitzvot</u> cover a variety of issues, including <u>food</u>, how to <u>worship God</u> and how to help the <u>poor</u>.

2) They were taken from the Torah by scholars, who made slightly different lists of them. The <u>standard</u> list was compiled by <u>Maimonides</u> in his <u>Mishneh Torah</u>. The mitzvot can be <u>divided</u> up in different ways:

- <u>248</u> of the mitzvot are <u>positive</u>, telling Jews what they should do. They're called <u>mitzvot aseh</u> in Hebrew.
- <u>365</u> mitzvot are <u>negative</u>, telling Jews what they shouldn't do. They're known as <u>mitzvot ta'aseh</u>.

- <u>Ritual</u> mitzvot list things Jews must or must not do to avoid offending God — they are between <u>a person</u> and <u>God</u>.
- <u>Moral</u> (ethical) mitzvot are about a Jew's dealings with <u>other people</u> — they are between <u>one person</u> and <u>another</u>.

3) The <u>Ten Commandments</u> are <u>important</u> mitzvot. The <u>first</u> is the central belief of Judaism (see p.31).

1. I am the Lord your God.
2. You shall have no other gods before me. You shall not make for yourself an image.... [or] bow down to them or worship them.
3. You shall not misuse the name of the Lord your God.
4. Remember the Sabbath day by keeping it holy.
5. Honour your father and your mother.
6. You shall not murder.
7. You shall not commit adultery.
8. You shall not steal.
9. You shall not give false testimony against your neighbour.
10. You shall not covet.

<u>Don't worship</u> <u>idols</u> (objects or pictures of God).

This means <u>don't lie</u> about <u>other people</u>.

Exodus 20:2-17 NIV

This means <u>don't be jealous</u> of what <u>other people have</u>.

4) Jews believe that humans have <u>free will</u>, so they're <u>responsible</u> for following the mitzvot. This means they can be <u>judged</u> on their actions by God. He will <u>forgive</u> someone who's <u>sorry</u> for their sins though.

5) Orthodox Jews <u>follow</u> the mitzvot <u>closely</u>. They try to go <u>further</u> than the mitzvot, so they don't <u>break one</u> by accident. Progressive Jews follow the mitzvot <u>less strictly</u> (see p.26). Some mitzvot can't be obeyed as they refer to the <u>Temple</u>, which no longer exists, but following as many as possible is a <u>key part</u> of many Jews' <u>relationship with God</u>. Doing so <u>unites</u> Jews and gives them an <u>identity</u> as <u>God's people</u>.

There are Other Important Principles

> "Every danger to human life suspends the [laws of the] Sabbath." Talmud Yoma 83a

1) <u>Pikuach nefesh</u> (saving a life) is <u>more important</u> than any mitzvot, except commandments 1, 2, 6 and 7. It follows the belief in the <u>sanctity of life</u> — life being <u>holy</u> because it's given by <u>God</u>. For example, a doctor can <u>break Shabbat</u> to <u>save</u> someone's <u>life</u>. Their life doesn't have to be in <u>immediate danger</u> — the action can be <u>preventative</u>. See p.50, 52 and 68 for more.

2) Jews believe people are the Earth's <u>custodians</u> — they have a <u>responsibility</u> to <u>look after</u> the world. This includes the idea of <u>tikkun olam</u> ('mending the world') — acting <u>morally</u> to improve life on Earth.

3) <u>Justice</u>, <u>charity</u> and <u>kindness</u> are important morals included in some <u>mitzvot</u>. <u>Gemilut hasadim</u> (acts of loving kindness) is a central principle of Judaism. The concept of <u>tzedakah</u> (charity) is also important — it should be given to make the world more <u>just</u>, so it's an <u>obligation</u> rather than a <u>choice</u>.

Key Beliefs in Judaism

You need to be able to compare <u>Jewish</u> beliefs about <u>life after death</u> with <u>Christian</u> ones, which are on p.6.

Jews have Different Beliefs about the Afterlife

1) The Torah focuses more on <u>life on Earth</u> than on an <u>afterlife</u> — Jews are encouraged to lead <u>good lives</u> for the sake of life on Earth, rather than the <u>hope</u> of what's to come.

2) The Tenakh talks about <u>Sheol</u>, where the souls of the dead live as <u>shadows</u> for <u>eternity</u>.

3) But ideas about the <u>afterlife</u> gradually developed — beliefs are now largely based on ideas in the <u>Talmud</u>.

- Many Jews believe life after death is spent in <u>Gan Eden</u> ('<u>Garden of Eden</u>' or Paradise) and/or <u>Gehinnom</u>.
- Some see Gan Eden as a place of <u>banquets</u> and <u>sunshine</u>. Others have a more <u>spiritual</u> view of it as a <u>closeness</u> to God. Only if you've lived a <u>blameless</u> life will you be sent <u>straight</u> to <u>Gan Eden</u> when you die.
- <u>Most souls</u> go to <u>Gehinnom</u> before they reach <u>Gan Eden</u>. Some see it as a place of <u>torment</u>, where people are <u>punished</u>. Some see it as a place for <u>purification</u>, where people are shown the <u>wrong</u> they did in this life. The truly <u>wicked</u> don't move on — some think they're <u>tormented</u> forever, others that their souls are <u>destroyed</u>.

4) God <u>judges</u> how good or evil people have been, to decide their <u>fate</u> in the afterlife. Some Jews see this as a <u>motivation</u> for <u>good behaviour</u> in this life, others argue that you should do good things simply because they are <u>good</u>.

> "God will bring every deed into judgment ... whether it is good or evil." Ecclesiastes 12:14 NIV

5) Some Progressive Jews <u>don't</u> believe in the afterlife, as it's not <u>explicitly</u> mentioned in the Torah. Others believe we <u>live on</u> in how we've <u>influenced others</u> during our lives.

6) The term <u>olam ha-ba</u> (the world to come) is also used for the afterlife. It's sometimes used to refer to the <u>Messianic Age</u> (see below), rather than where souls go straight <u>after death</u>.

7) Many Jews also believe they will eventually be <u>physically resurrected</u> — see below. Belief in <u>resurrection</u> is <u>important</u> in Judaism. <u>Maimonides</u> listed it as one of his 13 <u>principles of faith</u>.

A Messiah will bring Peace on Earth

> '<u>Messiah</u>' comes from the Hebrew '<u>mashiach</u>' which means '<u>anointed one</u>' — someone who is <u>chosen to rule</u>.

1) Many Jews believe that the <u>Messiah</u>, an inspirational leader, will bring an era of **perfect peace** and **prosperity** called the <u>Messianic Age</u>. He'll establish God's kingdom on Earth and <u>everyone</u> will acknowledge God. (<u>Unlike Christians</u>, Jews <u>don't</u> believe that <u>Jesus</u> was the <u>Messiah</u>.)

2) Jews believe that the Messiah will be <u>human</u> — not <u>divine</u> (god-like) as Jesus is for Christians (see p.2). He'll be a <u>male</u> descendant of the Jewish king <u>David</u> and will himself be "a King who will reign <u>wisely</u> and do what is <u>just</u> and <u>right</u>" (Jeremiah 23:5 NIV). He will spread <u>God's laws</u> throughout the world, <u>reunite</u> the <u>Jewish people</u> in Israel (the <u>Promised Land</u>) and rebuild the <u>Temple</u> there.

3) It is thought that the <u>prophet Elijah</u> will <u>appear</u> just <u>before</u> the <u>Messiah</u> comes.

4) It's believed that people will be <u>judged</u> by God and the Messiah on their <u>actions</u>. Some Jews believe <u>everyone</u> will be resurrected so they can be <u>judged</u>. Others think only the <u>righteous</u> will be resurrected to share in the Messianic Age.

> "Multitudes who sleep in the dust of the earth will awake: some to everlasting life, others to shame and everlasting contempt." Daniel 12:2 NIV

- <u>Orthodox Jews</u> believe that the <u>physical</u> body will be <u>resurrected</u>, intact, in the <u>Messianic Age</u>. Because of this, the body shouldn't be <u>cut</u> after death (<u>autopsies</u> are frowned upon) and <u>cremation</u> is <u>forbidden</u>. A Jewish <u>cemetery</u> is called the '<u>House of Life</u>' (<u>Bet ha-Chaim</u>), which reaffirms the view that the body will be resurrected.
- <u>Progressive Jews</u> believe that the <u>body</u> is simply a <u>vessel</u> for the <u>soul</u> (which they believe carries on <u>without</u> the body), and <u>reject</u> the idea of physical resurrection. So Progressive Jews accept <u>cremation</u> and <u>organ donation</u>.

5) Not all Jews believe a <u>Messiah</u> will come though. Many <u>Progressive</u> Jews believe instead that <u>people</u> themselves can bring about a <u>peaceful</u> and <u>prosperous</u> age on Earth through their own <u>good actions</u>.

Make sure you revise this page — or I will judge you...

Have a go at this exam-style question using what you've learnt on this page and page 6.

Describe two differences between Jewish and Christian teachings about the afterlife. [4]

Worship

You need to be able to compare Jewish worship (this page and p.31) with Christian worship — see p.8 and 10. A Jewish place of worship is called a synagogue, meaning 'assembly' or 'coming together'.

All Synagogues have the Same Four Features

There are no rules stating what a synagogue should look like on the outside.

1) The layout of the main (prayer) hall commemorates some aspects of the Temple in Jerusalem, which was the centre of Jewish worship before it was destroyed in 70 CE. All synagogues have these four features:

Aron Hakodesh (the Ark) a large cupboard or alcove with doors or a screen, on the wall facing Jerusalem. It's the centrepiece of the synagogue — it holds the Torah (see p.26) and symbolises the ark (box) that held the tablets God gave to Moses. Often, a copy of the 10 commandments is hung above the ark.

Sefer Torah (Scroll of the Torah) a parchment scroll kept inside the ark. It must be handwritten by a sofer (scribe). It's usually covered with a mantle (cloth), or sometimes by a case, which is ornately decorated.

Ner Tamid (Perpetual Light) a light above the ark which never goes out. It represents the menorah (see below) which was always alight in the Temple.

> "...keep the lamps burning before the Lord..." Exodus 27:21 NIV

Bimah or Almemar a raised platform with a reading desk. Orthodox synagogues usually have it in the centre, while Progressive ones often have it close to the ark. It represents the altar in the Temple.

2) There are no pictures of God or people in a synagogue. This is because the second of the Ten Commandments (see p.28) forbids idolatry (worshipping pictures or objects).

3) Some synagogues also have a menorah — a seven-branched candlestick.

4) Orthodox synagogues have separate sections for women. Progressive synagogues have mixed seating.

5) Synagogues are not only used for worship but are important centres for the Jewish community — they are used as meeting places for study groups and social clubs.

There are Three Daily Services

1) The Tenakh shows it's important to worship God together — for example, Psalm 116:14 NIV says "I will fulfil my vows to the Lord in the presence of all his people", i.e. in the presence of other Jews.

2) Attending synagogue can remind Jews of the importance of their faith and of their closeness to God. Some Jews believe God (Shekhinah, see p.27) is present when Jews worship together.

3) Orthodox synagogues hold services three times a day — shacharit (the morning service), minchah (afternoon) and ma'ariv (evening). Minchah is often just before sunset so that ma'ariv can follow straight afterwards (at sunset). Progressive synagogues tend not to have weekday services, although some do.

> Shacharit is the longest service (an hour), while minchah and ma'ariv last about half an hour each. They include blessings (thanks to God), songs of praise, prayers and sometimes a sermon from the rabbi. On Mondays, Thursdays, Shabbat and festivals, shacharit includes a Torah reading (sidrah) and a Nevi'im reading (haftarah).

4) The siddur (prayer book) is used during each service — it sets out the order of the daily prayers.

5) Ten people (known as a minyan) must be present for certain prayers to be said and the Torah to be read. In Orthodox Judaism these must all be men, but in Progressive Judaism they can be women too.

6) Services are often led by a rabbi — a religious leader responsible for teaching and advising the community. But any adult (male in Orthodox Judaism) with enough religious knowledge can do so. A hazzan (cantor — singer) leads the prayers, which are often sung or chanted. They might also lead the service.

7) The hazzan stands at the front of the hall. The hazzan prays in the same direction as everyone else in Orthodox services. If Progressive synagogues have a hazzan, they tend to face the congregation.

8) Progressive Jews pray in unison. Orthodox Jews pray at their own pace, often with varying movements.

9) Orthodox services are in Hebrew, except the sermon — Progressive ones are partly in the local language.

10) Progressive synagogues may have instruments or choirs to accompany singing, but Orthodox ones don't.

11) Jews face Jerusalem during prayer. There are times in prayer, e.g. during the Amidah (p.31), when Jews bend their knees and bow to show respect to God. Orthodox Jews often sway to help them concentrate.

Areas of Study 1, 2 & 3 — Jewish Beliefs and Living the Jewish Life

Worship

The Torah is Treated with Great Respect

The Torah can't be touched, so the reader uses a yad (pointer) to keep their place in the text.

1) Members of the congregation can be called to read from the Torah, which is an honour. It's known as aliyah (going up). There's a reader to do it for them if they don't know Hebrew well enough.

2) A Torah extract is read each week, so the whole Torah is read over 1 year (or 3 in Progressive Judaism).

3) During the service, the ark (see p.30) is opened and the Torah is carried through the congregation to the bimah. As it passes them, people will bow to, kiss or touch the Torah with their tallit (see below).

Prayer is Very Important

"Evening, morning and noon I cry out in distress, and he hears my voice." Psalm 55:17 NIV

1) Prayer is a central part of Jews' relationship with God — they believe God listens to their prayers. Prayers can include giving thanks or praise, confessing to sins, or asking God for something.

2) Many Jews pray three times a day even if they don't attend synagogue — it's a mitzvah to do so. They say the same prayers as in the services, but in a reduced form. This includes the Shema and Amidah.

- The Shema is a declaration of faith in only one God. It's in three parts, taken from the Torah (Deuteronomy 6:4-9 and 11:13-21 and Numbers 15:37-41). Jews should say it morning and night. The first sentence of the Shema is said when the Torah is taken from the ark.

"Hear, O Israel: the Lord our God, the Lord is one." Deuteronomy 6:4 NIV

- Many Jews have a copy of the first two parts of the Shema on every doorpost in their house (except the bathroom). It's written on a tiny parchment scroll called a mezuzah.

The Amidah ('standing prayer') is a set of 19 blessings. It begins by praising God, then asks for things such as justice, and ends with thanksgiving and asking for peace. It's said at weekday services — a short version is used for Shabbat and other festivals.

3) Women are traditionally seen as exempt from the mitzvah concerning services and prayer, but as a minimum it's thought they should say the Amidah twice a day. They often pray at home.

4) Full concentration on prayer is vital — it's known as 'kavanah', and without it prayers don't count.

5) Jews can pray spontaneously (make up their own prayers when they want) — this should be in addition to set prayers, which provide a structure for daily prayer. Many Jews say blessings before and after meals.

6) Jewish men often wear special clothing for prayer and worship. Tefillin are two boxes containing Torah passages, worn during shacharit (except on Shabbat and festivals). One is strapped to the upper arm and one to the head, reminding them to serve God with head and heart. A tallit (prayer shawl) is also worn during shacharit — it has fringes (tzitzit) tied in a special way, to remind Jews of the mitzvot.

7) Many men wear a cap called a kippah (yarmulke) as a sign of respect to God. Orthodox men wear them all day — Progressive and Conservative Jews tend to wear them only if praying or at the synagogue.

Shabbat (Sabbath) is Celebrated in the Synagogue

Shabbat is a sign of God's covenant with Jews (Exodus 31:13).

Shabbat is a day of rest to commemorate the seventh day of creation, when God rested after creating the universe. It begins at sunset on Friday and lasts until Saturday evening. It's a time for reflection and worship, away from the stress of daily life. It's also a chance for the community to get together — Shabbat services are well-attended family occasions. The services are similar to the weekday ones, with some additions:

Friday Evening	Saturday Morning	Saturday Afternoon/Evening
Progressive synagogues tend to have this at a set time rather than at sunset. The kiddush (see p.32) is said. Shabbat is welcomed with a set of hymns, psalms and prayers called Kabbalat Shabbat (Welcoming the Sabbath).	The main service of the week. There are Torah and Nevi'im readings, and hymns and prayers about the importance of the Torah. Orthodox Jews have an additional service called musaf afterwards.	The afternoon service includes a reading from the Torah, as well as prayers. It's followed by ma'ariv, which finishes with the havdalah (see p.32) to end Shabbat.

Prayer has to be focused and sincere — like your revision...

REVISION TASK

Shut the book, and write down as much as you can about the Shema and Amidah. Just testing!

Judaism	Family Life

The <u>home</u> is also an important place of <u>worship</u> and <u>ritual</u> for Jews — Judaism is a <u>family-focused</u> religion.

Shabbat is Celebrated in the Home

 Challot

1) The house is <u>cleaned</u> and <u>tidied</u> before Shabbat. Any <u>food</u> to be eaten on Shabbat is cooked <u>in advance</u>, because no '<u>work</u>' can be done on Shabbat. '<u>Work</u>' includes things like <u>cooking</u> or <u>gardening</u>. The <u>Torah</u> lists what 'work' is <u>forbidden</u>, but rabbis have updated it to <u>today's world</u>, e.g. to include <u>driving</u>.

2) A <u>family member</u> (usually <u>female</u>) lights two <u>candles</u> to mark the start of Shabbat. They say a blessing while <u>covering</u> their eyes. They may pass their hands over the candles to <u>welcome</u> Shabbat to the home.

3) At the <u>start</u> of the Shabbat meal, <u>kiddush</u> is said to set the Shabbat apart as <u>holy</u>. It includes reciting Genesis 2:1-3 (in which God rests after creation) and saying a blessing over <u>wine</u> which is then drunk.

4) After kiddush, Jews <u>wash their hands</u> in a set way. <u>Challot</u> are eaten — these are <u>two plaited loaves</u> to commemorate the double portion of '<u>manna</u>' (miraculous food) provided by God the day before each Shabbat during the <u>Exodus</u> (see p.28). A blessing's said over them before they're cut and dipped in salt.

5) <u>Parents</u> (traditionally the <u>father</u>) often <u>bless</u> their <u>children</u>. Shabbat's a key way they <u>learn</u> about Judaism.

6) The <u>havdalah</u> ('division') ceremony marks the <u>end</u> of Shabbat, separating it from the six days ahead. Blessings are said over sweet-smelling <u>spices</u>, a cup of <u>wine</u> and a <u>plaited candle</u> with several wicks.

Many Jews Follow Strict Dietary Laws

You might come across '<u>treif</u>', which is <u>Yiddish</u> for '<u>treifah</u>'.

1) The set of <u>food laws</u> written in the Torah is known as <u>kashrut</u> — have a look at Leviticus 11 and Deuteronomy 14:2-21. Permitted food is called <u>kosher</u> — everything else is <u>treifah</u> ('torn').

2) To be <u>kosher</u>, a mammal must have both <u>cloven</u> (split) hooves and <u>chew cud</u>. Sea creatures with both <u>fins</u> and <u>scales</u> are kosher, but <u>no</u> other seafood is. All <u>poultry</u> is <u>kosher</u>, but some other birds aren't.

3) Animals must be killed by a specially-trained person, with <u>a cut across the throat</u> using a sharp blade. <u>Blood</u> can't be eaten, so it must be drained from meat. <u>Meat</u> and <u>dairy</u> products can't be eaten <u>together</u>.

4) Some foods <u>can't</u> be eaten if they've been cooked only by someone who isn't <u>Jewish</u>.

5) <u>Orthodox</u> Jews keep <u>kashrut</u>. <u>Progressive</u> Judaism leaves it up to the <u>individual</u> — some <u>Progressive</u> Jews only observe <u>some</u> of the laws, or keep kashrut at <u>home</u> but eat <u>non-kosher food</u> elsewhere.

6) Keeping <u>kashrut</u> shows <u>self-control</u> and <u>obedience</u> to God — it's a religious <u>ritual</u> and part of the <u>mitzvot</u>. However, because of <u>pikuach nefesh</u> (p.28), kashrut can be <u>broken</u> if necessary for <u>medical</u> reasons.

Judaism has Rituals to Mark Different Life Stages

There are <u>Jewish rituals</u> to mark different <u>life stages</u>. These tend to <u>vary</u> between different strands of Judaism. This begins from <u>birth</u>, with the <u>brit milah</u> (circumcision) for boys or <u>simchat bat</u> (naming ceremony) for girls.

Brit milah — circumcision

1. Nearly all boys are <u>circumcised</u> (have their foreskin removed), regardless of which strand of Judaism they're born into. Boys <u>don't</u> have to be circumcised to be <u>Jewish</u>, but many people worry that their son will be <u>alienated</u> if he isn't circumcised.

2. It's a sign they belong to the Jewish <u>faith</u> and it's part of the <u>covenant God</u> made with <u>Abraham</u> (p.27) — God asked that "every male among you shall be circumcised" (Genesis 17:10 NIV).

3. It's usually done at home, <u>7</u> days after the baby's born (even if it's <u>Shabbat</u>). If the boy's <u>not healthy</u> enough, it happens <u>later</u>.

4. The <u>circumcision</u> is performed by a <u>mohel</u> (a Jewish person trained to do the procedure). The mohel and the father each say a <u>blessing</u> before it starts.

5. The brit milah is followed by saying the <u>kiddush</u> and giving the boy his <u>Hebrew name</u>. Then there's a <u>celebratory meal</u>.

Simchat bat — naming ceremony

1. This can also be known as the <u>brit bat</u> or the <u>zeved habat</u> (bat means daughter).

2. This developed <u>recently</u> so that there was an equivalent ceremony in the home to <u>welcome</u> the birth of a <u>girl</u>.

3. The ceremonies <u>vary</u> a lot, but they often involve <u>songs</u> of thanks, <u>blessings</u>, a <u>ritual</u> to welcome the girl into the <u>covenant</u> (e.g. lighting candles), an explanation of the <u>choice of names</u>, and the <u>kiddush</u>.

4. <u>Orthodox</u> Jews are less likely to do this. Instead, the girl is given her <u>Hebrew</u> name during a synagogue service. Her father will give a <u>Torah</u> reading.

Family Life | Judaism

The Bar or Bat Mitzvah is a Coming of Age Ceremony

In Progressive Judaism it's 13 for both genders.

1) At 13 a Jewish boy becomes bar mitzvah and at 12 a girl becomes bat mitzvah — a son or daughter of the commandments. It means they have to fulfil the mitzvot — they're responsible for living in a religious way.

2) They don't have to do anything to become bar or bat mitzvah — it's defined by their age — but there's often a ceremony to celebrate. The ceremony is also known as a bar or bat mitzvah.

3) The ceremony forms part of a synagogue service (often on Shabbat). The young person might lead some of the prayers, read from the Tenakh, give a speech or read some of the blessings. If they give a reading, they prepare for it beforehand by studying the relevant portion and learning to read it in Hebrew.

- In Orthodox Judaism, most girls don't have a bat mitzvah ceremony, as they don't have the same responsibilities towards worship as men (see p.31). There is continuing debate about whether this should change so they're treated equally.
- Instead, Orthodox girls have a bat hayil (daughter of valour) ceremony. It's held after one of the services, and all girls who have turned 12 in the previous year recite a religious passage or give a speech in front of family and friends.
- Nearly all Progressive Jews have a bar/bat mitzvah — as do Conservative Jews. They tend to be the same for boys and girls.

Marriage is Very Important in Judaism

1) Marriage is important in Judaism, because much of Judaism is focused on family and the home.

2) Marriage ceremonies are in two parts, called the kiddushin (the betrothal) and the nisuin (the wedding).

3) The wedding usually happens in a synagogue. It takes place under a huppah (canopy), which can be a simple tallit (p.31) or more elaborate. The huppah symbolises the home the couple will build together.

4) Firstly, blessings are said over a cup of wine, which the couple drinks, symbolising the life they will share.

5) The groom gives the bride a ring and says the wedding vow — this completes the kiddushin. At Progressive Jewish weddings, both the bride and the groom exchange rings and say the vow.

6) The ketubah (marriage contract) is read out. The traditional ketubah states the bride's right to be cared for by her husband and her entitlements in case of divorce or death (a bit like a prenuptial agreement). Progressive Jews have rewritten the ketubah to be a mutual statement of love and commitment.

7) The nisuin starts with seven blessings (sheva b'rakhot) said over wine, in which God is praised for creating the universe and humanity, and for the gift of children. There are also blessings for Israel and Jerusalem.

8) Finally, a glass is broken by stepping on it. There are various interpretations of this — it's thought to symbolise the destruction of the Temple (see p.30) or emphasise that love needs to be protected.

Jewish Mourning Rituals Allow People Time to Grieve

1) Mourning family members perform kriah — they make a tear in clothing or a ribbon, as a symbol of grief.

2) The funeral service often includes prayers, psalms and a eulogy (a speech praising the dead person).

3) The Kaddish, a prayer praising God, is said so people focus on God at a time they may feel far from him.

4) The seven days following the burial are known as shiva. Close family mourn during this time. Orthodox Jews (and some Progressive) don't leave the house, attend synagogue or work during shiva. Other mourners visit their house to comfort them and to form a minyan (see p.30) for the Kaddish.

5) The loss of a parent is particularly significant in Judaism. If someone has lost a parent they remain in mourning for a whole year — this is known as avelut. During this time, there are some restrictions, e.g. they won't go to parties. They also say the Kaddish every day for 11 months.

6) The Kaddish is also said on each Yahrzeit (anniversary of the death). On the eve of the Yahrzeit, many light a candle for 24 hours. It's a day of remembrance, during which some people fast.

7) Progressive Jews tend to choose which rituals to observe. Orthodox Jews usually observe them all.

There are a fair few Hebrew words on this page...

...so make sure you learn to spell them correctly — it could get you marks for SPaG (see p.93-95).

EXAM TIP

There are many festivals in the Jewish calendar. Of these, Rosh Hashanah and Yom Kippur are the most important holy days. They focus on judgement and atonement (making amends for wrongdoing).

The Meaning of Festivals Can Vary for Different People

1) Many members of all branches of Judaism tend to celebrate the festivals and do so in fairly similar ways.

2) They may see the festivals as being important for different reasons though. For some Jews, the social aspects of celebrating festivals in the synagogue may be just as important as the religious ones. Others may focus on the festivals' historical importance as much as their religious significance.

> Pesach (p.35) is a widely celebrated festival in the UK. This may be because it has historical significance for anyone of Jewish descent, regardless of how religious or orthodox they are. It's a good way of introducing children to Jewish history and ritual.

3) Differing beliefs may affect the meaning of the festival. E.g. Shavuot (p.35) celebrates the giving of the Torah — this makes it particularly important to Orthodox Jews, who think God gave it directly to Moses.

Rosh Hashanah is the Jewish New Year

Rosh Hashanah falls in September or October. It's a time for Jews to consider any wrongdoing in the past year and what they intend to do better in the next, in preparation for Yom Kippur.

> Leviticus 23 gives advice on the festivals and how Jews should observe them, including Rosh Hashanah: "you are to have a day of sabbath rest, a sacred assembly commemorated with trumpet blasts. Do not do any of your ordinary work" Leviticus 23:24-25 NIV

1) During the last month of the old year and on the day itself, a shofar (ram's horn) is blown. The shofar is a call for repentance (being sorry for the things you've done wrong) and spiritual reawakening.

2) As on Shabbat, no work is done and Jews spend most of the day in the synagogue. Prayers describing God's judgement and his role as 'king' are said, as well as ones hoping for forgiveness. The Torah is read.

3) Bread and apples dipped in honey are eaten, to symbolise the hope for a 'sweet' (pleasant) year to come.

4) It's thought God writes people's names in certain books on Rosh Hashanah. The truly good go straight into the 'Book of Life', but most go in the 'intermediate' book (there's a 'Book of Death' for the truly evil).

5) Those in the intermediate book can affect whether they'll end up in the Book of Life during the days of awe (the 10 days until Yom Kippur). The decision can be influenced by repentance — also known as teshuva, meaning 'turning' back to God. Prayer and good deeds (tzedakah) can also help.

6) The tashlich ('casting away') ceremony takes place — a prayer is said to ask God to remove the sins of his people. The ceremony is carried out next to water, e.g. a river or the sea.

Yom Kippur is a Day of Atonement

Yom Kippur is the holiest day of the year, so no work is done during it. It gives Jews the chance to ask God to forgive the sins they've committed over the past year.

1) It involves fasting for 25 hours — this helps Jews focus on spiritual rather than physical matters. Washing, bathing, using cosmetics, wearing leather shoes and having sex are all forbidden on Yom Kippur.

2) Worship in the synagogue is central to Yom Kippur. It's a mitzvah to attend all the services:

> • On Yom Kippur eve, the Kol Nidre ('all vows') prayer is said. It cancels all vows between a person and God in the coming year. It releases Jews from a focus on vows they might not keep, so they can concentrate on their true relationship with God.
> • The next day is spent in the synagogue, with readings from the Torah and prayers to confess any sins and show repentance.
> • The day ends with a service called the Neilah ('closing of the gates'), symbolising a final chance to repent as the gates of heaven are about to close and the Book of Life will be sealed. The shofar is then blown to mark the end of Yom Kippur.

Make sure you don't need to atone for a bad mark...

...by learning this page thoroughly. Shut the book, write the headings 'Rosh Hashanah' and 'Yom Kippur', then scribble down as much as you can remember about each.

Festivals

Pesach, Shavuot and Sukkot are known as the 'Pilgrim Festivals', as Jews used to travel to the Temple in Jerusalem to celebrate them. They're also called 'harvest festivals', as they all originally had links with harvest.

Sukkot Comes Five Days After Yom Kippur

A sukkah. —→
Sukkot is the plural.

1) Sukkot lasts eight or nine days (see below) and is a festival of rejoicing.

2) During Sukkot, Jews live in a tent-like structure called a sukkah. This is a reminder of how God "made the Israelites live in temporary shelters when [he] brought them out of Egypt" (Leviticus 23:43 NIV). In the UK, Jews may just eat in their sukkah, as the autumn is cold.

3) At home or in synagogue, an etrog and a lulav are waved each morning while blessings are said (Leviticus 23:40). Etrogs are like lemons, and a lulav is made of date palm, willow and myrtle.

4) On the first six days of Sukkot (except Shabbat), Jews circle the bimah (p.30) once, each holding an etrog and lulav. On the seventh day, they do so seven times with the Torah scrolls. Afterwards, they hit the willow against the floor — its falling leaves represent sins being shed.

5) Simchat Torah marks the end of the cycle of Torah readings. The Torah is carried round the bimah seven times and the last and first Torah portions are read. For non-Israeli Orthodox Jews, it's the 9th day of Sukkot. For Israelis and Progressive Jews, it's the 8th day, which is also the festival of Shemini Atzeret. On Shemini Atzeret, Jews pray for rain now harvest is over.

Pesach (Passover) Commemorates the Exodus

Pesach is in March or April.

1) Pesach commemorates the events leading up to the Israelites' escape from slavery in Egypt, as well as the Exodus itself (see p.28). Pesach means 'to spare' or 'to pass over', referring to the night when the angel of death killed the Egyptians' first-born sons, but 'passed over' the Israelites without harming them.

2) It lasts 7 or 8 days. On the first night or first 2 nights, it's celebrated with seder — a service and meal.

3) Each food symbolises a part of the Exodus story, which is retold by the head of the family during seder using a book of ritual called the Haggadah. Exodus 12:3-8 states what food to include in seder.

- Karpas — a vegetable dipped in salt water, to remind Jews of the pain and tears caused by slavery.
- Matzah (unleavened bread) — bread made from flour, water and no yeast, which Jews made for the Exodus. Anything made from grain and water that has 'risen' (fermented) is called 'chametz' and can't be eaten during Pesach.
- Maror (bitter herbs) — a bitter vegetable, usually raw horseradish, is eaten to remind Jews of the bitterness of slavery.
- Baytsah (egg) — the egg's hard-boiled and roasted. It symbolises the sacrifices once offered in the Temple.
- Z'roah (lamb bone) — this isn't eaten (neither is the egg) but it symbolises the lamb sacrificed on the night of the Exodus.

Shavuot Celebrates the Giving of the Torah at Mount Sinai

1) Shavuot takes place fifty days after Pesach and lasts two days (though only one in Israel). It celebrates two events — the start of the harvest, and the Torah being given to the Jews by God.

2) Many Jews stay up the whole of the first night of Shavuot to study and celebrate the Torah.

3) The Ten Commandments are read in the synagogue on the first day. The Ketuvim story of Ruth, a convert to Judaism, is significant to Shavuot — it shows the importance of commitment to the covenant.

4) No one can really agree why, but it's traditional to eat dairy food on Shavuot.

5) Jews decorate their homes and synagogues with flowers and plants as a symbol of the harvest. This is partly to symbolise the way Mount Sinai burst into flower after the Torah was given. It's also because Shavuot used to be the time the Jewish people would bring their wheat and fruit harvests to the Temple.

> "Count fifty days ... and then present an offering of new grain to the Lord." Leviticus 23:16 NIV

Harvest the knowledge from this page and learn it...

...sorry. Anyway, moving on, have a go at this exam-style question:

Outline three aspects of Sukkot.   [3]

Areas of Study 1, 2 & 3 — Jewish Beliefs and Living the Jewish Life

Revision Summary

Right, we've covered an awful lot and it's now time to find out how much of that went in... These questions are similar to the ones you'll get in the exam, so should get you used to how much you're supposed to write.

If there's anything you can't answer, go back through the section and have another go when you've re-read it. For some questions — you'll be told which ones — there are extra marks for spelling, punctuation, grammar and specialist terminology, so check your writing carefully and make sure you've used technical terms.

The clue's in the question here — they're worth 3 marks, so you need to make three brief points.

1) Outline the contents of the three parts of the Tenakh.

2) Outline three of the commandments included in the Decalogue.

3) Outline three important moral principles in Judaism.

4) Outline three features of the Jewish marriage ceremony.

5) Outline three examples of Jewish mourning rituals.

6) Outline three aspects of worship on Yom Kippur.

7) Outline the meaning of three elements of the seder meal.

These are 4 mark questions. To get full marks, you need to make two points and develop them.

8) Explain two Jewish attitudes towards the Torah.

9) Explain two reasons why the covenant between God and Moses is important for Jews.

10) Explain two reasons why belief in the Messiah is important for Jews today.

11) Explain two ways in which Orthodox and Progressive synagogue services are different.

12) Explain two Jewish attitudes to kashrut.

5 marks now — they just keep ramping up. You also need to include an example from Jewish teachings in your answer.

13) Explain two Jewish teachings about the characteristics of God.

14) Explain two Jewish beliefs about God's covenant with Abraham.

15) Explain two Jewish beliefs about resurrection.

16) Explain two ways in which Shabbat is important to Jews.

> For the longer answer questions, make sure your writing is accurate and well organised — you want the points you make to be obvious to the examiner.

This is the biggy — worth 15 marks (3 marks are for SPaG and specialist terminology). You'll always get a list of things you must include, so use it to plan your answer before you start writing. Make a list of arguments for and against so you don't miss any out in your answer — you need to include both sides.

17) 'The best way for Jews to build a relationship with God is by saying set daily prayers.'
Evaluate this statement. Give arguments that support the statement and arguments that disagree with the statement. You must include:
   • examples from Jewish teachings
   • different Jewish points of view
   • a conclusion.

> Have a look at the advice on writing essays in the 'Do Well in Your Exam' section.

Sexuality and Sexual Relationships | All religions

While different faiths may have similar views about sex, there's a bigger divide among views on homosexuality.

Islam, Christianity and Judaism have Similar Attitudes to Sex

1) Traditionally, all three religions teach that the only correct context for sexual activity is within marriage — sex outside of it is seen as a sin. This means cohabitation (living together unmarried) isn't approved of.

In Judaism, Maimonides' list of mitzvot says sexual relationships shouldn't happen without a ketubah and kiddushin (p.33) — see Sefer Hamitzvot no. 355.	Qur'an 23:7 states that "whoever seeks beyond [marriage] then those are the transgressors".	The Catechism of the Catholic Church says "Sexuality is ordered to the conjugal love of man and woman" (2360). 'Conjugal' means 'within marriage'. It also says that sex is 'unitive' and 'procreative' — to bring married couples together as one and for having children.

2) Christians, Muslims and Jews are urged to keep sex within marriage for positive reasons as well — marriage is believed to make sex more special. All three religions stress the importance of enjoying sex. The Song of Solomon in the Bible and Ketuvim contains poems celebrating sexual desire and relationships.

3) 'Strict' members of all three faiths think the principle of only having sex within marriage still applies. More liberal members might see this as outdated, although they still tend to see marriage as the ideal.

4) Promiscuity (having multiple sexual partners) is often seen as wrong in all three religions. But many British people think it's acceptable, especially now contraception (see p.38) is widely available — though a large number of sexual partners is seen more negatively.

5) Atheists and humanists tend to accept sex outside of marriage. Humanists accept it as long as it causes no harm to anyone. Generally, sex outside of marriage is considered normal in British society.

Homosexuality is a Disputed Topic

> The first same-sex marriages in the UK took place in 2014 — see p.39-41 for different religions' views.

Homosexuality is attraction to members of the same sex. Heterosexuality is attraction to the opposite sex.

1) Many people in British society consider both heterosexuality and homosexuality to be natural and normal.

2) The Christian, Muslim and Jewish scriptures seem to say that homosexual sex is wrong — though the relevant bits are interpreted differently by some. They only condemn sex between men, not between women, which is hardly mentioned. (Though it's often frowned upon because male homosexuality is.)

> The story of Sodom (see Genesis 19:3-25) is used by Christianity, Islam and Judaism to argue against homosexuality. The city's destroyed after the men in Sodom demand sex with two male angels God sent, which some people use to show that homosexuality's wrong. The angels say God sent them to destroy the city because of sin, so others say he was going to destroy it anyway and it wasn't because the men wanted sex with them.

3) The texts don't condemn people who have homosexual feelings but don't act upon them. This means some people who are homosexual and religious opt for celibacy (they don't have sexual relationships).

4) Some argue that as the scriptures were written in a different cultural context from ours, we can't apply their standards today. Generally, the religions condemn homophobia and they're becoming more accepting of homosexuality, but it isn't seen as ideal and many see homosexual sex as a sin.

The Catechism of the Catholic Church says "Under no circumstances can [homosexual acts] be approved" (2357). It urges homosexual people to stay celibate but says they shouldn't face any discrimination.	The Anglican Church is split on the topic. There are some openly gay clergy in the Church of England, but conservative members don't approve of homosexuality. 1 Corinthians 6:9-10 suggests it's a sin.	Progressive Jews usually accept homosexuality. Homosexual people can become Progressive rabbis. Orthodox Jews tend to be against it — homosexual sex is forbidden in Leviticus 18:22 NIV, which calls it 'detestable'.	Many Muslims think the Qur'an bans homosexuality, due to the Sodom story (e.g. Qur'an 7:81 "you approach men with desire, instead of women ... you are a transgressing people"). Some Muslims disagree and argue that these teachings should be reinterpreted.

Within each religion there are different views...

...e.g. Orthodox and Progressive Jews differ when it comes to homosexuality. You often have to give two views in the exam and you get marks for the level of detail, so learn them well.

Contraception

Within each religion, views on contraception can vary a lot — some believers accept its use, some don't.

Contraception Prevents a Woman Becoming Pregnant

Using contraception is sometimes called 'family planning'.

1) Contraception is also known as birth control and is used to stop a woman conceiving. It can be temporary (e.g. the contraceptive pill or condoms) or permanent (sterilisation).

2) Most atheists and humanists have no objection to contraception. They think it's better if people only have children if they really want them. Contraception allows people to choose when to have sex, by limiting the risk of pregnancy. Some types also reduce the risk of STIs (sexually transmitted infections).

3) People applying situation ethics look for the most loving option — they would be likely to support contraception if it means only children who will be loved are born, and people are protected from STIs.

4) Some Christians, Muslims and Jews object to forms of contraception that might destroy a fertilised egg, such as the morning after pill — this is because they see it as being the same as abortion (see p.51).

5) Many religious people don't believe in sterilisation, which prevents people ever having children.

Christian Denominations have Different Opinions

1) The Catholic Church says anything 'deliberately contraceptive' is 'intrinsically wrong' (Humanae Vitae 14). Married couples should 'transmit human life' (Catechism of the Catholic Church 2367), i.e. have children.

2) Many individual Roman Catholics disagree with this stance, especially because of concerns about STIs.

3) The Church says contraception may lead to promiscuity (p.37) and sees some methods as abortion. It does allow natural contraception — only having sex at the less fertile times in a woman's menstrual cycle.

4) Other Christian Churches have different views. The Anglican, Methodist and Presbyterian Churches are in favour of contraception, suggesting that it lets parents plan their family in a responsible way.

Orthodox and Progressive Jews tend to have Differing Views

1) Judaism traditionally teaches that a child is a gift from God, and contraception interferes with God's plans to bless couples with children.

> "A man shall not abstain from [propagating] the race unless he already has children."
> Talmud Yevamot 61b

2) Most Orthodox Jews only accept contraception for compassionate reasons, e.g. if pregnancy could be physically or psychologically harmful to the mother or an existing child.

3) Some find contraception within marriage acceptable if the couple do plan to have children later on.

4) Progressive Jews find contraception more acceptable and leave the decision to each individual.

5) Sex should be as natural as possible so hormonal contraceptives like the pill are generally preferred to barrier methods like condoms. But some agree with barrier methods as a means of preventing STIs.

There are Different Attitudes to Contraception within Islam

1) Some Muslims see contraception as wrong — they might refer to the hadith Sahih al-Bukhari 34:432, which says conception is Allah's will and suggests people shouldn't try to avoid it. Other Muslims believe that another hadith, Sahih al-Bukhari 62:136, supports the use of contraception.

2) It's the right of both husband and wife to try for children, so both partners must agree to contraception.

3) Reasons for using contraception are usually focused on whether another child may cause harm to the mother, any existing children or to the potential child, e.g. if the family can't afford to feed another child.

4) Only 'reversible' methods are allowed, though — sterilisation and vasectomies are usually not accepted.

Remember that religious views focus on marital sex...

Have a go at this exam-style question — answer in the context of the religion you've studied.

Explain two religious beliefs about contraception.   [4]

Marriage and Divorce

Marriage in the UK — Things have Changed

1) The number of marriages taking place in the UK each year has been decreasing over the last 40 years. People are also tending to get married later in life, and many people have children without being married.

2) Same-sex marriage is legal in England, Scotland and Wales. Many see this as good as it creates equality.

3) Although many non-religious people still see marriage as important, others see it as unnecessary. It's now more common (and acceptable) for people to cohabit (live together) — either before marrying or instead of getting married. Cohabiting couples don't have the same legal rights as married ones though.

4) Divorce is also far more common. Non-religious people often see it as sensible if the couple don't get on, as they'll be happier if they divorce. Some argue parents fighting can harm children more than divorce. People might apply situation ethics (looking for the most loving outcome in each situation) — even if they value marriage highly, they might see divorce as the best option in some situations. However, many religious people see marriage as very important, and try to avoid divorce if at all possible.

Christians think Marriage is Important and Holy

> Pope Francis said marriage is 'indispensable' to society (Not Just Good, but Beautiful).

1) The Christian faith values marriage very highly — marriage reflects the union of Jesus with his followers.

2) Marriage is a covenant (contract) between two people to offer love, support and commitment, and to have children. Christians see marriage as sacred — they talk about the 'sanctity of marriage'.

3) Many accept cohabitation, especially as preparation for marriage. Some don't — they disagree with sex outside marriage. The Catholic Church tends to be against it, but Pope Francis has recognised it can be hard for people to marry, e.g. for financial reasons — but they should be encouraged to marry eventually.

4) Faithfulness in marriage is important — adultery is forbidden in the Ten Commandments (Exodus 20:14).

Christians are Divided Over Same-Sex Marriage

1) The decision to legalise same-sex marriage in the UK was criticised by the Catholic Church and the Church of England. Many members of the clergy are against it.

2) But some Church of England clergy hold blessings for same-sex couples after they marry in civil (non-religious) ceremonies.

> "The Church of England affirms, according to our Lord's teaching, that marriage is ... a union... of one man with one woman." Canon B30

3) It's splitting the Anglican Church. Supporters of same-sex marriage say Christians should be loving to all and should support anyone who wants to marry. Those against it say it's a sin. They also think it's wrong because one of the main purposes of marriage is having children.

4) The Catholic Church is more strongly against homosexual relationships and same-sex marriage.

Different Christian Churches have Varying Attitudes to Divorce

1) There are different views about divorce — many think it breaks the sanctity of marriage.

The Roman Catholic Church says it's impossible to divorce (Catechism of the Catholic Church 2382). Marriage is a sacrament — God made the couple one flesh, which can't be undone. However, a marriage can be annulled (declared void) if the couple never had sex or if a partner didn't consent to or understand the marriage, or refused to have children.	The Church of England says divorce is possible and accepts that some marriages fail. Divorcees can re-marry in church if they find a minister willing to marry them. Some Church members disagree with this. Nonconformist Churches (e.g. Baptists and Methodists) will usually re-marry divorcees, but an individual minister can refuse to do so if it goes against their conscience.

2) Jesus himself was anti-divorce, but in favour of forgiving people's sins.

Matthew 19:8-9 NIV says divorce and remarriage are only allowed if someone's partner's been unfaithful.	"A man [and] his wife ... will become one flesh. ... what God has joined together, let no one separate." Mark 10:7-9 NIV	In John 8:2-11, Jesus forgives a woman who's committed adultery. But he tells her, "Go now and leave your life of sin" (NIV).

3) Some Christians view an unhappy marriage as a waste of two lives, and so see divorce as preferable.

Now have a go at the Revision Task at the bottom of p.40.

Marriage and Divorce

Marriage is very important in Islam — Muslims are advised to marry.

Marriage is Strongly Recommended in Islam

1) Marriage provides companionship, love and stability. Muslims believe marriage is Allah's will — it says in Qur'an 24:32 "marry the unmarried among you" and 30:21 "He created for you ... mates that you may find tranquillity in them; and He placed between you affection...".

2) Islam is family-oriented, so marriage is important. It's a secure environment for having children (procreation). Cohabitation often isn't accepted as it tends to involve sex outside of marriage.

3) According to a hadith, Muhammad said that marriage was half of a Muslim's faith.

4) Qur'an 4:1-24 clearly sets out rules for who people can marry and how much different people inherit.

5) Nikah is the name for marriage under shari'ah — Islamic law. To have the marriage recognised as legal in Britain, couples must also have a civil wedding ceremony.

6) Some Muslims have arranged marriages. This is where the parents will choose a marriage partner for their child. However, both potential partners have the right to say no to marrying their parents' choice.

7) Polygamy is criticised by many Muslims, but others believe the Qur'an allows it. A man should only take multiple wives if he can treat them equally. Some criticise the fact it's only allowed for men. Polygamy is illegal in the UK, but polygamous marriages are accepted if they took place elsewhere.

8) Adultery is a sin — the Qur'an calls it "evil" (Qur'an 17:32). Some Muslim countries punish it severely.

Same-Sex Marriage is a Controversial Topic in Islam

1) Many Muslims are against same-sex marriage as they believe homosexual sex is forbidden by the Qur'an (see p.37). The Muslim Council of Britain spoke against the law legalising same-sex marriage in the UK, arguing it was unnecessary because civil partnerships gave same-sex couples equal rights anyway and that same-sex marriage undermined the definition of marriage as between a man and a woman.

2) Some Muslims see it as wrong because marriage is partly for having children. However, some Muslims do support same-sex marriage. They argue that homosexuality is normal and that it's good for same-sex couples to have the chance to be married, as marriage is important in Islam.

3) Others have argued that, since Muslims are a minority in Britain, they should help out another minority by supporting same-sex marriage, regardless of their individual views on homosexuality.

Divorce is the Last Resort, but it's Accepted

"Of all the lawful acts the most detestable to Allah is divorce." (Sunan Abi Dawud 12:2173)

1) Divorce is permitted, but only as a last resort. If things aren't going well, an arbiter from each family should be appointed to try to sort things out.

2) Muslims see reconciliation as particularly important when the couple have children.

3) Qur'an 2:226-241 lays out the conditions under which divorce can happen. In both Sunni and Shi'a Islam, it's possible for a man to divorce his wife by saying 'I divorce you' three times. Some Sunni Muslims believe all three can be said at the same time, but not everyone agrees with this. In Shi'a Islam, 'I divorce you' must be said once a month for three months, and two people must witness it.

4) Both believe in having an iddah (waiting period, often of three months) to allow time for reflection. The waiting period also ensures the woman is not pregnant.

5) A woman can divorce a man in this way (divorce 'by talaq') if it was written into her marriage contract. Otherwise she has to apply to a shari'ah court for a divorce 'by khul' (if her husband agrees to divorce) or a tafreeq divorce (if the husband doesn't agree). After divorce, men and women are free to re-marry.

6) As Islamic law isn't part of British law, these kinds of divorce dissolve the nikah, but don't count as a legal divorce if the couple also had a civil marriage — they would have to get a civil divorce too.

Now try this task for the religion you're studying...

Summarise Christian or Muslim beliefs and teachings on marriage and divorce in your own words.

Marriage and Divorce

The family is a <u>key</u> part of the Jewish <u>faith</u>, so <u>marriage</u> is <u>important</u> within Judaism.

Marriage is Important in Judaism

1) To Jews, <u>marriage</u> is an <u>emotional</u>, <u>intellectual</u> and <u>spiritual</u> union. Many see it as the proper context for <u>sex</u> (seen as natural and God-given) and <u>having children</u> (procreation), but it is also for <u>companionship</u>.

2) Marriage is seen as a <u>sacred</u> thing — the word for the first part of the wedding ceremony, <u>kiddushin</u>, means <u>sanctification</u>. God <u>recommends</u> marriage — in Genesis 2:18 he says "It is not good for the man to be alone" (NIV) and then creates Eve to accompany Adam.

> "He who finds a wife finds what is good and receives favour from the Lord." Proverbs 18:22 NIV

3) <u>Adultery</u> is seen as <u>sinful</u>, as it goes <u>against</u> the <u>7th commandment</u> (Exodus 20:14).

4) Marriage and children <u>continue</u> the Jewish <u>faith</u>, as it's passed on through the <u>family</u>.

5) This means there's often some <u>anxiety</u> over '<u>marrying out</u>' — marrying someone who <u>isn't Jewish</u>. Jews who have '<u>intermarried</u>' are <u>less likely</u> to carry on Jewish <u>customs</u> and <u>practices</u>. '<u>Intermarriage</u>' is more <u>accepted</u> than it used to be though.

6) <u>Orthodox</u> Jews don't tend to <u>cohabit</u> because sex outside of marriage is seen as wrong. <u>Progressive</u> Jews see cohabitation in a more <u>positive</u> light, but ideally the relationship should be <u>stable</u> and <u>long-term</u>.

7) Technically, the Torah <u>allows</u> polygamy for <u>men</u> — Abraham had <u>two</u> wives, for example. But almost no Jews today are in <u>polygamous</u> marriages.

Same-Sex Marriage is a Divisive Topic in Judaism

1) <u>Liberal</u> and <u>Reform</u> Judaism both backed same-sex marriage <u>before</u> it became <u>legal</u> in the <u>UK</u>, and <u>both</u> hold same-sex weddings in their <u>synagogues</u> now that it's legal.

2) Jews who <u>support</u> same-sex marriage refer to Genesis 1:27, "God created mankind in his own image" (NIV) — they say being <u>homosexual</u> can't be wrong, as people have been <u>created</u> homosexual.

3) Many <u>Masorti</u> Jews <u>support</u> same-sex marriage. They have created a <u>shutafut</u> (<u>partnership</u>) ceremony for same-sex marriages or civil partnerships — this is different from the traditional <u>kiddushin</u>.

4) <u>Individual rabbis</u> in all <u>3</u> movements can choose <u>not</u> to hold same-sex weddings if they <u>want</u> to though.

5) <u>Orthodox</u> Jews <u>don't</u> tend to support same-sex marriage, believing it goes <u>against</u> the teachings of the <u>Torah</u> on homosexual sex. There's a <u>growing recognition</u> though among some Orthodox Jews that homosexual Jews need to be <u>welcomed</u> in synagogues and <u>supported</u>.

Divorce is Allowed, but it's the Last Resort

1) Jews <u>accept</u> that some marriages don't work out, and that it's <u>better</u> for a couple to <u>divorce</u> than to stay together and be <u>unhappy</u>. But <u>divorce</u> is a last resort after all attempts at <u>reconciliation</u> have <u>failed</u>.

2) The <u>Torah</u> teaches that a husband and wife "become one flesh" (Genesis 2:24 NIV) when they <u>marry</u>, so divorce is <u>difficult</u> and shouldn't be entered into <u>lightly</u>. However, Maimonides' <u>Mishneh Torah</u> (Ishut 24) sets out <u>conditions</u> for when divorce should happen, e.g. if a man knows his wife has committed <u>adultery</u>.

3) Traditionally, a <u>woman cannot</u> initiate divorce. This has caused an issue for <u>Orthodox</u> women who can't get their husband to agree to a divorce, as they <u>can't remarry</u> in a <u>Jewish ceremony</u> without a <u>get</u> (<u>divorce certificate</u> issued by Jewish courts). Women in this situation are known as <u>agunot</u> (<u>chained women</u>). <u>Wives</u> can also <u>refuse consent</u> for a divorce, but this happens <u>less often</u>.

4) <u>Reform</u> synagogues recognise <u>civil divorces</u>, but people may want a <u>religious divorce</u> too. A Reform Jewish court <u>can</u> issue a <u>get</u> even if the husband won't agree. Reform Jews <u>don't need</u> a <u>get</u> to remarry.

There's a lot to take in here...

...so go back over anything you're not sure about. Then test out your new knowledge by jotting down two different Jewish ideas on each of these topics: marriage, same-sex marriage, and divorce.

REVISION TASK

Families

As the saying goes, 'you can choose your GCSEs, but you can't choose your family'. Or something like that...

Family is Important to Christians, Jews and Muslims

1) Ideally, a stable family can give a child a sense of identity and a feeling of security. They'll learn how to behave, how to give and receive love, and about right and wrong.

2) Many Christians, Jews and Muslims think it's best for a child to have a father and a mother present (ideally the child's biological parents), so that they grow up with one role model of each sex. Ideally, the couple would be married, as it's believed this provides more stability.

3) For religious people, family life can be a way of introducing their children to their faith.

Christianity and Catholic Christianity

- Family life is important for most Christians. It's seen as a way to build a stable society.

  > "family is 'the first and vital cell of society'." Pope John Paul II, Familiaris Consortio 42 (Catholic teachings on family)

- Many Christians believe it's important to have children and educate them in the faith — see for example Catechism of the Catholic Church 2226 and this quote.

  > "bring [your children] up in the training and instruction of the Lord." Ephesians 6:4 NIV

- This might include activities at home such as reading the child Bible stories, or teaching them about prayer by saying grace (giving thanks) before meals.

- Children become part of the faith at baptism, and this develops as they attend church and prepare for confirmation (see p.9). Many churches provide Sunday schools, which teach Christian ideas through Bible stories. Catholic children attend catechism classes to prepare them for their first confession and communion.

- Festivals such as Christmas and Easter have a strong emphasis on celebration within the family.

- Children are asked to honour their parents — to look after and respect them (Exodus 20:12).

Judaism

- Family life is also very important to Jews, as it's through the family that the Jewish religion and customs are passed on. Children are seen as a divine gift — Psalm 127:3 NIV says "Children are a heritage from the Lord". Orthodox Jews consider anyone whose mother is Jewish to be Jewish — Progressive Jews say the father can 'pass on' Jewishness as well.

- Children should look after their parents — honouring your parents is a mitzvah (Exodus 20:12).

- Many Jewish rituals happen in the home, such as celebrating Shabbat or keeping kashrut (see p.32) so family life is important for educating children about the Jewish faith.

- Rituals like brit milah (male circumcision) and simchat bat (a girl's naming ceremony) connect the child to the faith. Their bar/bat mitzvah ceremony (p.33) requires them to learn about Judaism.

- Talmud Bava Batra 21a explains how teachers were introduced to educate children about the Torah from age 6 or 7. This ensured that knowledge about the Torah was passed from generation to generation. Now, children often attend classes at a heder (a religious school run by the synagogue) to learn Hebrew, and study the Torah and Talmud. This helps them be able to participate in prayers and services.

Islam

- Many Muslims think family life teaches people to be kind, considerate and affectionate. Strong family ties help strengthen the Muslim community — the ummah.

- The Qur'an asks people to care for their parents — "We have enjoined upon man, to his parents, good treatment" (Qur'an 46:15). Muslims place importance on the extended family too.

- Rituals such as aqiqah (a naming ritual) and the bismillah ceremony, which marks the start of the child's religious education, help connect the child to the faith.

- Following Muslim food laws by having halal food in the home helps introduce the child to Islam.

- Mosques often have schools (madrasahs) to teach children about Islam. They learn Arabic so they can read the Qur'an and say prayers. They're also taught from the hadith and sunnah (see p.19).

It's never simple, is it...

Explain two reasons why family is important in the religion you're studying.
Include an example from a source of wisdom and authority. [5]

EXAM QUESTION

Area of Study 1 — Marriage and the Family

Families

Family Life in the UK has Changed

1.8 children is the average...

1) For a long time, the nuclear family was seen in Britain as the ideal family model. Traditionally, a nuclear family was a married man and woman and their children. Religious families are more likely than the UK average to follow this model.

2) Today, the term may include same-sex parents, unmarried couples, and reconstituted (or blended) families (where divorcees with children find new partners). Single-parent families are more common too.

3) Some people worry about children with same-sex parents, as they'll only have role models from one gender. But many believe same-sex couples can provide a stable, loving home, which is what's important.

4) An extended family includes grandparents etc. They might live together, which is more common as people live longer, house prices rise and parents work. For example, parents, children and grandparents might share a home to save money. The grandparents can be looked after but also help care for the children.

Christians Try to Welcome and Support Different Families

1) Some Christians' views on divorce and homosexuality make it difficult for them to accept certain types of family. The Catholic Church is more strongly against same-sex parenting than many other denominations. But whatever their opinions, many Christians focus on making sure blended families and single or same-sex parents feel welcome in church. They consider it important that the family remains connected to the church, particularly so that any children will still be brought up in a Christian way.

2) Churches try to support families in the local parish (area) in many ways, such as by providing counselling and offering classes to parents to help them raise their child in the Christian faith. Churches also provide support at important times in family life through rites of passage such as baptisms, weddings and funerals.

3) Jesus showed people the importance of children: "Let the little children come to me... for the kingdom of heaven belongs to such as these" (Matthew 19:14 NIV). Churches hold family worship, e.g. where children might take part in a service and the music is enjoyable for children.

4) Catholic churches support families in various ways: If you're studying Christianity, just read the first point in the box below.

- Pope John Paul II said that Catholics should take "solicitous care to make sure that [divorcees] do not consider themselves as separated from the Church" (Familiaris Consortio 84). However, divorced Catholics aren't allowed to take communion (see p.8), which could mean they feel unwelcome in church.
- Participating in church worship and the sacraments brings families together. The Catechism of the Catholic Church (2226) says that "The parish is the Eucharistic community and the heart of the liturgical life of Christian families".
- The Family Group Movement is a Catholic organisation that brings people of all ages and situations together, united by their beliefs. Members meet up regularly to do activities together and support one another.
- SVP (St Vincent de Paul Society) is a charity which offers support to whoever needs it, including families.

Jewish Views Tend to Vary, but Families are Supported

1) Single parents aren't considered the ideal but many Jews try to make them feel welcome in the community. It can be harder for single parents to have time and money to take a full part in synagogue and Jewish life.

2) It's sometimes more difficult for divorced parents in Orthodox, and especially ultra-Orthodox, communities. Family is so important that divorcees can be seen as going against the faith. Women without a get (see p.41) who have a new relationship might be seen as adulterers, and their children seen as illegitimate.

3) Progressive and Conservative Jews tend to be more accepting of divorcees, blended families and same-sex parents. They focus on each individual being happy.

4) The Jewish community believes it's important to support families:

- Some synagogues hold services with games and songs which allow children to participate. Synagogues might also hold gatherings for families to spend time together, or classes for parents.
- The Jewish community supports families during key moments in life, through rites of passage such as bar and bat mitzvahs, weddings and funerals. Organisations and rabbis offer counselling for, e.g. bereavement.

Islam & General	Families & Gender Equality

Muslim Views are Changing About Families

1) Some Muslims are accepting of divorced people and blended families, while others are less so.

2) Many Muslims would frown upon same-sex parents because they see homosexuality as wrong. Other Muslims believe that, whatever their personal opinion, they should be accepting of same-sex parents because no one is without sin, so they shouldn't judge. Others are in favour of same-sex parents.

3) The extended family is important in Islam, particularly for offering love and support.

4) The ummah can help to support families. The Qur'an teaches that the ummah should be united together in their faith: "And hold firmly to the rope of Allah all together and do not become divided" (Qur'an 3:103). It supports families at important times through rites of passage, such as funerals, and offers counselling.

5) Men and women worship separately. Women may pray at the mosque less often than men, so boys will often go with their fathers. During Id ul-Adha and Id ul-Fitr (p.24), often the entire family worships at the mosque. Some mosques have groups for parents and children, which exposes the children to the faith.

Men and Women Often Have Different Roles in the Family

For all religions, read the rest of this page.

1) Taking care of the family and home has often been seen as the 'woman's role', with the man's role being to earn money to support the family. Having different roles doesn't necessarily mean men and women are unequal, but these fixed ideas make it hard for either gender to do the opposite role. These traditional roles were, and often still are, supported by Christianity, Islam and Judaism (p.45).

2) These fixed roles mean many men don't get the chance to look after and spend time with their children. When a baby is born, the standard paternity leave for men is 2 weeks — many see this as too little. Shared parental leave (SPL) was introduced in the UK in 2015, giving parents the option to share the time allocated to the mother for maternity leave. But very few men have taken SPL so far.

3) Many women find it difficult to return to work after having children — many find their male colleagues have been promoted in the meantime, or they struggle to afford childcare so they can return to work.

Discrimination Based on Gender is Widespread

Religious views on gender roles have shifted over time as well — see p.45.

1) Gender discrimination is a problem in British society, although the situation's gradually improving. Fixed ideas about men's and women's roles are slowly giving way to an acceptance that you shouldn't define people by gender, and that the idea of certain roles is unnecessary and bad for both genders.

2) Gender stereotypes — e.g. women being more emotional or men being more confident — are now seen by many people as false and damaging to both genders. For example, many people think it's bad that men might feel less able to show or express their emotions because it's thought not to be 'manly' to do so.

3) Some people argue there is still a long way to go before women are treated equally to men, e.g. as well below half of MPs are women. Others think the genders are now treated equally. A minority of people argue that it's now men who have it worse, e.g. because women are now more likely to go to university.

There are Problems with Equality in the Workplace

1) Women have always worked, but in the past they were prevented from doing many jobs, by law or by other people. Some had to stop work when they married.

2) Women were often paid less than men for the same job, or only offered jobs with less responsibility and lower pay. This is still the case, but it's less common now because it's been made illegal through various laws, which were brought together in the Equality Act 2010.

3) Despite these laws, there are professions in which one gender is underrepresented. Nursing or midwifery are seen as women's jobs, while building or firefighting are seen as men's. Women are also underrepresented in positions of authority, e.g. as politicians or company directors.

4) Many women still face discrimination at work, such as not being considered for promotion or being sexually harassed, although it's illegal. It can be hard to prove it happened because of their gender — or even to find out it's happening. E.g. it's hard to tell if you're being paid less than someone else in the same job.

Area of Study 1 — Marriage and the Family

Gender Equality

The Bible is a bit Unclear on the Status of Women

1) The Bible gives different messages on the subject of gender discrimination. Some of Jesus's followers were women, e.g. Mary and Martha (Luke 10:38-42), and he treated them equally.

2) Galatians 3:28 says "There is neither ... male [nor] female, for you are all one in Christ Jesus" (NIV). But 1 Timothy 2:12 says: "I do not permit a woman to teach or to assume authority over a man; she must be quiet" (NIV), which suggests that men and women aren't equal.

> For most of Christian history, women weren't allowed to be priests. This is no longer the case — women can now be ministers in most Protestant denominations, and Anglican priests and bishops. But they can't be Roman Catholic or Orthodox priests.

3) The Bible also says wives should do as their husbands tell them. But many Christians say this reflects the ideas of society at the time, and doesn't correspond with Jesus's attitude towards women.

> "Wives, submit ... to your own husbands as you do to the Lord. For the husband is the head of the wife as Christ is the head of the church..." Ephesians 5:22-23 NIV

4) Many Christians now believe men and women should be equal. The Catechism of the Catholic Church 1938 mentions "sinful inequalities" and says Catholics fight against this.

5) Pope John Paul II said "society should create and develop conditions favouring work in the home" for women (Familiaris Consortio 23). Other denominations are less focused on traditional gender roles.

Jewish Men and Women are Often Seen as 'Separate but Equal'

1) Genesis 1:27 ("male and female he created them" NIV) is often used to state that men and women are seen as equals before God, although different, and with different responsibilities.

2) Judaism doesn't suggest that women should not be able to follow their chosen career. However, there is still a belief that motherhood is a privilege, and women should devote some of their life to it.

3) Orthodox Jews aim to uphold Jewish tradition, so are more likely to suggest women stay at home as wives and mothers. Women play an important role in celebrating Shabbat and teaching children about the faith. Many ultra-Orthodox women work at least part-time though, so their husbands can study the Torah.

4) Reform and Liberal Judaism are committed to full gender equality, e.g. they have female rabbis (p.26).

In Islam, Men and Women are Equal but have Different Roles

1) Men and women have an equal obligation to Allah in terms of prayer, fasting, pilgrimage and charity.

> "Indeed, the Muslim men and Muslim women, the believing men and believing women, the obedient men and obedient women ... the charitable men and charitable women, the fasting men and fasting women... and the men who remember Allah often and the women who do so — for them Allah has prepared forgiveness and a great reward." Qur'an 33:35

2) The Prophet Muhammad had several wives. He treated them equally, and told others to treat their wives well, but all his wives were expected to act modestly. His first wife worked before they were married.

3) Some teachings might suggest men are superior, e.g. "Men are in charge of women by [right of] what Allah has given one over the other and what they spend [for maintenance] from their wealth" (Qur'an 4:34). But they're usually taken to mean that men and women have different roles in the community — men are responsible for providing for the family, and women for the home.

4) Many Muslims believe it's OK for women to work. But some believe women should only work if essential or in traditionally female roles, e.g. midwifery. Some see it as a distraction from looking after the family.

5) Wearing modest clothing, often including a head covering, is an important part of Islam for many Muslim women. Many others don't consider it part of their faith. Some people see it as a way of oppressing women and believe Muslim women are forced to wear it. Many Muslim women argue it's their choice, and that any ban on head coverings would be just as oppressive, as it takes away that choice.

Hmmm... it's a tricky issue.

Learn specific examples to give in your answer, such as jobs where women or men are underrepresented.

Revision Summary

You might think you're done with this section... but I'm afraid there are a few questions for you to do first, just to see how much went in. These questions are similar to the questions you'll have in the exam, so you can get used to what you're meant to do and how much you should write.

If you're not sure about any of the answers, have another read of the section and then try again.

Answer each of these questions <u>in the context of the religion you've studied</u>.

These questions are worth 3 marks, so you need to write down three brief points.

1) Outline three ways in which the religious community supports families.

2) Outline three types of family.

3) Outline three religious beliefs about sexual relationships.

4) Outline three beliefs about the purpose of family.

5) Outline three religious beliefs about marriage.

If you want top marks in these 4 mark questions, you'll need to make sure your answers are well-developed.

6) Explain two reasons why some believers disagree with contraception.

7) Explain two religious attitudes to same-sex marriage.

8) Explain two religious beliefs about non-traditional families.

9) Explain two religious beliefs about sex outside of marriage.

10) Explain two ways that children can be introduced to their faith.

> For the 4 and 5 mark questions, be sure to write a concise, well-organised answer — make your points clear to the examiner.

And add 1 more — these questions are worth 5 marks.
You should also include an example from a source of wisdom and authority.

11) Explain two ways in which religious believers respond to divorce.

12) Explain two religious beliefs about homosexuality.

13) Explain two religious beliefs about gender equality.

And the big one — this is a 12 mark question. Use the bullet point list below to help you plan your answer — the list gives you the things you need to include. Remember, you'll need to make sure you've covered arguments for and against the statement.

14) 'Marriage is a lifelong union between one man and one woman.'
Evaluate this statement.
Give arguments that support the statement and arguments that disagree with the statement.
You must include:

- examples of teachings within the religion you've studied

- non-religious opinions

- a conclusion.

> Take a look at the 'Do Well in Your Exam' section — it gives advice on writing essays.

The Origins of the Universe | All religions

No one saw exactly how the <u>Earth</u> came to be like it is... but science and religion both have their <u>theories</u>.

Scientific Arguments — There are Two Main Types

Cosmological Theories — How the Universe Began

Chief amongst these is the <u>Big Bang</u> theory. It says that the Universe began in an <u>explosion</u> of matter and energy. Matter from this explosion eventually formed stars, planets and <u>everything</u> else. The Universe still seems to be expanding — important <u>evidence</u> for this theory.

Evolutionary Theories — How Living Things Changed

<u>Charles Darwin</u> argued that life on Earth originated from simple cells. Life <u>evolved</u> (gradually changed) over millions of years into a huge variety of forms, and those <u>best adapted survived</u> — 'survival of the fittest'. According to this theory, people evolved from <u>apes</u>, not Adam and Eve.

<u>Non-religious people</u> look to <u>science</u> for <u>answers</u>. They believe that the universe and human life came about by <u>chance</u>. They say that since people evolved from <u>apes</u>, they <u>can't</u> have been created by <u>God</u>.

Religions have their own Ideas about all this...

Some religious people believe <u>only</u> in the stories written in <u>scriptures</u>. Others believe that <u>science</u> tells them <u>how</u> the world was created, but <u>religion</u> explains <u>why</u>. They believe that God <u>caused</u> the Big Bang, and evolution is the <u>way</u> he made humans.

Christian Ideas

1) <u>Genesis</u> chapter 1 says God created everything over <u>six days</u>. On the seventh day he <u>rested</u>. Genesis chapters 1 and 2 describe how God created <u>people</u> in <u>his image</u>, and made <u>woman</u> from <u>man</u> (see p.3).

2) Some believe the Bible gives a <u>literal</u> account of what happened. People who <u>disagree</u> with evolution claim there's a <u>lack</u> of <u>proof</u> backing up the theory — <u>fossils</u> don't show the <u>full process</u> of evolution.

3) However, lots of Christians view the creation story as <u>symbolic</u> and also believe in scientific theories. The <u>Big Bang theory</u> was actually first put forward by a Roman Catholic priest, <u>Georges Lemaître</u>, so religion and science <u>don't</u> have to be completely <u>separate</u>.

4) In fact, many believe that <u>science</u> and <u>religious</u> ideas can exist in <u>harmony</u>. Both the <u>Church of England</u> and the <u>Roman Catholic Church</u> have recognised the <u>benefits</u> of the two working together.

> "Collaboration between religion and science is mutually beneficial..." General Synod of the Church of England, 2010

> "Evolution in nature does not conflict with the notion of Creation..." Pope Francis, Pontifical Academy of Sciences, October 27 2014

Jewish Ideas

1) The <u>Jewish creation story</u> is in Genesis and is the <u>same</u> as the <u>Christian</u> one (see p.3).

2) Jews interpret this story in <u>different ways</u>. Ultra-orthodox Jews believe it is <u>literally</u> true, and would find it <u>difficult</u> to accept <u>scientific arguments</u>.

3) Others would argue that the <u>Torah</u> account is a <u>metaphor</u>, and are <u>open</u> to scientific evidence.

> "So God created mankind in his own image..." Genesis 1:27 NIV

Islamic Ideas

1) The Muslim creation story is <u>similar</u> to that in Genesis: "It is Allah who created the heavens and the earth and whatever is between them in six days" (Qur'an 32:4).

2) The Qur'an says Allah "began the creation of man from clay" (Qur'an 32:7) and <u>breathed</u> life and a <u>soul</u> into the first man, <u>Adam</u> — and all humans <u>descend</u> from him.

3) Some see the descriptions of <u>creation</u> in the Qur'an as <u>agreeing</u> with <u>science</u>. E.g. the Qur'an says "Have those who disbelieved not considered that the heavens and the earth were a joined entity, and We separated them..." (Qur'an 21:30) — this could be understood to <u>support</u> the <u>Big Bang theory</u>.

No monkeying around now, there's a lot to learn here...

Jot down all the beliefs you've learnt about the origins of the universe for the religion you're studying.

(REVISION TASK)

General	# The Environment and Stewardship

Religious believers think people should <u>look after</u> the environment because it was created by God.

The World is Important Because God Created It

Many believers <u>value</u> the world and what's in it because it is <u>God's creation</u>.
They see God's hand in things such as <u>beautiful countryside</u>, a <u>wild sea</u> or a
<u>butterfly's wing</u>. But people <u>don't</u> always take good <u>care</u> of the world we live in...

Humans have Damaged the Environment

Global Warming

- <u>Gases</u> in the atmosphere, called '<u>greenhouse gases</u>', help keep the Earth <u>warm</u>.
- Over the past century, the amount of greenhouse gas in the atmosphere
  has <u>increased</u>, and measurements show that the Earth has <u>got hotter</u>.
  This is called <u>global warming</u>. Higher temperatures make <u>ice melt</u>, which
  causes <u>sea levels</u> to <u>rise</u>. This could lead to <u>flooding</u> in low-lying areas.
- It is mainly caused by the <u>fuels</u> used to generate energy, like <u>oil</u>, <u>coal</u> and <u>gas</u>.

Natural Resources

- A <u>natural resource</u> is anything found naturally that's <u>useful</u> to humans.
- The Earth's population is <u>increasing</u> and people use more <u>raw materials</u> and more <u>energy</u>
  every year. If people carry on like this, many <u>natural resources</u> will eventually <u>run out</u>.
- <u>Fertile land</u> for growing crops is also rapidly <u>declining</u>. Each year, <u>overgrazing</u>
  and <u>irresponsible farming methods</u> turn more fertile land into <u>desert</u>.

Pollution

- Pollution from chemicals can <u>contaminate</u> the environment.
- <u>Sewage</u> and <u>chemicals</u> can pollute lakes, rivers and seas. These pollutants <u>harm</u>
  the plants and animals that live in and around the water, including humans.
- People use <u>toxic chemicals</u> for farming. They also bury <u>nuclear waste</u>
  underground, and dump a lot of <u>household</u> and <u>industrial waste</u> in landfill sites.
  The toxic chemicals can <u>kill</u> plants and animals, and cause <u>cancer</u> in humans.
- <u>Smoke</u> and <u>gases</u> from vehicles and industry can pollute the <u>air</u>,
  cause <u>health problems</u> in humans and damage the <u>ozone layer</u>.

There are Many Ways to Tackle these Problems

1) Many people, both religious and non-religious, work to <u>reduce</u> and <u>repair</u> the harm caused to
   the <u>environment</u>. They think that it's <u>important</u> to look after the planet for <u>future generations</u>.

2) Many religious believers feel it's their <u>duty</u> to <u>look after</u> the environment.
   God <u>gave</u> people the Earth, but expects them to <u>care</u> for it — this idea is called
   <u>stewardship</u>. See the next page for more details on different religious beliefs.

3) Lots of people try to be environmentally friendly by <u>recycling</u> things like <u>paper</u> and <u>plastic</u>.
   They may also take <u>public transport</u> or <u>walk</u> to cut down on pollution caused by vehicle fumes.

4) There's a <u>limit</u> to the <u>Earth's resources</u>, so many people believe it's <u>important</u> to be able to
   <u>manage</u> the resources currently available and to find alternative, <u>sustainable</u> options too.

5) Some also <u>campaign</u> to better inform others about the <u>damage</u> being done to the environment.

Recycle some of this information by using it in the exam...

EXAM TIP

You've probably been told this a hundred times, but always read the questions carefully.
The 12 and 15 mark questions will list points you need to include in your answer, so pay close attention.

The Environment and Stewardship

Christians Believe in Looking After the Environment

1) In Genesis 1:26, God said humans could "rule over the fish in the sea and the birds in the sky, over the livestock and all the wild animals..." (NIV). This power is known as <u>dominion</u>. Some people think it means humans can use the environment <u>however</u> they want.

> "humanity's dominion cannot be understood as licence to abuse, spoil, squander or destroy what God has made..." Christian Declaration on Nature, Assisi 1986

2) However, many Christians believe that God made them <u>stewards</u> of the <u>environment</u>. They have no right to <u>abuse</u> God's creation, and they have a <u>responsibility</u> to protect it.

> "The Lord God took the man and put him in the Garden of Eden to work it and take care of it." Genesis 2:15 NIV

3) Some Christians believe that everything is <u>interdependent</u> (i.e. everything depends on everything else), so driving species of animal or plant to <u>extinction</u>, or harming the <u>planet</u>, eventually ends up harming <u>people</u>.

4) The <u>damage</u> humans do to the environment <u>clashes</u> with their role as <u>stewards</u>. Christian organisations such as <u>CAFOD</u>, <u>Christian Aid</u> and <u>Tearfund</u>® are concerned with putting this responsibility into <u>practice</u>. They put pressure on <u>governments</u> and <u>industry</u> to think more about how people are <u>abusing</u> the <u>planet</u>.

Judaism also Teaches Stewardship

1) Jews <u>value</u> the world because it is <u>God's</u> and he created it: "The earth is the Lord's, and everything in it, the world, and all who live in it; for he founded it on the seas and established it on the waters" (Psalm 24:1-2 NIV).

2) Jews believe in the concept of <u>stewardship</u>. Concern for the <u>natural world</u> is often seen as being at the <u>heart</u> of Jewish teaching.

> "...it is our Jewish responsibility to put the defence of the whole of nature at the very centre of our concern." Jewish Declaration on Nature, Assisi 1986

3) God's creations should <u>remain</u> as he intended, and humans have <u>no right</u> to abuse them. The Jewish Declaration on Nature also stated that "humanity was given dominion over nature, but was commanded to behave towards the rest of creation with justice and compassion". Some think everything is <u>interdependent</u>, with <u>trees</u> being particularly <u>important</u>. Since the creation of <u>Israel</u> in 1948, <u>millions</u> of trees have been <u>planted</u> to aid the <u>reclamation</u> of the desert and help <u>rebuild</u> the <u>nation</u>.

4) Jews also believe that as <u>custodians</u>, they're responsible for making the world <u>better</u> — this is called <u>tikkun olam</u> ('mending the world'). Tikkun olam isn't <u>just</u> about the environment — it's a general <u>ideal</u> that includes helping the <u>poor</u>, and behaving <u>morally</u>.

Muslims are Khalifah of the Earth

1) The Earth is seen as being a <u>product</u> of the <u>love of Allah</u>, so Muslims should treat it with <u>love</u>.

2) Muslims believe they have been appointed <u>khalifah</u> (vice-regents or trustees) of the Earth. This is the idea that while they're on Earth they should take <u>responsibility</u> for the world (<u>stewardship</u>), and make it the sort of place Allah wants it to be.

3) This means Muslims have an <u>obligation</u> to protect the environment. Muslims might carry out their duty as khalifah by being <u>careful</u> with the <u>resources</u> they use, and <u>encouraging others</u> to take care of the environment too.

4) The <u>Prophet Muhammad</u> (called Allah's Apostle here) said that planting a tree is a <u>good</u>, <u>charitable deed</u>:

> "Allah's Apostle said, 'There is none amongst the Muslims who plants a tree or sows seeds, and then a bird, or a person or an animal eats from it, but is regarded as a charitable gift for him.'" Sahih al-Bukhari 39:513

5) At the <u>Day of Judgement</u>, Muslims believe <u>questions</u> will be asked of them. They will be required to <u>answer</u> for any <u>ill-treatment</u> of the planet and its resources.

Look after the environment — it's the natural thing to do...

Define stewardship in your own words, then write a few points about how people might carry it out.

Animal Rights

There is a variety of views on whether animals should be used for the benefit of humans.

Animal Experimentation and Vegetarianism are Key Issues

1) Animals are sometimes used to test products used by humans or for medical experiments. Some people see this as cruel. Others look at the issue in a utilitarian way — utilitarianism is the idea that decisions should be made based on what has the best balance of good and bad outcomes. This can be used to argue that animal testing is acceptable if it could help many people, even if animals suffer.

2) Animals are also used for food. Some say that humans are built to consume meat. Other people argue that hurting animals is wrong, so it's better to be vegetarian or vegan.

Christians believe Animals should be Treated Well

1) Some people might argue that dominion gives humans the right to do what they want with animals, but others say stewardship means caring for God's creatures. Christianity teaches that animals should be treated with kindness, but that they can be used to benefit mankind (as long as their suffering is considered): "The righteous care for the needs of their animals" (Proverbs 12:10 NIV). Many would say only human life is sacred, as only humans were created in the image of God.

2) The Catholic Church tolerates animal testing, but only if it benefits mankind (e.g. if the experiments lead to the development of life-saving medicines).

> "Medical and scientific experimentation on animals is a morally acceptable practice if it remains within reasonable limits and contributes to caring for or saving human lives. It is contrary to human dignity to cause animals to suffer or die needlessly." Catechism of the Catholic Church, 2417-2418

3) Some Christians think it's always wrong to cause suffering to animals to increase our scientific knowledge, particularly since medicines don't always have the same effect on humans as they do on animals. Some denominations, e.g. the Society of Friends (Quakers), are against any ill-treatment of animals.

4) Unlike some other religions, Christianity has no specific food laws. So vegetarianism (not eating meat) and veganism (not eating or using any animal products) are matters for individuals to decide about. The Bible talks about eating meat, so many Christians believe it's fine.

Judaism has Laws about Eating Meat

1) The Noahide Laws, a set of rules Jews believe people should follow, forbid cruelty to animals. The Torah contains specific food laws — only certain animals can be eaten, and the ones that are allowed must be slaughtered in a humane fashion. Foods that are allowed are called kosher (see p.32).

2) The Torah teaches people to treat animals in a sustainable way. Deuteronomy 22:6-7 says that a person can take young birds from a nest, but should not take the mother.

3) Experiments on animals may be tolerated if they result in a benefit for mankind, but only as a last resort. Jews believe in pikuach nefesh — the idea that human life must be saved, even if that means going against other Jewish laws (see p.28). This can be used to argue in favour of animal testing.

Islam Teaches that Animals Should Never be Mistreated

1) The idea of khalifah affects how Muslims treat animals (see p.49). Animals are part of Allah's creation, which Muslims are entrusted to look after.

> "It is Allah who made for you the grazing animals... you eat." Qur'an 40:79

2) Cruelty to animals is forbidden, as is their use simply for pleasure.

3) Muslims believe in showing compassion for all creatures — animals must be slaughtered humanely for the meat to be halal (Arabic for 'allowed').

> "Allah's Apostle said, 'Whoever keeps a dog, one Qirat of the reward of his good deeds is deducted daily, unless the dog is used for guarding a farm or cattle.'" Sahih al-Bukhari 39:515

4) Muslims will generally only allow animal testing if it is done to produce genuine medical advances for humans. The animals should be treated humanely, and no unnecessary pain should be inflicted on them.

Animal rights shouldn't be left out...

Summarise what the religion you're studying teaches about the treatment of animals.

Abortion and Euthanasia

Arguments about abortion and euthanasia revolve around who can <u>decide</u> when life <u>begins</u> and <u>ends</u>.

Abortion and Euthanasia are Controversial Issues

> Abortion is when a <u>foetus</u> is removed <u>prematurely</u> from the womb <u>before</u> it can <u>survive</u>. It's <u>legal</u> in England, Scotland and Wales and can take place until the <u>24th week</u> of pregnancy. Abortions can take place <u>after</u> this time if there's a <u>danger</u> to the <u>health</u> of the mother or foetus.

> <u>Euthanasia</u> is killing someone to <u>relieve suffering</u>, often from an incurable illness. <u>Active</u> euthanasia is when a patient <u>requests</u> help to die, often using <u>drugs</u> — it is <u>illegal</u> in the <u>UK</u>, but legal in some countries, e.g. <u>Belgium</u>. In <u>passive</u> euthanasia, medical treatment that might extend someone's life is <u>withdrawn</u> — they might <u>refuse</u> further treatment, or a <u>life-support machine</u> might be turned off if there is no hope of recovery. This is <u>legal</u> in the <u>UK</u>.

1) Christianity, Islam and Judaism teach that <u>all life</u> is created by <u>God</u>. As God's creation, all life <u>belongs</u> to God and is therefore <u>holy</u>. This is the '<u>sanctity of life</u>' argument.

2) Based on this, many religious people believe that people <u>don't</u> have the <u>right</u> to <u>interfere</u> with when life <u>ends</u>, or to <u>prevent</u> the beginning of a <u>new life</u>. Many support <u>hospices</u> — a hospice is a place where <u>terminally ill</u> people can be well <u>cared for</u>.

3) Other people take into consideration a person's <u>quality of life</u> (how <u>able</u> they are to live a <u>normal</u> life).

Many Christians see Abortion as Undesirable

1) Abortion is a very <u>complicated</u> and <u>emotional</u> issue, but generally speaking, Christianity teaches that abortion is <u>undesirable</u> as God "created mankind in his own image" (Genesis 1:27 NIV).

2) However, the <u>Roman Catholic Church</u> goes so far as to say that abortion is <u>murder</u>, as it teaches that human life <u>starts</u> as soon as the egg is fertilised at <u>conception</u>.

> "...all direct abortion... [is] to be absolutely excluded as lawful means of regulating the number of children." Humanae Vitae, section 14

3) Many argue abortion is wrong because God <u>cares</u> a lot about <u>children</u>. Jesus said "Let the little children come to me, and do not hinder them, for the kingdom of God belongs to such as these" (Luke 18:16 NIV).

4) Not all Churches see it in such black and white terms. The Church of England believes that abortion is <u>permissible</u> in <u>certain circumstances</u>, such as when the pregnancy puts the <u>mother's life</u> at <u>risk</u>. The Society of Friends (the <u>Quakers</u>) argues that the <u>life</u> of the unborn child <u>cannot</u> be valued <u>above</u> that of the woman. Many Christians argue that allowing a woman to <u>choose</u> is a way of showing <u>Christian compassion</u> — whether they agree with the choice made or not.

5) The Bible <u>doesn't</u> actually mention abortion, but it connects <u>life</u> with <u>breath</u>, e.g. in the creation of Adam — so it could be argued that the foetus is only <u>alive</u> when it breathes <u>independently</u>. Other Christian writings (e.g. the <u>Didache</u>, a 2nd century manual of Christian teaching) are quite specifically <u>against</u> it.

Some Christians are Strongly Against Euthanasia

> "...an act or omission which... causes death in order to eliminate suffering constitutes a murder gravely contrary to the dignity of the human person and to the respect due to the living God, his Creator." Catechism of the Catholic Church, 2277

1) <u>Roman Catholics</u> are the most <u>strongly opposed</u> to euthanasia. They believe that anything that intentionally causes death is <u>wrong</u>. So even those who are <u>unlikely</u> to recover consciousness should be kept <u>alive</u>.

2) Some Christians view euthanasia as going against the commandment "You shall not murder" (Exodus 20:13 NIV). Some might argue that only <u>God</u> should <u>decide</u> when a person's life <u>ends</u>, as he gave them life in the first place.

3) Many Christians believe suffering is <u>part of life</u>. Job was made to <u>suffer</u> by Satan, but <u>refused</u> to <u>end</u> his life: "Shall we accept good from God, and not trouble?" (Job 2:10 NIV).

4) Euthanasia could be seen to <u>ruin</u> the natural course of death, when a <u>soul</u> starts to make its way to God.

5) Many Christians feel they must <u>care</u> for sick people, and euthanasia <u>goes against</u> this. Local churches often have links with <u>hospices</u> — Christians would argue hospices allow a person to feel <u>valued</u> as they reach the end of their life.

**Catholic Christianity
Christianity, Judaism**

Abortion and Euthanasia

Some Christians Support Passive Euthanasia

1) Some Christians suggest that the use of 'extraordinary treatment' (e.g. life-support machines which are keeping someone alive artificially) is not always the best approach — they suggest the easing of suffering through passive euthanasia is a way of demonstrating Christian compassion.

2) However, many only agree with euthanasia if the dying person chooses it for themselves.

3) Anglican denominations are against active euthanasia. However, they agree that terrible distress should not be suffered at all costs, and that death may be considered a blessing rather than continuing life-extending treatment. They argue that a person's quality of life must also be considered.

Judaism Allows Abortion in Some Cases

1) As a general rule, Judaism is opposed to abortion that is carried out for non-medical reasons. Human life is part of the universe that God created, and he "created mankind in his own image" (Genesis 1:27 NIV). An unborn child is part of that creation.

> "For you created my inmost being; you knit me together in my mother's womb." Psalm 139:13 NIV

2) Some Jews might argue that it is up to God to decide when life starts and ends (see below).

3) However, Judaism does not teach that the life of an unborn child is more valuable than that of the mother — the foetus isn't seen as a human until birth. Many Jews accept that, in certain cases, abortion should be allowed. Most rabbis allow abortion if pregnancy becomes physically or mentally dangerous for the woman concerned, or if the child is likely to be severely disabled and unable to lead a full life. But it cannot be carried out simply for convenience.

> "...anyone who saves a life is as if he saved an entire world." Mishnah Sanhedrin 4:5

Judaism Teaches That Only God Can Decide When People Die

1) Jewish teaching is generally opposed to the practice of euthanasia. There are some rabbis who have come out in support of it, but most Jews see life as a sacred gift from God. They believe people do not have the right to decide when a life should end.

2) Many see euthanasia as going against pikuach nefesh (see p.28) — Jews should do all they can to save human life, not bring about its end.

3) The relief of pain and suffering is a key part of Jewish teaching. So although euthanasia is seen as wrong if it involves actively doing something to cause someone's death, it may be possible to withhold treatment, if this treatment would cause further distress. Reform Jews would agree with this idea, but ultra-orthodox Jews are strongly against stopping treatment.

4) The words of Rabbi Moses Isserles are sometimes used to argue that it may be reasonable to switch off a life-support machine that's keeping someone alive: "If there is anything which causes a hindrance to the departure of the soul... then it is permissible to remove it."

5) The Jewish sacred text, the Nevi'im, contains an example of euthanasia. Abimelek is hit by a stone:

> "...a woman dropped an upper millstone on his head and cracked his skull. Hurriedly he called to his armour-bearer, 'Draw your sword and kill me, so that they can't say, "A woman killed him." ' So his servant ran him through, and he died." Judges 9:53-54 NIV

To avoid being killed by a woman, which would have been seen as embarrassing, he gets a man to kill him instead. This could be seen as supporting the right to die in a dignified way, but the text doesn't condone or condemn the action, and most don't see it as giving support for euthanasia.

It's tricky, emotional stuff...

For this question, answer in the context of the religion you've studied:
Outline three beliefs about euthanasia.   [3]

Abortion and Euthanasia

Islam Allows Abortion Before Ensoulment in some Circumstances

Muslims believe that people's lives are sacred (see p.51). The Qur'an teaches that "whoever kills a soul... it is as if he had slain mankind entirely" (Qur'an 5:32). This means that abortion is generally seen as wrong.

1) The passage on the right sums up Islamic teaching on abortion. But there are circumstances in which it is permissible.

> "And do not kill your children... We provide for them and for you. Indeed, their killing is ever a great sin." Qur'an 17:31

2) When the mother's life is in danger, abortion is lawful. The potential life in the womb is not as important as the actual life of the mother.

3) When a foetus gets its soul, this is called ensoulment. Islam teaches that this happens after 120 days, when "the soul is breathed into his body" (Sahih al-Bukhari 55:549).

4) This means that within the first 120 days, abortion can be allowed if the mother's life is at risk, or if the baby would be born with a serious defect, though not all Muslims agree with this. After 120 days, abortion is only allowed to save the life of the mother.

5) Some Muslim women argue that they should be free to choose what happens to their bodies. Those that disagree claim that Qur'an 81:8-9 says unborn children will want to know why they were killed.

Muslims are Usually Against Euthanasia

1) Euthanasia is seen as wrong by most Muslims: "do not kill yourselves [or one another]" (Qur'an 4:29).

2) Muslims believe that their lives are Allah's and he has a plan for every living person — he has decided how long each person will live on this Earth, and they do not have the right to interfere with that plan.

3) Islam teaches that life on Earth is a test. Allah knows why people suffer, and they do not have good reason to end their own lives, no matter how bad that suffering is. Instead, those who are suffering should turn to Allah, pray and wait — Allah is merciful, and all will be revealed on the Day of Judgement.

> "O you who have believed, seek help through patience and prayer. Indeed, Allah is with the patient." Qur'an 2:153

4) As a result, Muslims support hospices, but often they try to look after the ill person at home — this allows them to be surrounded and taken care of by their family, friends and neighbours.

> "...when disaster strikes them, [they] say, 'Indeed we belong to Allah, and indeed to Him we will return.' Those are the ones upon whom are blessings from their Lord and mercy." Qur'an 2:156-157

5) However, when a patient has a terminal illness with no hope of improvement, Islam allows doctors to stop 'unnecessary' treatment.

There are Many Non-Religious Views on Abortion and Euthanasia

1) Many atheists support abortion as it gives women control over what happens to their bodies. Humanists prioritise quality of life over sustaining life, and look at the impact on the woman first.

2) There is some debate surrounding the time limit on abortions. Since some babies born prematurely at 24 weeks or less are surviving, some feel that the timeframe for abortions should be shortened. Others feel that there shouldn't be a time limit on abortions at all.

3) There is more of a divide in opinions when it comes to euthanasia. Some support it when a person will die from an illness or where they are suffering from an incurable illness. They feel that ending someone's suffering through euthanasia is the kindest thing to do.

4) However, some people fear that legalising euthanasia would potentially lead to people feeling pressured into it. Some also feel that doctors should work to protect lives, not the opposite.

5) Some people might apply situation ethics — looking for the most loving option in each situation, rather than applying the same rules in every instance. This might lead them to support abortion or euthanasia where it seems to be the kindest option.

Abortion and euthanasia are complicated topics...

...so go back over the pages if you need to. If you're studying Islam, do this question when you're ready: Explain two Muslim teachings on euthanasia.   [4]

EXAM QUESTION

The Afterlife

There's <u>more information</u> on the afterlife on p.6 for Christianity, p.20 for Islam and p.29 for Judaism.

Most Religions Teach that there is an Afterlife

1) Many people believe that, although your <u>body</u> may die and decay, your <u>soul</u> can live on — in other words, you move on to a different kind of <u>existence</u>. This is the basic idea of <u>life after death</u>.

2) Most religions teach that something happens to the soul <u>after death</u>. Some religions teach that the soul is <u>rewarded</u> or <u>punished</u> for the <u>actions</u> of the person on Earth. Others believe the soul is <u>reincarnated</u>. Christians, Muslims and Jews believe that life on Earth isn't <u>everything</u> — a <u>better life</u> awaits them. It's still <u>important</u> though, and is <u>preparation</u> for the afterlife.

<u>CHRISTIANITY</u> teaches that people go to <u>heaven</u> or <u>hell</u>, depending on how God <u>judges</u> their actions — trying to live life according to Christian <u>teachings</u> and believing in <u>Jesus</u> will allow them to receive <u>God's grace</u> and go to <u>heaven</u>. Catholics believe that some go to <u>Purgatory</u> — a place where <u>sins</u> are <u>paid for</u> before going to heaven (see p.6).

"And God raised us up with Christ and seated us with him in the heavenly realms in Christ Jesus... For it is by grace you have been saved..." Ephesians 2:6-8 NIV

"...one who had repented, believed, and done righteousness, it is promised by Allah that he will be among the successful." Qur'an 28:67

<u>MUSLIMS</u> believe the afterlife means going to <u>jannah</u> (paradise) or <u>jahannam</u> (hell). After a person dies, their soul goes to <u>barzakh</u> to <u>await judgement</u> (see p.20). On <u>Yawm ad-Din</u> (the Day of Judgement), everyone's actions will be judged. Muslims believe Allah "...will assemble you for the Day of Resurrection..." (Qur'an 45:26). Those who Allah deems <u>good</u> go to <u>jannah</u>, and the <u>bad</u> to <u>jahannam</u>.

Lots of <u>JEWS</u> believe in <u>Gan Eden</u> (paradise) and <u>Gehinnom</u>, a place where people are <u>punished</u> for bad things they've done (see p.29). Most people will <u>move</u> from Gehinnom to Gan Eden, but <u>evil</u> people will stay for <u>eternity</u>. Some believe they'll eventually be <u>resurrected</u>, when God "will swallow up death for ever" (Isaiah 25:8 NIV). This is part of <u>Maimonides'</u> 13 principles of faith. However, Jews tend to <u>concentrate</u> on <u>this life</u>, rather than what might happen after death.

3) There are many <u>arguments</u> used by both <u>religious</u> and <u>non-religious</u> people to <u>support</u> life after death:

- The <u>paranormal</u> (things science can't explain, which are thought to have a spiritual cause, e.g. <u>ghosts</u>) is sometimes used as evidence. Some people (<u>mediums</u>) claim they can <u>talk</u> to the <u>dead</u>.
- Some people claim to have evidence of <u>reincarnation</u> (they lived a previous life, died, and were reborn in a new body). Lots of research has been carried out with young <u>children</u> who claim to remember <u>past lives</u>.
- People say they've had a <u>near-death</u> or <u>out-of-body experience</u> where they've spoken to long-dead <u>family members</u>.
- Some believe there must be <u>more</u> after <u>life on Earth</u>. They might see going to heaven or paradise as a <u>reward</u> for people who've been <u>good</u> all their lives — it must exist to <u>compensate</u> for the <u>unfairness</u> of life on Earth.

Some People Don't Believe in Life After Death

1) Many people believe that when you die, that's it — you <u>cease to exist</u>. They might argue that there isn't any <u>concrete evidence</u> that there is life after death, so the <u>logical</u> answer is that it <u>doesn't exist</u>. They think people's <u>memories</u> of previous lives <u>aren't real</u> — they could've been <u>suggested</u> to the person.

2) They might say that believing in an afterlife is just a way of <u>helping</u> people deal with <u>death</u> — the idea provides <u>comfort</u>.

3) They could also argue that the idea of an afterlife is used by religions to put <u>pressure</u> on people to <u>follow</u> their teachings and <u>live</u> their lives in a certain way.

4) Believers would <u>disagree</u> with these arguments, since their own beliefs come from <u>sacred texts</u>.

5) Christians might argue that Jesus's <u>resurrection</u> shows that there's life after death: "He was put to death in the body but made alive in the Spirit" (1 Peter 3:18 NIV). However, <u>non-believers</u> may say that the stories of Jesus's resurrection are <u>made up</u>.

It might not seem like it now, but there is life after exams...

EXAM TIP

For 12 mark questions, be sure to finish with a conclusion, based on the arguments you've considered.

Revision Summary

Those were some pretty big issues that you've just read about — now let's see how much you can remember. These questions will let you get a feel for how the exam will be, and how much writing is involved.

If there's anything you can't answer, go back through the section and have another go when you've re-read it.

Answer each of these questions <u>in the context of the religion you've studied</u>.

Let's get the ball rolling with some 3 mark questions. 3 marks = 3 short points.

1) Outline three arguments people might give in support of life after death.
2) Outline three ways believers could protect the environment.
3) Outline three scientific ideas about how the universe and human life began.
4) Outline three religious beliefs about how the world was created.
5) Outline three ways in which people damage the environment.

Moving up to 4 marks. Make two points, but this time develop them further to get an extra mark for each.

6) Explain two religious teachings about the sanctity of life.
7) Explain two ways in which believers might respond to animal experimentation.
8) Explain two reasons why religious people might accept scientific arguments about creation.

5 marks up for grabs now. You'll need to refer to a source of wisdom and authority for top marks.

9) Explain two religious teachings about stewardship.
10) Explain two reasons why some believers are against abortion.
11) Explain two religious beliefs about the treatment of animals.
12) Explain two religious beliefs about life after death.

Make sure that you write clearly and organise your answer well for the longer answer questions.

And last but not least — the 12 mark question. The question will always come with bullet points that you should include in your answer, so use them to make a plan before you begin. Think about arguments in favour of and against the statement, and pack your answer full of information. You'll need to answer in the context of the religion you've studied.

13) 'Euthanasia can be the most compassionate way to help someone who is terminally ill.'
   Evaluate this statement.
   Give arguments that support the statement and arguments that disagree with the statement.
   You must include:
   • examples of teachings from the religion you've studied
   • different opinions within the religion you've studied
   • appropriate ethical arguments
   • a conclusion.

Turn to the 'Do Well in Your Exam' section for more about writing essays.

All religions | Justice, Good and Evil

Working for <u>justice</u> and trying to live <u>good lives</u> are important for many religious believers.

Justice is Important for Many People

1) <u>Justice</u> is the idea of each person getting what they <u>deserve</u> and maintaining what's <u>right</u>. It includes <u>punishing</u> the <u>guilty</u> and protecting the <u>innocent</u>. For victims of crime, justice might mean seeing the offender <u>pay</u> for what they did through <u>punishment</u>, and being made to <u>realise</u> the impact of their <u>actions</u>.

2) Justice is important to religious and non-religious people. Most believe justice is <u>essential</u> for countries to <u>run</u> properly and to ensure that people <u>follow</u> the <u>law</u>. Religious people believe that <u>God/Allah</u> is <u>just</u>:

> <u>CHRISTIANS</u> believe justice is <u>important</u> — everyone should be treated <u>fairly</u> as God created people to be <u>equal</u>. Christians see <u>God</u> as <u>just</u>, and think that they should be too: "And what does the Lord require of you? To act justly..." (Micah 6:8 NIV). They believe that, after a crime is committed, <u>justice</u> can be <u>restored</u> by giving the <u>offender</u> a <u>punishment</u> for their actions.

> <u>ISLAM</u> teaches Muslims to work for justice, and to treat others <u>justly</u> and <u>equally</u>. It is an important part of <u>shari'ah</u> (Islamic law). Muslims believe that they should <u>always</u> strive for <u>justice</u> to take place: "O you who have believed, be persistently standing firm in justice, witnesses for Allah, even if it be against yourselves or parents and relatives" (Qur'an 4:135). Many also believe that those who <u>fight</u> for justice will be <u>rewarded</u> in the <u>afterlife</u>, but those who don't will be sent to <u>jahannam</u> (hell).

> <u>JEWS</u> must follow the <u>mitzvot</u> set out in the <u>Torah</u>, and there have been <u>courts</u> (<u>Bet Din</u>) ensuring these laws are followed since long ago. Jews believe that everyone is equal, and they are <u>encouraged</u> to work for justice: "You must purge the evil from among you... Show no pity: life for life, eye for eye, tooth for tooth, hand for hand, foot for foot" (Deuteronomy 19:19-21 NIV). This means that the <u>victim</u> needs to be <u>compensated</u> by the criminal for <u>justice</u> to truly be done.

People Should Do Good and Avoid Evil

1) Christianity, Islam and Judaism all teach people to live <u>good lives</u>. This includes <u>following</u> religious <u>teachings</u>, e.g. by helping other people. The good things that people do will <u>please God/Allah</u>. Religious people believe they should <u>avoid</u> sin and evil, as their actions will be <u>judged</u> when they die.

2) Many believe that there are <u>two</u> types of evil. <u>Moral evil</u> is when suffering occurs because of <u>human actions</u>, e.g. <u>murder</u> and <u>rape</u>. <u>Natural evil</u> is suffering caused by the <u>world</u>, e.g. <u>floods</u> and <u>earthquakes</u>.

3) Both crime and punishment are connected to <u>suffering</u>. Religious people are normally against most <u>crimes</u> because of the <u>suffering</u> they cause. In some sacred texts, <u>suffering</u> is described as a <u>punishment</u> for the <u>sins</u> people have committed or as a <u>test</u> from God — <u>read p.7 and p.79</u> for more information.

> - In <u>CHRISTIANITY</u>, the <u>sheep</u> and <u>goats</u> parable (Matthew 25:31-46) says that everyone will be <u>judged</u> and <u>separated</u> into the <u>good</u> (the sheep) and the <u>bad</u> (the goats). Jesus said that <u>helping</u> another person is like helping <u>him</u>. If you <u>ignore</u> someone in need of help, it's like <u>ignoring him</u>: "...whatever you did not do for one of the least of these, you did not do for me" (Matthew 25:45 NIV). The people who haven't helped will <u>suffer</u> because of this.
> - Many Christians believe that <u>evil</u> and <u>suffering</u> is caused by humans <u>misusing</u> their <u>free will</u> — they believe that the <u>original sin</u> people are born with makes them <u>capable</u> of sin (see p.7). Some say <u>Satan</u> tempts people to sin.

> - <u>ISLAM</u> teaches that Allah is <u>merciful</u> and those who have done <u>good things</u> will be <u>rewarded</u>, but he will make people who do <u>bad things</u> suffer for them.
> - If people <u>intend</u> to do something <u>good</u>, that will <u>help</u> them on the <u>Day of Judgement</u>, but if they intend to do something <u>bad</u>, it <u>won't</u> count against them (see p.20).
> - Many Muslims believe that the <u>devil</u>, <u>Iblis</u>, tries to make humans turn to <u>evil</u>.

> "He admits whom He wills into His mercy; but the wrongdoers - He has prepared for them a painful punishment." Qur'an 76:31

> - The <u>JEWISH</u> sacred texts explain how to <u>behave</u> in a <u>good</u> way.
> - Jews believe that <u>evil</u> and <u>suffering</u> is the result of humans <u>taking advantage</u> of the <u>free will</u> they were allowed by God.
> - But God will <u>forgive</u> people if they commit <u>sin</u>: "I will have mercy on whom I will have mercy, and I will have compassion on whom I will have compassion" (Exodus 33:19 NIV).

4) Non-religious people reject the idea that <u>God</u> causes suffering. They might feel religion isn't worth the suffering it can sometimes <u>cause</u>, e.g. as an <u>excuse</u> for <u>terrorism</u>, or through <u>persecution</u> of believers.

Why is justice important? Just is...

...that won't get you any marks. Summarise why justice is important in the religion you're studying.

Crime

Crime happens on a <u>daily</u> basis for many reasons. Many <u>religious organisations</u> work to put an <u>end</u> to it.

Many Crimes Break Religious Laws and Teachings

1) There are many <u>different types</u> of crime, including <u>murder</u>, <u>theft</u> and <u>hate crimes</u>.

2) Christianity, Islam and Judaism are against these as they break <u>religious moral laws</u>.

3) <u>Christians</u> and <u>Jews</u> are strongly against <u>murder</u> and <u>theft</u> as they <u>break</u> two of the <u>Ten Commandments</u>. In <u>Islam</u>, the Qur'an also <u>condemns</u> murder and theft.

4) Murder, often seen as the <u>worst</u> crime, goes against the idea of <u>sanctity of life</u> (the belief that life is <u>sacred</u>) held by <u>all</u> three religions.

5) Crimes such as <u>theft</u> and <u>hate crimes</u> disregard religious teachings that people should be treated <u>equally</u>, as the offender shows <u>no concern</u> for the victim.

> A hate crime is any type of crime committed against someone because of their ethnicity, religion, etc.

Crime is Caused by Lots of Different Factors

Most religious believers would agree that if someone does something <u>illegal</u>, they <u>deserve</u> to be <u>punished</u>. But the cause of crime <u>isn't</u> as simple as someone just being <u>bad</u> — there are many different <u>reasons</u> why a person might <u>commit</u> a <u>crime</u>:

1) **POVERTY** — People who are poor might turn to <u>crime</u> out of <u>desperation</u>. They might <u>steal food</u> or <u>money</u>, or earn <u>money</u> illegally, e.g. selling stolen goods.

2) **UPBRINGING** — Some people might become criminals if they've had a <u>troubled</u> <u>childhood</u>, or if they've <u>grown up</u> around crime and it's become <u>normal</u> to them.

3) **MENTAL ILLNESS** — This can lead people to commit crimes because, e.g. they may not fully <u>understand</u> the <u>difference</u> between what's <u>legal</u> and <u>illegal</u>. Others may be easily <u>persuaded</u> into committing a crime.

4) **ADDICTION** — Being dependent on something such as <u>drugs</u> or <u>alcohol</u> can lead to people doing illegal things to <u>fund</u> their <u>addiction</u>.

5) **GREED** — Someone might <u>steal</u> or <u>earn</u> money <u>illegally</u> to get something they <u>want</u> but can't afford.

6) **HATE** — A person might do something illegal because someone else has <u>treated</u> them <u>badly</u>, or because they're driven by <u>prejudice</u>, e.g. racism.

7) **OPPOSITION TO UNJUST LAW** — A law might be <u>broken</u> as a <u>protest</u> if it's seen as unfair. In the 1950s and 60s many people, such as <u>Rosa Parks</u>, broke laws that treated black people <u>unfairly</u> in the <u>USA</u>.

> Many feel that the <u>reason</u> behind the crime should be taken into <u>consideration</u>, and many religious people would want to <u>help</u> the <u>individual</u> as well as tackle the <u>bigger issues</u> that cause crime. However, certain causes would be more likely to get <u>sympathy</u> than others, e.g. <u>poverty</u> would be seen as more <u>reasonable</u> than <u>greed</u>. Many think that breaking a law that is <u>unfair</u> or that goes <u>against</u> religious law is <u>acceptable</u>.

Christians Work to Prevent Crimes

1) Christians are <u>strongly against</u> crime — they're told to <u>care</u> for others: "Love your neighbour as yourself" (Mark 12:31 NIV). Committing a crime such as <u>theft</u> or a <u>hate crime</u> doesn't treat the victim as an <u>equal</u>. Murder is seen as <u>destroying</u> something <u>created</u> by God.

2) Christians have <u>defied laws</u> to fight for what's <u>right</u>, e.g. Martin Luther King (see p.66). In this case, Christians may <u>support</u> breaking laws: "We must obey God rather than human beings!" (Acts 5:29 NIV).

3) Many Christians would <u>help</u> people who are e.g. struggling in <u>poverty</u>, in order to tackle the <u>source</u> of crime. They might donate to <u>charity</u> or help out in <u>food banks</u>, among other things.

4) <u>Christian groups</u> also play their part to try to <u>prevent</u> crime: For <u>Catholic Christianity</u>, just read the <u>purple</u> box.

> The <u>Prison Fellowship</u> is a Christian organisation in England and Wales that helps prisoners by <u>praying</u> for them, through <u>group activities</u>, and helping maintain <u>contact</u> with their <u>families</u>. They try to make prisoners see how they have <u>affected victims</u> of their crimes and <u>stop them</u> from <u>committing crime</u> again when they leave prison, e.g. through <u>restorative justice</u> (see p.59).

> <u>Street Pastors</u>, who help people out at night (see p.13), have helped to <u>lower</u> crime rates and <u>prevent violence</u>.

Now try the <u>Revision Task</u> at the bottom of p.58.

Islam & Judaism

Crime

Elements of both Islam and Judaism help to <u>prevent</u> crime.

Muslims Believe Crime Interrupts the Relationship with Allah

1) Muslims believe that on <u>Yawn ad-Din</u> (the Day of Judgement — see p.20), those who've committed crimes might <u>not</u> be sent to <u>jannah</u>.

2) Many Muslims also believe that a life of crime <u>doesn't</u> allow believers to <u>focus</u> on what really <u>matters</u> — their <u>faith</u> and connection with <u>Allah</u>.

"Allah orders justice and good conduct and giving to relatives and forbids immorality and bad conduct and oppression." Qur'an 16:90

3) <u>Murder</u> is seen as one of the <u>worst</u> crimes: "whoever kills a soul... it is as if he had slain mankind entirely" (Qur'an 5:32). Crimes such as <u>theft</u> and <u>hate crimes</u> defy Islamic <u>teachings</u> about people being <u>equal</u>.

4) Muslims hope that <u>key elements</u> of their religion help to <u>reduce</u> the likelihood of <u>crime</u>. For example, <u>compulsory</u> charitable donations (<u>zakah</u> — see p.22) help to tackle poverty. Alcohol, drugs and gambling are <u>banned</u>, reducing the chance of <u>addiction</u>. Parents are taught to follow <u>teachings</u> in the Qur'an to give their child the best possible <u>upbringing</u>, which should <u>prevent</u> them from turning to crime. Some <u>mosques</u> offer help for families too.

5) Islam teaches Muslims to <u>speak out</u> against <u>unjust laws</u> that go against Allah's teachings, so many would <u>understand</u> someone breaking an unjust law in <u>protest</u> against it.

6) In <u>shari'ah courts</u>, the <u>circumstances</u> surrounding the crime are looked into <u>thoroughly</u>, so the defendant is punished <u>accordingly</u>.

7) Some Muslims work to try to <u>reduce</u> crime by <u>helping prisoners</u> and <u>ex-offenders</u>:

The <u>Muslim Chaplains Association</u> offers <u>religious guidance</u> in <u>prisons</u> in the UK. It aims to <u>reform</u> prisoners and <u>stop</u> them from committing crimes after they are <u>released</u>, e.g. by helping them to <u>reintegrate</u> into society again. It also tries to keep ex-offenders <u>connected</u> to <u>chaplaincies</u> in their local <u>community</u> so they continue to receive <u>support</u> after prison.

<u>Mosaic</u> is a charity that pairs <u>young people</u> approaching the <u>end</u> of their prison sentence with a <u>mentor</u>. As they adjust to life outside of prison, the mentor will <u>help</u> them with things like finding a <u>job</u> and somewhere to <u>live</u> — with the aim that this should <u>prevent</u> them from returning to a life of <u>crime</u>.

Judaism Forbids Murder and Theft in the Noahide Laws

1) The <u>Noahide Laws</u>, which Jews believe that <u>everyone</u> in the world should follow, state that <u>murder</u> and <u>theft</u> are <u>forbidden</u>. Crimes such as <u>hate crimes</u> go against Jewish teachings on <u>equality</u>.

2) Crime goes against <u>God's teachings</u> — Judaism teaches that people who <u>disobey</u> God will be <u>punished</u> by him.

"...the Lord's anger will burn against you, and he will shut the heavens so that it will not rain and the ground will yield no produce, and you will soon perish..." Deuteronomy 11:17 NIV

3) Some <u>aspects</u> of Judaism work to <u>reduce</u> the chances of crime. For example, Jewish <u>financial aid</u> (<u>tzedakah</u>) is donated to charity and helps to combat <u>poverty</u>. Jewish parents are told to <u>guide</u> their <u>children</u> and to make sure they know what's <u>right</u> and <u>wrong</u>.

4) Many Jews would <u>protest</u> against <u>unjust laws</u>, and perhaps <u>break</u> them, as there are <u>examples</u> in the <u>Torah</u> of defying the law for what is right. In Exodus 1:16-17, two <u>midwives</u> were told by the king to <u>kill</u> Hebrew baby boys, but they <u>didn't</u> follow his instructions.

5) Some <u>rabbis</u> work with the <u>Jewish Prison Chaplaincy</u> in order to provide support for Jewish prisoners. The <u>support</u> offenders receive can help them to <u>turn their backs</u> on crime when they leave prison.

There's lots to learn here, so have another read if you need...

REVISION TASK

Then have a go at writing a short paragraph about what the religion you're studying teaches about crime, and what people of that faith do to try to prevent crime.

Forgiveness — All religions

Forgiveness is <u>important</u> to many religious believers — seeking God/Allah's forgiveness, and forgiving others.

Forgiveness can Reunite People and Prevent Reoffending

1) Forgiveness means stopping being <u>angry</u> with someone who's done something <u>wrong</u>. It is very important for many religious believers. They believe God is <u>merciful</u> towards people who <u>genuinely</u> seek his <u>mercy</u> and that they should <u>reflect</u> God's forgiving nature in their <u>own behaviour</u>.

2) Many believe it's important to <u>forgive</u> criminals so they can be <u>reconciled</u> with the <u>community</u>. If they leave prison <u>isolated</u> from others, with <u>no job</u> and <u>little prospects</u>, <u>reoffending</u> might seem like the <u>only option</u>. Forgiveness allows <u>both</u> victims and perpetrators to <u>move on</u>. However, most religious people believe that <u>criminals</u> should still be <u>punished</u> for what they've done.

3) Forgiveness can be <u>shown</u> in many ways. <u>Lesser offences</u> no longer stay on people's <u>records</u> <u>permanently</u>, and there are <u>schemes</u> that give ex-offenders <u>skills</u> and a <u>job</u> when they're released.

4) <u>Restorative justice</u> is where an offender might <u>meet</u> people who've <u>suffered</u> because of the crime they committed. Actually meeting the people they've hurt can help offenders to <u>realise</u> the <u>extent</u> of the <u>damage</u> they've done, try to <u>make up for</u> their actions and <u>discourage</u> them from <u>reoffending</u>. It helps the <u>victim</u> to work towards <u>forgiving</u> the offender.

Christianity Teaches that Forgiveness Comes from Love

1) Jesus taught that <u>God</u> is always ready to <u>forgive</u> and that Christians must <u>accept</u> that forgiveness, and forgive <u>others</u> in turn. The <u>Lord's Prayer</u> includes a verse about forgiveness (Matthew 6:12).

2) Jesus told people to seek <u>reconciliation</u> in any disagreements <u>before</u> offering a <u>gift</u> to God at the temple: "First go and be reconciled to them; then come and offer your gift" (Matthew 5:24 NIV). He also taught people to forgive "not seven times, but seventy-seven times" (Matthew 18:22 NIV).

3) Forgiveness is closely related to <u>repentance</u>. Christians believe that God's forgiveness can only come when they <u>repent</u> of their sins (i.e. say sorry, and turn their backs on them).

Islam Teaches that Allah is Forgiving

1) Muslims can seek <u>retribution</u> (see p.60) for injuries, but they're encouraged to <u>forgive</u> instead. Whenever the <u>Qur'an</u> describes <u>punishment</u>, it talks about <u>forgiveness</u> too.

2) Muslims believe that they must be <u>merciful</u> so that <u>Allah</u> will do the <u>same</u> to them on <u>Yawm ad-Din</u> (the Day of Judgement).

> "But if you pardon and overlook and forgive - then indeed, Allah is Forgiving and Merciful." Qur'an 64:14

3) They believe that wrongdoing should be forgiven if the offender is <u>sorry</u> and tries to <u>make amends</u>.

4) The <u>Prophet Muhammad</u> was forgiving, as told in the Hadith — Muslims believe in <u>following</u> his <u>example</u>.

5) But some <u>crimes</u> are seen as so <u>awful</u> that forgiveness isn't an option, e.g. <u>shirk</u> (see p.17).

Jews Should Follow God's Example and Be Forgiving

1) Jews believe that <u>God</u> is <u>forgiving</u> and <u>merciful</u>, so they <u>must</u> forgive other people too: "...for with the Lord is unfailing love and with him is full redemption" (Psalm 130:7 NIV).

2) For the festival of <u>Yom Kippur</u>, Jews ask for <u>forgiveness</u>, both from <u>people</u> they've hurt and from <u>God</u> (see p.34). Jews believe that you can only be forgiven by the <u>one</u> you've <u>hurt</u>, so God can only forgive a sin against God, <u>not</u> another person.

3) Jews should allow criminals to <u>repent</u> for what they've done and <u>seek forgiveness</u>:

> "Let the wicked forsake their ways and the unrighteous their thoughts. Let them turn to the Lord, and he will have mercy on them, and to our God, for he will freely pardon." Isaiah 55:7 NIV

Answer this question for the religion you've studied...

Explain two reasons why forgiveness is important to religious people. Give a sacred text reference. [5]

EXAM QUESTION

General, Christianity, Catholic Christianity	# Punishment & Treatment of Criminals

Punishment can be used to 'get back' at someone for committing a crime, or to prevent crime in the future.

Criminals Have the Right to Be Treated Fairly

1) The European Convention on Human Rights gives the accused the right to have a fair trial. A trial is considered fair when it is carried out publicly in an unbiased court, and the accused has the opportunity to present their version of events. In the UK, the person is considered 'innocent until proven guilty'.

2) Being tried before a jury (a panel made up of members of the public) is not compulsory in the UK under the Human Rights Act, but many consider it to be one of the main ways to ensure a trial is fair.

3) If found guilty, the sentence given varies depending on the severity of the crime — these include prison and community service. Believers are often in favour of community service — it allows the offender to repay their debt to society yet still lead a normal life, which should help to ensure they don't reoffend.

4) In some countries corporal punishment and torture are forms of punishment:

> - Corporal punishment is when physical pain is delivered by e.g. beating or flogging the offender. It's not used in Europe.
> - Torture is illegal in the UK under the European Convention on Human Rights, but it is used as a punishment in some countries. Torture is often carried out to extract information or confessions from suspected criminals
> - Many religious people would say that torture goes against the sanctity of life argument — life comes from God and is sacred.
> - People who use situation ethics may decide torture is justified in some cases if the information it provides could save many lives.

Punishment can have Various Aims

Retribution

Some people think of punishment as a way of taking revenge on a criminal, of making them 'pay' for what they've done. Critics of this way of thinking argue that revenge doesn't put right the wrong — that it's better to look for a more constructive solution.

Protection

If a criminal is considered dangerous, this is the idea that their punishment should protect the rest of society, e.g. imprisonment. Not many people would disagree with this, but some would argue that you protect society best by reforming offenders.

Reformation

Punishment should aim to change criminals so they won't reoffend again — the idea being that nobody is inherently bad. Many religious people feel this allows offenders to repent and seek forgiveness from God for their actions. Programmes to reform criminals include counselling and giving them work in the community.

Deterrence

The idea that if a punishment is sufficiently bad in some way (e.g. expensive, embarrassing, restricting, painful) it will put people off committing the crime — they understand the consequences. Critics argue that people don't stop to think about punishment before they commit a crime, especially if they've taken drugs or alcohol, so deterrence doesn't work.

Christianity Supports Fairness and Human Rights

1) Christians believe people should be given a fair trial — which could be through trial by jury: "Speak up and judge fairly; defend the rights of the poor and needy" (Proverbs 31:9 NIV).

2) Jesus told people to look at their own behaviour before criticising others. In John 8, a woman who was accused of adultery was saved by Jesus when he said: "Let any one of you who is without sin be the first to throw a stone at her" (John 8:7 NIV). No-one did, and it reminds Christians that everyone sins.

3) Christians believe in treating criminals mercifully: "...if someone is caught in a sin, you who live by the Spirit should restore that person gently" (Galatians 6:1 NIV).

4) Christians think that criminals should be punished for what they've done in a just way, but some think that life in prison should be difficult in order to make offenders think twice about crime. Some think punishment should be "eye for eye" (Leviticus 24:20 NIV), so focus on retribution. Others believe they should "turn... the other cheek" (Matthew 5:39 NIV), and so look more towards reformation.

5) Many Christians don't support torture or corporal punishment because Jesus was against violence (Matthew 26:52), and many support human rights. Christians are particularly aware of the cruelty of physical punishment, as Jesus was beaten and made to wear a crown of thorns before his death.

Now try answering the exam question on p.61.

Area of Study 2 — Crime and Punishment

Punishment & Treatment of Criminals

There are many different views on punishments, but most Muslims and Jews believe in treating people fairly.

Islamic Law is Different to UK Law

1) Some Muslim countries have legal systems that are similar to many Western countries, but some use shari'ah. Shari'ah courts are different to UK courts. Juries aren't used — instead, the judge decides if the accused is guilty. Solicitors often aren't present — the accused represents themselves in court.

2) The Qur'an says that the punishment should fit the crime: "...an eye for an eye..." (Qur'an 5:45). But Qur'an 2:178 explains that the offender can sometimes compensate the victim financially.

3) Many Muslims believe in reformation, and punishment should give criminals the opportunity to see the error of their ways.

> "Allah wants to make clear to you [the lawful from the unlawful] and guide you to the [good] practices of those before you and to accept your repentance." Qur'an 4:26

4) The Qur'an teaches that prisoners should be treated fairly:

> "And they give food in spite of love for it to the needy, the orphan, and the captive" Qur'an 76:8

5) However, some argue that treating prisoners harshly can be more effective in reforming them. Some Muslims are against community service as they believe it's too easy and doesn't stop reoffending.

6) Shari'ah allows corporal punishment. The Qur'an mentions punishments such as whipping that are carried out publicly — the aim of this is to deter the criminal, but some believe this form of punishment can reform offenders too, and offers retribution. However, some Muslims believe corporal punishments are too severe, and don't respect the offender's human rights.

7) Most Muslims don't agree with torture, but some might allow it if it could prevent greater suffering.

Fairness is Important in Judaism

1) Human rights are important to many Jews, and Judaism teaches that offenders should be treated fairly:

> "One witness is not enough to convict anyone accused of any crime or offence they may have committed. A matter must be established by the testimony of two or three witnesses." Deuteronomy 19:15 NIV

2) Fair trials are important in Judaism, and many Jews support having juries involved in trials.

3) In Israel, juries aren't used — the case is decided by one judge, or sometimes three judges. Solicitors defend the accused in court, and can help those arrested before they talk to the police.

4) Jewish people believe that punishment is important. They value punishment in terms of deterrence, protection and retribution: "When justice is done, it brings joy to the righteous but terror to evildoers" (Proverbs 21:15 NIV). But the majority of Jews also believe that punishment should give offenders the chance to reform.

5) The Torah says that the punishment should match the crime: "Anyone who injures their neighbour is to be injured in the same manner: fracture for fracture, eye for eye, tooth for tooth" (Leviticus 24:19-20 NIV). The Torah also explains that "Whoever sheds human blood, by humans shall their blood be shed" (Genesis 9:6 NIV).

6) But many Jews think the punishments set out in the Torah are too harsh — most understand "eye for eye" as meaning that the severity of the sentence given to the offender should be appropriate for the crime committed, rather than that violence should be used.

7) Lots of Jews are concerned about the condition of prisons and prisoners' wellbeing. Most disagree with torture, but some might argue that it's tolerable if the information uncovered could protect lots of people. Pikuach nefesh requires that Jews do all they can to save lives (see p.28).

Don't do the crime if you can't do the time...

Answer the question below in the context of the religion you've been studying.
Explain two religious attitudes to the aims of punishment.   [4]

All religions	# The Death Penalty

The death penalty is <u>killing</u> someone as punishment for a crime — it's also called <u>capital punishment</u>.

The Death Penalty Isn't Used Much Nowadays

1) Capital punishment has been <u>abolished</u> in many countries, including most of Europe and South America. Elsewhere, it only tends to be used for <u>very serious</u> crimes, e.g. <u>murder</u>, <u>espionage</u> (spying) and <u>treason</u>.

2) <u>Religious</u> and <u>non-religious</u> people might make some of these <u>arguments</u> for and against the death penalty:

For the Death Penalty	Against the Death Penalty
• The risk of death might act as a <u>better deterrent</u> to violent criminals than a prison sentence. • If you execute a murderer, it's <u>impossible</u> for them to <u>kill again</u>. Imprisoned murderers have been known to <u>order</u> killings from jail, or to <u>reoffend</u> when released on parole. In cases like these, the <u>suffering</u> of the criminal could potentially <u>protect</u> many people. • <u>Utilitarianism</u> (or the <u>principle of utility</u>) is the idea that the <u>best</u> course of action creates the best <u>balance</u> of <u>good</u> and <u>bad</u> results, e.g. it could be used to argue that killing criminals, although bad for them, would be good for the <u>majority</u> of society.	• Killing as punishment is <u>just as bad</u> as murder — many <u>religious people</u> and <u>Humanists</u> are against <u>any</u> form of killing. • It doesn't give the offender the chance to <u>reform</u>. • There have been cases where someone has been proved <u>innocent after</u> having been executed. • Life is <u>special</u> and should be <u>preserved</u> — many religious people believe in the <u>sanctity of life</u>. • Many religious believers think <u>God alone</u> can decide when to <u>end</u> someone's <u>life</u>.

3) <u>Christians</u> and <u>Jews</u> might be against the death penalty because the <u>Ten Commandments</u> forbid killing.

4) Some people might use <u>situation ethics</u> to decide on a <u>case-by-case</u> basis if the death penalty should be applied. This could lead to people being <u>for</u> the death penalty in <u>some</u> cases, but <u>against</u> it in <u>others</u>, depending on, e.g. the <u>severity</u> of the crime and the <u>background</u> to the case.

Christians have Mixed Views on Capital Punishment

1) Many <u>Christians</u> are opposed to <u>capital punishment</u>, as it doesn't allow for <u>reform</u>, or show <u>mercy</u>. <u>Jesus</u> said to set aside "eye for eye" (Matthew 5:38 NIV) and told people to "love your enemies" (Matthew 5:44 NIV). Many are against the <u>violent nature</u> of the death penalty.

2) However, some Christians in the <u>United States</u> (where capital punishment is <u>legal</u>) believe that the death penalty is a <u>good</u> thing. They say it <u>protects</u> the innocent. They might refer to <u>biblical texts</u> such as "Whoever sheds human blood, by humans shall their blood be shed" (Genesis 9:6 NIV) and "Anyone who strikes a person with a fatal blow is to be put to death" (Exodus 21:12 NIV).

Islamic Law Allows the Death Penalty

1) The Qur'an outlines crimes punishable by <u>death</u>, but <u>encourages</u> victims' families to take <u>compensation</u>.

2) Muhammad said that death could be a punishment in <u>three</u> cases: "the married adulterer, a life for life, and the deserter of his Din (Islam)" (Sahih Muslim 16:4152). This is reflected in <u>shari'ah law</u>.

3) However, some Muslims believe that <u>Allah</u>, not humans, should decide when <u>life ends</u> — they <u>don't</u> agree with capital punishment.

Many Jews are Against Capital Punishment

1) Exodus 21:12-17 outlines crimes <u>punishable</u> by death, such as <u>kidnapping</u>. Someone who "schemes and kills someone deliberately" (Exodus 21:14 NIV) could face the <u>death penalty</u>. Many Jews <u>disagree</u> with this — people can <u>pay</u> for their <u>actions</u> and seek <u>forgiveness</u>. The death penalty is an option in <u>Israel</u>, but is <u>hardly</u> used.

2) Mishnah Makkot 1:10 suggests that the death penalty should be <u>avoided</u>. A court "that would execute somebody once in seven years would be considered destructive". The <u>Talmud</u> put many <u>restrictions</u> on using the death penalty so it was nearly <u>unusable</u>.

Learn all the different arguments about the death penalty...

You must discuss both sides of the argument for 12 mark questions — don't just stick to your own views.

EXAM TIP

Revision Summary

And that wraps up another section — time to see how you got on. The questions below are a similar style to the questions you'll be answering in the actual exam.

If there's anything you can't answer, go back through the section and have another go when you've re-read it.

Answer each of these questions <u>in the context of the religion you've studied</u>.

For these 3 mark questions, keep it short and snappy with 3 brief points.

1) Outline three aims of punishment. *Retribution, rehabilitation, protection*

2) Outline three examples of causes of crime. *Addiction, poverty & need*

3) Outline three arguments against capital punishment. *Murder, against reform, sanctity of life*

4) Outline three conditions that make a trial fair.

5) Outline three ways that an offender might be punished. *Prison, community service, death penalty*

6) Outline three ways that forgiveness can be shown.

These 4 mark questions require you to develop your points for full marks.

7) Explain two religious beliefs about evil and suffering.

8) Explain two ways that religious people can help to prevent crime.

9) Explain two religious attitudes to crime.

Make sure your longer answers are well organised and clearly written so the examiner can easily see your points.

And the questions continue — this time for 5 marks.
You should include an example from a source of wisdom and authority.

10) Explain two reasons why justice is important to many religious believers.

11) Explain two religious beliefs about why people should live good lives.

12) Explain two religious beliefs about the treatment of people accused of crimes.

13) Explain two reasons why many religious believers feel that punishment is important.

Saving the best for last — the 12 mark question. The question will have bullet points that you need to include, so you can use these to make a plan. Jot down arguments for and against the statement so you don't forget any when you actually start writing your answer.

14) 'The death penalty is never a suitable punishment.'
   Evaluate this statement.
   Give arguments that support the statement and arguments that disagree with the statement.
   • examples of teachings from the religion you're studying
   • non-religious arguments
   • appropriate ethical arguments
   • a conclusion.

Head over to the 'Do Well in Your Exam' section for help with writing essays.

Peace and Conflict

World peace — a pretty tall order, but there are a lot of people <u>striving</u> for it...

Peace is the Absence of Conflict and Violence

1) <u>Peace</u> means that everyone in the world lives in <u>harmony</u>, and there is <u>no conflict</u>.

2) Many organisations, such as the <u>United Nations</u> (UN), work to find <u>peaceful solutions</u> to disputes and to <u>end all wars</u>, all over the world.

3) Christianity, Islam and Judaism all <u>encourage</u> believers to work towards <u>achieving peace</u> in the world.

Pacifism

- A <u>pacifist</u> is someone who has strongly held beliefs that <u>war</u> and physical <u>violence</u> are <u>wrong</u>. Pacifists believe that <u>all</u> disputes should be settled <u>peacefully</u>.

- There were pacifists in Britain who <u>refused</u> to fight in the world wars. These '<u>conscientious objectors</u>' went to prison rather than go against their beliefs — they were <u>prisoners of conscience</u>. They suffered <u>humiliation</u> in prison, and after they'd been released.

- There are different <u>degrees</u> of pacifism — some people are against violence <u>under any circumstances</u>, whereas others may <u>disagree</u> with violence, but understand that sometimes violence is the <u>least horrible</u> option.

Violence Has Many Different Forms

1) <u>Crime</u> is a source of a lot of violence, e.g. <u>assault</u> or <u>murder</u>.

2) Violence can occur during <u>protests</u> — a protest is when a group of people join together to <u>campaign</u> for a cause they support. While many protests occur <u>peacefully</u>, some protests become <u>violent</u> if protesters don't feel their views are being heard.

3) <u>Terrorism</u> is when a person or group deliberately seeks to cause <u>fear</u> and inflict <u>suffering</u> on other people through <u>violence</u>, sometimes for <u>political</u> reasons. The attack on the <u>World Trade Center</u> by the terrorist organisation <u>al-Qaeda</u> in New York in September 2001 was the <u>worst</u> terrorist attack in history.

4) <u>War</u> is when two or more groups or countries <u>fight</u> one another. It's <u>usually</u> decided by <u>governments</u>.

5) War and terrorism have caused many <u>deaths</u>. Lots of religious people believe in the <u>sanctity of life</u> argument, that life is given by <u>God</u> and is <u>sacred</u>, so war and terrorism are in <u>direct conflict</u> with this.

Wars Can Have Many Causes

Most wars have causes that are a <u>combination</u> of lots of different factors:

1) <u>RELIGION</u> — this has been the cause of many <u>conflicts</u> in the past and the present (see p.65-68).

2) <u>SELF-DEFENCE</u> — wars started to <u>combat</u> a threat from another country or to <u>stop</u> them from attacking first, e.g. a <u>pre-emptive strike</u>.

3) <u>TRIBALISM</u> — this tends to trigger wars where a <u>group</u> of people fight for their own <u>independent</u> state.

4) <u>HONOUR</u> — wars fought to defend the <u>honour</u> and <u>dignity</u> of a country, or to <u>save face</u>.

5) <u>GREED/ECONOMICS</u> — <u>acts of aggression</u> (attacking without provocation) are <u>condemned</u> by the UN, so purely economic wars driven by greed (e.g. raids and invasions to gain territory or goods) are few and far between. Economic factors still have an impact though — <u>poverty</u> and <u>economic imbalances</u> can make wars <u>more likely</u>.

6) <u>RETALIATION</u> — a war might be started in <u>revenge</u> for something, e.g. <u>World War One</u> started after Franz Ferdinand, Archduke of Austria, was <u>assassinated</u>.

I'll give you a peace of advice...

In questions 1(d) and 3(d) in your exams, you can scoop an extra 3 marks for spelling, punctuation, grammar and specialist terms. Brush up on these by heading over to the 'Do Well in Your Exam' section.

EXAM TIP

Peace and Conflict

Some wars are seen as necessary and 'just'. Others are sometimes seen as being fought for God.

Many People Think There Can Be 'Just Wars'

1) Although most people see peace as being ideal, many recognise that sometimes a war has to be fought. Just War theory is a philosophical theory, developed from ideas of Christian philosophers — such as St Thomas Aquinas in the 13th century. The ideas have now been adopted by people of many different beliefs. The theory explains the conditions that must be met for a war to be classed as necessary:

- There must be a good reason for the war, e.g. self-defence or to help innocent people under threat.
- All other options have been attempted to avoid war.
- It must be started by a proper authority — such as an elected government or president.
- A war must have a reasonable chance of success. Fighting an unwinnable war is considered a waste of lives.
- Any harm caused by fighting the war mustn't be as bad as the harm it's trying to prevent.

There are also conditions for fighting a war justly. These are:

- Discrimination: war should discriminate between combatants and civilians — it's not seen as 'just' to deliberately target civilians.
- Proportionality: the military advantage gained by an attack must outweigh any harm to civilians.

2) Religious and non-religious people might turn to situation ethics to decide if a war is 'just'. They'd look at all the factors surrounding the case, and choose what they think would most likely bring about peace.

People Who Fight in Holy Wars Believe They're Supported by God

1) A holy war is one where people believe that God is 'on their side'. Wars are mentioned in both the Old Testament and the Tenakh, and in the Qur'an.

2) In the past, holy wars have been fought over territory or to convert people, e.g. the crusades in the 11th to 13th centuries. However, holy wars can be declared for different reasons, such as to protect a religion.

3) Religion has been a factor in modern wars too (though often not the only factor). Although the civil war in Syria didn't start over religion, Sunni and Shi'a Muslims have fought on opposite sides. Jews and Muslims are on opposing sides in the conflict in Palestine.

4) Atheists and humanists, who don't believe in God, have criticised religion for causing conflict and wouldn't support starting a war over religion — but neither would many religious people. Some atheists and humanists also identify as pacifists, and don't agree with conflict being used at all.

Christians Believe People Should Be Peaceful

1) Many of Jesus's teachings show that peace is the ultimate goal for all human beings.

2) Isaiah 9:6 referred to the Messiah as the "Prince of Peace" (NIV) — Christians believe Jesus was the Messiah and God wanted him to create peace on Earth.

3) For Christians, Jesus's command to "Love your enemies" (Luke 6:27 NIV) is very important in the way they live their lives. He said that people shouldn't follow the Old Testament teachings about retaliation:

"You have heard that it was said, 'Eye for eye, and tooth for tooth.' But I tell you... If anyone slaps you on the right cheek, turn to them the other cheek also." Matthew 5:38-39 NIV

This implies that Christians shouldn't meet violence with violence.

4) This is evident in Matthew 26:47-56. Even though Judas had betrayed him, Jesus didn't condone anyone being violent. Jesus said "all who draw the sword will die by the sword" (Matthew 26:52 NIV), suggesting that people who engage in conflict will die because of it.

5) In his Sermon on the Mount, Jesus said "Blessed are the peacemakers" (Matthew 5:9 NIV). He also told his followers "Peace I leave with you; my peace I give you" (John 14:27 NIV).

Peace and Conflict

Many Christians Follow Jesus's Teachings and Work for Peace

1) Some Christians put Jesus's teachings into action and work to put an end to violence in the world.

> Dorothy Day was a Catholic activist who followed Jesus's pacifist teachings. She protested against the Spanish Civil War, WW2, violence and nuclear weapons in the USA (see p.69). She co-founded 'The Catholic Worker', a newspaper which was firmly anti-war and eventually evolved into a pacifist group of campaigners.

> The Catholic Archbishop Oscar Romero worked for peace during turbulent times in 1970s El Salvador. He raised awareness of the suffering and violence people were being subjected to by the military and the police. He helped those affected by the cruelty, fought for their rights and promoted peace between opposing groups. He was killed for his beliefs in 1980.

2) Some, such as Dorothy Day, believe that Jesus's teachings mean Christians should be pacifists. The Society of Friends (Quakers) is opposed to war under all circumstances.

3) Because of their belief in peace, Christians tend to use passive resistance against injustice — campaigning without violence.

> Dr Martin Luther King was a Baptist minister who dedicated his life to trying to change the way black people were treated in the USA. He organised peaceful marches, rallies and boycotts, and in 1965 blacks were given equal voting rights with whites.

> Thomas Merton was a Catholic monk and a famous pacifist. In the 1960s, his writings influenced many in the civil rights movement for racial equality and he was against the violence of the Vietnam War.

4) Most Christians wouldn't support violent protests, but some might think it's sometimes justified — when Jesus saw that some people were exploiting the temple, he "overturned the tables of the money changers and the benches of those selling doves" (Matthew 21:12 NIV) in protest at what they were doing.

Some Christians Recognise Just Wars

1) Although war goes against the teachings of Jesus, most Christian denominations accept that there can be such a thing as a 'just war'. They would agree with the conditions of the Just War theory (see p.65). It doesn't mean that the war is right — it's just not the worst option.

2) Some interpret this verse as meaning the government has the right to use violence to ensure peace:

> "...if you do wrong, be afraid, for rulers do not bear the sword for no reason. They are God's servants, agents of wrath to bring punishment on the wrongdoer." Romans 13:4 NIV

Some believe that sometimes war is the only way to find peace, e.g. against an evil regime. Christians are taught to "Love your neighbour" (Mark 12:31 NIV) — this could involve defending people in war.

3) The Catechism of the Catholic Church (2265) says that "Legitimate defence can be not only a right but a grave duty for one who is responsible for the lives of others". However, due to the advanced weaponry used in modern-day wars (see p.69) and the horrendous impact that war has had in Syria, the Catholic Church is reconsidering its stance on just war.

4) Christians are strongly against the indiscriminate killing involved in terrorism.

Holy Wars are Now Rejected By Nearly All Christians

1) In the 11th, 12th and 13th centuries, Christians went on crusades to 'free' the Christian holy places in Palestine. The wars caused a lot of devastation.

2) In the past, holy wars were fought to convert other people to Christianity. Jesus told his disciples "Do not suppose that I have come to bring peace to the earth. I did not come to bring peace, but a sword" (Matthew 10:34 NIV). Many think Jesus wasn't actually talking about violence here — he meant that spreading the Christian message would cause divisions between believers and non-believers.

3) The vast majority of Christians don't believe in the idea of a holy war any more. Although it's for different reasons, their stance on holy war would be the same as an atheist's (see p.65).

Just war — just learn it...

Explain two Christian beliefs about just war. Refer to sacred texts.   [5]

Peace and Conflict

Islam Teaches People to be Peaceful

1) Islam promotes living a peaceful existence — the Qur'an teaches that people should be kind to others, even if they don't treat them well. Muslims believe Allah sees everything and will judge people.

> "And the servants of the Most Merciful are those who walk upon the earth easily, and when the ignorant address them [harshly], they say [words of] peace." Qur'an 25:63

> "If you should raise your hand against me to kill me - I shall not raise my hand against you to kill you. Indeed, I fear Allah, Lord of the worlds." Qur'an 5:28

2) Muslims believe they should play their part to bring about peace. They can do this through prayer, campaigns or by working with people from other religions to create peace in the community.

3) The majority of Muslims disagree with pacifism, as war is sometimes justified in the Qur'an: "Fight in the way of Allah those who fight you but do not transgress. Indeed. Allah does not like transgressors" (Qur'an 2:190). It means they can fight in self-defence, but should only do what's absolutely necessary.

4) Some are against all war and violence as they believe peaceful action is always best, and is key to Islam.

5) The Arab Spring in 2011 saw many Muslims in countries such as Egypt demanding more political power for ordinary people. Many demonstrations were carried out peacefully, with a focus on passive resistance. Islam teaches people to protest against injustice, but not in violent ways.

In Islam, a Just War is Known as Military Jihad

1) Jihad means 'striving' or 'struggle', and the concept is often misunderstood. There are two types of jihad — greater and lesser jihad (see p.23). Lesser jihad is the 'struggle' to improve the world, and war is an example of it, but it must be fought only as a last resort. The Qur'an teaches that people can fight: "Allah will punish them by your hands and will disgrace them and give you victory over them..." (Qur'an 9:14).

2) The part of jihad involving military action is known as Harb al-Maqadis (holy war). It's a war considered to be justified by God to protect Muslims and their religion. Some believe the Qur'an says that war is an acceptable option to defend Islam: "Those who believe fight in the cause of Allah" (Qur'an 4:76).

3) Sunni and Shi'a Muslims have similar views on jihad nowadays. Both consider it a key part of their religion as it's covered in the Qur'an — in Shi'a Islam it's also formally recorded as one of the Ten Obligatory Acts (see p.21). In the past, Twelver Shi'a Muslims believed that jihad could only be declared when the last Imam came out of hiding (see p.16), but jihad for defensive purposes was still allowed.

4) Military jihad has very strict rules — these are the conditions in Islam for a just war. There are many similarities with Just War theory:

- It is justified to bring about freedom from tyranny, restore peace, combat oppression, or right injustice.
- Jihad must be in the name of Allah, and according to his will. It must be declared by a religious leader.
- If an Islamic country has been assaulted, then war is justified.
- In the past, jihad was used to spread Islam and gain more land. However, now many Muslims believe jihad must not be used to colonise, suppress or impose Islam on non-believers.
- The hadith Muwatta Malik 21:10 also sets out some conditions for battle: "Do not kill women or children or an aged, infirm person. Do not cut down fruit-bearing trees. Do not destroy an inhabited place".
- If the opposition wants to end the war, then Muslims must accept it: "And if they incline to peace, then incline to it [also]..." (Qur'an 8:61).

5) Some believe that if they do fight for Allah, they'll be rewarded in the afterlife "And he who fights in the cause of Allah and is killed or achieves victory — We will bestow upon him a great reward" (Qur'an 4:74).

6) Some Muslims believe that just wars can no longer exist because of, e.g. the use of WMDs (see p.69).

7) The term 'jihad' is sometimes used by Islamic terrorists to justify their acts of terror. However, nearly all Muslims are strongly against this — they don't consider the terrorists to be real Muslims.

Learn all the conditions for a just war in Islam...

Explain two Muslim beliefs about just war. Refer to sacred texts. [5]

EXAM QUESTION

Judaism	**Peace and Conflict**

Judaism Teaches that Peace is Very Important

1) The universal greeting among Jews is 'shalom' (peace). Jews don't support war unless it's essential — the Torah teaches that peace should be the first approach, and war shouldn't be started without good reason.

2) Trying to bring about peace is very important in Judaism, and it features in many Jewish prayers. Peace is believed to be given by God.

3) Jews expect that a Messiah will come and bring peace to Earth (see p.29). Micah 4:3 prophesies that when this happens, weapons will be unnecessary and will be turned into ploughshares (the blade of a plough): "They will beat their swords into ploughshares and their spears into pruning hooks" (NIV). Isaiah 2:4 demonstrates how Jews hope that war will end: "Nation will not take up sword against nation, nor will they train for war any more" (NIV).

4) Jews are against terrorism, and hope God will defend the weak from terrorists: "defending the fatherless and the oppressed, so that mere earthly mortals will never again strike terror" (Psalm 10:18 NIV).

5) Most Jews aren't pacifists, but non-violence is seen as a good choice if it's the only way to survive, or if using violence would be pointless. This is why Jews generally don't respond violently to anti-Semitism. Only non-violent protest against injustice would be encouraged.

> Emanuel Ringelblum provided food and tried to improve conditions in the ghettos of Warsaw (under German control at the start of WWII). He collected accounts of the atrocities that happened and hid them underground — some information eventually reached other countries in Europe. He defied the Germans without resorting to violence.

Violence is Sometimes Allowed

1) Pikuach nefesh (the duty to save life) means Jews must try to save someone who's in danger of being murdered — even if they must kill the murderer. However, they should use the minimal necessary force.

2) According to the Talmud and the Torah, a person can kill someone else in self-defence if their own life is under threat: "Whoever sheds human blood, by humans shall their blood be shed" (Genesis 9:6 NIV).

3) These ideas can apply to war, and many Jews believe that sometimes war is needed to bring about peace.

There are Two Types of War — Obligatory and Optional

1) War is split into two types — milchemet mitzvah (obligatory war) and milchemet reshut (optional war).

2) Milchemet mitzvah are thought to be commanded by God, so could be thought of as holy war. In the Old Testament, God supported the Israelites in war — King David praised God for his help: "The Lord... shot his arrows and scattered the enemy" (2 Samuel 22:14-15 NIV). Milchemet mitzvah might be:

> - a war fought in self-defence, or a pre-emptive strike in order to avoid being attacked.
> - a war to help neighbouring countries — so that your own country is not invaded.

These conditions are similar to Just War theory.

3) In recent times, wars have been fought by the state of Israel. Many Jews see these as milchemet mitzvah. Some see them as defending the Promised Land that was given to Abraham by God.

4) Milchemet reshut refers to wars described in the Tenakh to expand Israel's territory. Maimonides said they could only be fought while the Temple existed — many think they can't be fought today.

5) There were conditions on milchemet reshut, e.g. in Deuteronomy 20. One condition was peace must be offered first: "When you march up to attack a city, make its people an offer of peace" (Deuteronomy 20:10 NIV). It includes rules about the treatment women of children, and cutting down trees too.

6) Although some of these aren't in line with Just War theory, they've been developed into modern ideas about just war, such as protecting non-combatants and not causing unnecessary destruction.

Mitzvah or reshut? Make sure you know which is which...

Explain two Jewish beliefs about when war is justified.
Include an example from a source of wisdom and authority. [5]

Weapons of Mass Destruction | All religions

Another heavy topic I'm afraid...

Weapons of Mass Destruction Cause a Huge Amount of Damage

1) Some wars have used <u>weapons of mass destruction</u> (WMDs). These are weapons that can destroy large areas of land and/or lots of people all at once, e.g. <u>chemical</u>, <u>biological</u> and <u>nuclear</u> weapons. They're <u>indiscriminate</u> — they harm soldiers and civilians alike.

2) <u>Chemical</u> and <u>biological</u> weapons are <u>banned</u> by international law — using them is considered a <u>war crime</u>. There are many arguments <u>for</u> and <u>against</u> possessing <u>nuclear weapons</u>:

> - Nuclear weapons serve as a <u>deterrent</u> to ensure peace — a country might <u>not</u> attack another if that country has nuclear weapons. Many countries give this as the <u>reason</u> for <u>keeping</u> nuclear weapons. In the 1900s, several conflicts were <u>settled</u> or <u>sidestepped</u> because nuclear weapons posed too big a <u>risk</u>.
> - Some have a <u>utilitarian</u> perspective — the best course of action is the one that brings about the best <u>balance</u> of positive and negative results. The <u>USA</u> bombed Hiroshima and Nagasaki in Japan in <u>WW2</u> as they thought that using nuclear weapons would <u>save</u> the most <u>lives</u> overall, and <u>end</u> the war <u>faster</u>.
> - Nuclear weapons could be used by a country in order to <u>defend</u> itself if under attack.

> - Nuclear weapons are <u>costly</u>. Many people argue that <u>funds</u> could be <u>better spent</u>, e.g. on healthcare.
> - Many religions believe in the <u>sanctity of life</u> — life was given to humans by God and should be <u>respected</u>. <u>Widespread suffering</u> caused by nuclear weapons completely goes against this.
> - Believers who agree with <u>Just War theory</u> might argue that the <u>indiscriminate nature</u> of nuclear weapons (they would kill innocent people) could <u>never</u> be classed as <u>just</u>.
> - Earth is <u>God's creation</u> — using nuclear weapons would <u>destroy</u> what God trusted humans to take <u>care</u> of.

Many Religious Believers are Against WMDs

Christian views

- Some Christians use <u>Jesus's teachings</u> about <u>peace</u> to argue against nuclear weapons. <u>All</u> Christian denominations are <u>against</u> using them.
- However, some think nuclear weapons help to <u>keep the peace</u> as countries are afraid of starting a nuclear war.

Muslim views

- Many Muslims are against WMDs as they don't follow the conditions of <u>lesser jihad</u> (see p.67) — <u>innocent people</u> would get hurt or killed.
- <u>Pakistan</u> (a Muslim country) has nuclear weapons, but other Muslim countries have come out <u>against</u> possessing WMDs.

"...whoever kills a soul... it is as if he had slain mankind entirely." Qur'an 5:32

Jewish views

- The Talmud says that if something will inflict harm on over a <u>sixth</u> of the population, then it's <u>not allowed</u>.
- The <u>Purity of Arms</u> rule is followed by the <u>Israeli Defence Forces</u>. It says they will only use their weapons as much as is considered <u>reasonable</u>, they <u>won't hurt</u> people who aren't involved in the conflict and will try <u>not</u> to <u>damage</u> buildings. The sweeping damage caused by WMDs <u>doesn't</u> fit with these constraints.
- Although actually using WMDs <u>couldn't</u> be <u>justified</u>, Jews believe that a country could <u>say</u> that they'll use nuclear weapons, but <u>without</u> ever intending to <u>use</u> them, to <u>stop</u> something <u>bad</u> happening. They might support this idea with the <u>sanctity of life</u> argument. Israel has <u>never</u> revealed <u>whether</u> it has nuclear weapons.

1) Both <u>Christians</u> and <u>Jews</u> might turn to Deuteronomy 20. It suggests that <u>women</u> and <u>children</u> should be <u>spared</u>, and <u>unnecessary damage</u> shouldn't be caused: "When you lay siege to a city for a long time... do not destroy its trees by putting an axe to them, because you can eat their fruit" (Deuteronomy 20:19 NIV). The <u>total destruction</u> that WMDs would cause goes <u>against</u> this.

2) Some <u>atheists</u> are in favour of WMDs to <u>deter</u> an opponent and to potentially <u>use</u> — they don't believe their <u>actions</u> will be <u>judged</u>. Others are strongly <u>anti-WMDs</u> as they believe people only live <u>one life</u> on Earth. <u>Humanists</u> have <u>opposed</u> the use of WMDs due to the <u>huge number</u> of people that would <u>suffer</u>.

Make sure you know arguments for and against WMDs...

...plus non-religious views and ethical arguments too. These will all help edge you closer to top marks.

All religions — Peacemaking

Finding peace and resolving conflicts is <u>important</u> to Christians, Jews and Muslims.

Justice, Forgiveness and Reconciliation are Key to Peacemaking

1) <u>Justice</u> is the idea of each person getting what they <u>deserve</u>, and maintaining what's <u>right</u>. Believers think that God is <u>just</u> — he treats and judges people <u>fairly</u> as he created everyone <u>equally</u>. Justice leads to a <u>fairer society</u> — if people feel they're treated equally, there's more chance of <u>peace</u>.

2) <u>Forgiveness</u> is when a person <u>stops</u> feeling <u>hurt</u> by something another person has done to them. Another of God's characteristics is that he is <u>merciful</u> — he forgives people for the things they've done wrong. As God is merciful towards them, <u>believers</u> feel that they should <u>forgive</u> other people, and that forgiveness is the <u>only</u> way true peace can be achieved.

3) <u>Reconciliation</u> is bringing people together that previously were in conflict to make <u>peace</u>.

Christians Believe That God is Fair and Forgiving

1) Christians believe that <u>justice</u> is very important, since people are <u>equal</u> in the eyes of God. Christians have a <u>duty</u> to look after other people, and try to <u>guide</u> them to do what's right and <u>repent</u> of their sins.

2) They believe they should follow God's <u>example</u> and be just to <u>others</u>: "...what does the Lord require of you? To act justly and to love mercy and to walk humbly with your God" (Micah 6:8 NIV). The parable of the <u>sheep</u> and <u>goats</u> shows God treats people well if they've done the same to others.

3) <u>Forgiveness</u> is important to Christians — <u>read p.59</u> to learn more about it. They believe they should <u>seek</u> God's forgiveness and <u>forgive</u> people who've hurt them.

> "Blessed are the merciful, for they will be shown mercy." Matthew 5:7 NIV

4) If they <u>repent</u>, and put their <u>faith</u> in God, God forgives people and they are <u>reconciled</u> with him. Christians believe the same sort of <u>reconciliation</u> is needed between people to create peace.

Muslims Try to Forgive and Reconcile as Muhammad Did

1) Muslims believe strongly in <u>justice</u> and that they should treat all people <u>fairly</u> and <u>equally</u>. They consider maintaining justice to be part of their role as '<u>khalifah</u>' — <u>vice-regents</u> of Allah's creation.

2) Islam teaches that <u>Allah</u> and the <u>Prophet Muhammad</u> are forgiving — <u>have a read of p.59</u>.

3) Muslims are encouraged to work to restore <u>peace</u>. They believe it's important to <u>reconcile</u> fractured relationships — this is something that the <u>Prophet Muhammad</u> did.

> "And not equal are the good deed and the bad. Repel [evil] by that [deed] which is better; and thereupon the one whom between you and him is enmity [will become] as though he was a devoted friend." Qur'an 41:34

Jews Must Work for Justice and Ask for Forgiveness

1) <u>Justice</u> is a major part of Judaism — Jews believe in <u>fairness</u>. Pirkei Avot 1:18 (part of the <u>Talmud</u>) says that "By three things is the world sustained: law, truth and peace."

2) Many Jews believe that <u>true peace</u> can only happen when everyone is treated <u>fairly</u> and any people in conflict are <u>reconciled</u>.

> "Learn to do right; seek justice. Defend the oppressed." Isaiah 1:17 NIV

3) <u>Seeking forgiveness</u> from God and people you've wronged is very <u>important</u> in Judaism. In <u>conflict</u> situations, asking for forgiveness and forgiving others is an important step to <u>reconciliation</u>. <u>Turn to p.59</u> to find out more about forgiveness in Judaism.

Learn it all — the examiner isn't as forgiving as God...

Write 'Justice', 'Forgiveness' and 'Reconciliation' along the top of a piece of paper. Underneath, write down what you've learned on this page for the religion that you're studying.

Peacemaking

Many religious organisations work towards <u>peace</u> and help people in countries devastated by war.

Religious Believers Can Work for Peace Directly and Indirectly

1) Many religious believers feel they must act to create <u>peace</u> — see p.66 for some examples. Some might be <u>directly</u> involved in peacemaking by working for organisations which offer <u>relief</u> to war-torn areas.

2) Some religious charities <u>campaign</u> for help for groups in conflict to <u>rebuild</u> their <u>relationship</u>. For example, <u>Christian Aid</u> has urged governments to find a <u>compromise</u> in the Israel/Palestine conflict.

3) Religious people can also help to create peace <u>indirectly</u>, e.g. by <u>donating</u> money to charitable causes and by holding <u>protests</u> and <u>demonstrations</u> against conflicts. Some may work to ensure that people have equal <u>human rights</u>, which could help to <u>avoid</u> conflict.

Christian Charities Work for Peace and Help Victims of War

In the <u>Sermon on the Mount</u>, Jesus says "Blessed are the peacemakers, for they will be called children of God" (Matthew 5:9 NIV). Many feel that it's important to <u>help people</u> caught up in <u>conflict zones</u> and to try to bring <u>peace</u> to the area.

- <u>Pax Christi</u> is a Catholic organisation that works for peaceful conflict <u>resolution</u>. They try to bring people back <u>together</u> who've been in <u>conflict</u> with one another.
- They believe in <u>avoiding</u> conflict and the <u>violence</u> that comes with it. They campaign for governments to spend <u>less money</u> on weapons and armed forces. They also disagree with <u>nuclear weapons</u>, and work for nuclear <u>disarmament</u>.

Muslims Can Give Money to Support Peacemaking

1) Muslims believe it's important to try to create a <u>peaceful world</u>. They believe that this is part of their role as <u>khalifah</u>.

2) Individuals can help to make the world more <u>equal</u> through <u>zakah</u> — <u>2.5%</u> of their yearly savings should be given to the <u>needy</u>, no matter how rich or poor they are. Zakah could be <u>donated</u> to a number of different <u>charities</u> which are involved in <u>peacemaking</u> and supporting <u>victims of war</u>.

- The <u>Muslim Peace Fellowship</u> is a group of Muslims who want to promote <u>peace</u>, <u>justice</u> and <u>non-violence</u>.
- It strives to do <u>good</u> through <u>Islam</u> — the group promotes peace <u>through</u> faith, and works to bring about changes that make society <u>fair</u> and <u>compassionate</u> to <u>everyone</u>. They do this by <u>raising awareness</u> through events, prayer and working with other faiths.

- <u>Islamic Relief UK</u> is a group inspired by their <u>faith</u> to try to help as many people as possible.
- They help people affected by <u>war</u> — in <u>Syria</u> they've given people essentials such as <u>food</u> and <u>healthcare</u>. They also help people in <u>neighbouring countries</u> who've <u>fled</u> their homes because of the <u>conflict</u>.

Many Jews Work for Peace in Israel

1) Jews believe that <u>peace</u> is something that God gives the <u>world</u>. Many Jews <u>protest</u> for peace and try to create a <u>fairer world</u>, since they believe that peace is only really possible when <u>everyone</u> is treated <u>justly</u>.

2) Charity through <u>financial aid</u> is called <u>tzedakah</u>. Everyone is expected to contribute <u>10%</u> of their wealth — this money can <u>help</u> people <u>affected</u> by war and help to create <u>equality</u> to <u>avoid</u> war.

The <u>Jewish Peace Fellowship</u> is a pacifist organisation, founded to help <u>conscientious objectors</u> in WWII. The organisation believes that military action <u>never</u> solves conflicts, and that <u>active non-violence</u> (e.g. negotiations, promoting social justice) is the only way to settle disputes. They're helping to <u>resolve</u> the conflict in <u>Israel</u> and <u>reconcile</u> the people there.

<u>Natal</u> (Israel Trauma Center for Victims of Terror and War) helps people in <u>Israel</u> who've been affected by the <u>conflict</u> there. It aims to <u>care</u> for and <u>treat</u> people suffering from <u>health problems</u> related to <u>war</u>, e.g. post traumatic stress disorder.

Peace, love, charity... and a nice revision task to end with...

How do religious believers work for a more peaceful world? Jot down as many ways as you can.

Revision Summary

That was a lot of information to take in there, so now test yourself to see how you got on. These questions are similar to the ones that you'll be answering in the exam, so you know what it'll be like on the day.

If there's anything you can't answer, go back through the section and have another go when you've re-read it.

Answer these questions <u>in the context of the religion you've studied</u>.

The exam will start off with some straightforward 3 mark questions.

1) Outline three causes of conflict.

2) Outline three conditions of Just War theory.

3) Outline three concepts that are important in peacemaking.

4) Outline the work of three Christians who campaigned for peace. ← Only answer this question if you're studying <u>Catholic Christianity</u> or <u>Christianity</u>.

5) Outline three ways that charities work for peace and help victims of conflict.

6) Outline three reasons why holy wars have been fought in the past.

4 marks now — make 2 points, but this time develop them for full marks.

7) Explain two ways in which religious people can work for peace.

8) Explain two reasons why justice is important for religious believers.

9) Explain two religious teachings about forgiveness.

10) Explain two religious attitudes to pacifism.

Make sure your writing is well structured and accurate in the longer questions — your points have to be clear to the examiner.

Next up, some 5 mark questions. You should include an example from a source of wisdom and authority.

11) Explain two religious teachings about conflict.

12) Explain two religious beliefs about holy war.

13) Explain two reasons why peace is important to believers.

Hang on to your hat — it's the 12 mark question. The question will come with a list of things to include, so use it when you start planning your answer. Write a list of arguments for and against the statement and make sure you've included them all.

14) 'Nuclear weapons deter countries from attacking each other and ensure peace.'
    Evaluate this statement.
    Give arguments that support the statement and arguments that disagree with the statement.
    You must include:
    • examples of teachings from the religion you've studied
    • different opinions within the religion you've studied
    • appropriate ethical arguments
    • a conclusion.

If you need advice on writing essays, have a look at the 'Do Well in Your Exam' section.

Design and Causation | All religions

The belief that God <u>created</u> the world is an <u>important part</u> of <u>many religions</u>, and often strengthens <u>faith</u>.

Different People Believe for Different Reasons

1) About <u>84%</u> of the <u>global population</u> belongs to a religion (source Pew Research Centre). The rest don't have specific religious beliefs, or have <u>no spiritual beliefs</u>. There are <u>many reasons</u> for being <u>religious</u>:

- People want to find out <u>why</u> life is as it is. Some people are convinced the '<u>design</u>' or '<u>causation</u>' arguments <u>explain</u> this.
- Some are drawn to the <u>purpose</u>, <u>structure</u> and <u>comfort</u> religion provides, or simply by the desire to have <u>something</u> to <u>believe</u>. Some people's faith is <u>strengthened</u> by the <u>feelings</u> they experience during <u>worship</u> and as part of a religious <u>community</u>.
- People brought up by religious <u>parents</u> or in a religious <u>community</u> are more <u>likely</u> to believe in a <u>god</u>.

2) There are <u>various reasons</u> why people might reject religion: they believe there's <u>no proof</u> there's a <u>god</u>, or that religion causes too much <u>strife</u> between people, or that the <u>evil</u> in the world shows there's no <u>god</u>.

3) <u>Atheists reject</u> the idea of a <u>divine being</u>. <u>Agnostics</u> believe it's <u>impossible</u> to know <u>either way</u> for <u>certain</u>.

The Design Argument: 'The Universe Must Have Had a Designer'

1) Belief that God <u>created</u> the universe is a <u>central</u> part of <u>belief in God</u> — not only does the universe's existence <u>prove</u> God's existence, but believers think it shows some of his <u>characteristics</u>, e.g. his <u>power</u>.

2) Many Christians, Muslims and Jews believe a god <u>exists</u> because of '<u>design</u>' arguments. The idea is that the <u>intricate workings</u> of the <u>universe</u> can't have come about by <u>chance</u>. There must have been some kind of <u>designer</u> — a <u>god</u>. The Bible, the Qur'an and the Torah <u>support</u> this argument:

> The <u>Qur'an</u> says <u>aspects of nature</u> are <u>evidence</u> <u>Allah</u> is the <u>creator</u>. "In the creation of the heavens and earth, and the alternation of the night and the day ... and ... the winds and the clouds ... are signs for a people who use reason." (Qur'an 2.164)

> The <u>Bible's</u> argument is <u>similar</u>. Romans 1:20 says "since the creation of the world God's invisible qualities — his eternal power and divine nature — have been clearly seen, being understood from what has been made" (NIV).
>
> "God created the heavens and the earth" Genesis 1:1 NIV — Torah/Bible

3) Some think aspects of <u>nature</u> support this idea. For example, <u>snowflakes</u> form <u>complex</u> shapes that are <u>unique</u> to each <u>individual</u> snowflake. The <u>distribution</u> of <u>petals</u> and <u>seeds</u> on many <u>plants</u> and the <u>spiral</u> shape of some shells follow <u>mathematical</u> rules.

4) <u>William Paley's watchmaker argument</u> says that if you came across an intricate <u>watch</u>, you wouldn't think it was made <u>by chance</u> — you would assume it had been <u>designed</u>. The same must be true of <u>complex structures</u> in <u>nature</u>. A common example people give is the <u>human eye</u>, which is made up of <u>many parts</u> — it's so <u>sophisticated</u>, they believe it <u>must</u> have had a designer.

5) <u>Scientists</u> say the <u>conditions</u> that led to the <u>creation</u> of the <u>universe</u> and <u>life</u> were extremely <u>specific</u>. The <u>fine-tuning</u> argument says this shows there was a <u>designer</u> — they couldn't have occurred by <u>chance</u>.

Some People Aren't Convinced by These Arguments

1) <u>Charles Darwin</u> explained how species <u>developed</u> by <u>adapting</u> themselves to the <u>conditions</u> around them through '<u>survival of the fittest</u>'. <u>Species</u> or <u>individuals</u> that have <u>characteristics</u> that are <u>beneficial</u> for <u>survival</u> are <u>more likely</u> to live, while those that <u>aren't</u> well-adapted are <u>more likely</u> to <u>die out</u>. This helps to explain how species have <u>developed</u> their <u>characteristics</u> through <u>time</u> — known as <u>evolution</u>.

2) In <u>2009</u>, a survey found <u>37%</u> of people in <u>Britain</u> thought evolution was 'beyond reasonable doubt'.

3) Some Christians, Muslims and Jews believe evolution <u>doesn't</u> contradict the <u>design argument</u> — <u>God</u> or <u>Allah</u> must have 'designed' <u>evolution</u>. <u>Darwin</u> didn't see it as <u>conclusive</u> proof <u>against</u> God's existence.

4) Some <u>disagree</u> with evolution. They may struggle most to <u>reconcile</u> evolution with the belief that God created <u>humans</u> in his own <u>image</u> — it may seem <u>unlikely</u> he did so by <u>slowly evolving</u> humans from <u>apes</u>.

5) <u>Scientists</u> can explain things such as why <u>plants</u> and <u>shells</u> often have <u>spiral</u> patterns — shells have <u>evolved</u> to do so because it means the animal <u>inside</u> a shell can keep <u>living</u> in it as it <u>grows</u>.

6) Some people believe God <u>created</u> the universe but has not had any <u>further involvement</u> with it. Some believe that there's <u>no evidence</u> the '<u>designer</u>' and <u>creator</u> still <u>exists</u>.

Design and Causation

Ideas about <u>causation</u> have been used over the <u>centuries</u> as evidence that a divine being <u>exists</u>.

Causation: 'There Must Have Been a First Cause'

1) The <u>cosmological argument</u>, also known as the <u>First Cause</u> argument, is founded on a <u>chain of logic</u>.

2) Everything that <u>happens</u> is <u>caused</u> by <u>something else</u>. An event <u>now</u> was caused by an <u>earlier</u> event, that was caused by an <u>even earlier</u> event, etc. If you trace this <u>chain</u> back in time, there are <u>two</u> possibilities:
   - The chain goes back <u>forever</u> — i.e. the universe has <u>always</u> existed, it's <u>eternal</u>.
   - You eventually reach a <u>starting point</u> — an <u>uncaused</u> cause or 'First Cause'.

3) Some think the 'First Cause' was <u>God</u>, as only he is <u>eternal</u> and has enough <u>power</u> to create the universe.

4) The <u>scriptures</u> in Christianity, Islam and Judaism describe how <u>God</u> created the <u>universe</u>. Believers may use the <u>cosmological</u> argument (along with the design argument) as <u>evidence</u> to <u>support</u> this idea.

Christians Believe God Created the Universe

1) <u>Christian</u> teachings on creation are taken from Genesis 1-2, which says God created <u>everything</u> — see p.3. Some take the description in Genesis <u>literally</u>. Others think it's more <u>symbolic</u>, and might look to <u>science</u> too.

2) <u>Thomas Aquinas</u>, a 13th century monk, developed <u>Five Ways</u> to prove God <u>exists</u>. They've been <u>influential</u> in <u>Christianity</u>. Three of them have a <u>similar logic</u> to the <u>cosmological</u> argument:

• <u>Nothing</u> can <u>move</u> by itself — everything needs <u>something</u> to <u>move</u> it. • This means the <u>first</u> thing that <u>ever</u> moved needed something to <u>move</u> it. • This <u>first mover</u> is <u>God</u>.	• <u>Nothing</u> can <u>create</u> itself. • There can't be a <u>chain</u> of <u>creation</u> that's been happening <u>forever</u>. • So there must have been a <u>first cause</u> — God.	• <u>Contingent</u> beings are beings that are <u>caused</u> to <u>exist</u>. • It's <u>necessary</u> for there to be a <u>being</u> which has <u>created</u> contingent beings. • This <u>necessary being</u> must be God.

The Qur'an States that Allah Created the Universe

1) <u>Muslims</u> believe <u>Allah</u> created the world — Qur'an 79:27 says "Allah constructed it". The Qur'an says <u>Allah</u> made Adam from <u>clay</u> and breathed <u>life</u> and a <u>soul</u> into him — and that all humans <u>descend</u> from Adam.

2) The Muslim theologian <u>al-Ghazali</u> wrote in his book al-Iqtisad fil'Itiqad that <u>everything</u> that starts to exist was <u>caused</u> to <u>exist</u>. The <u>universe</u> started to exist, so it had a <u>cause</u> — <u>Allah</u>. The focus on the universe having <u>started</u> to exist (i.e. not being <u>infinite</u>) is a <u>key part</u> of the theory, known as the <u>kalam cosmological argument</u>. Al-Ghazali believed the <u>universe</u> was made up of <u>chains of events</u> that Allah had <u>predetermined</u>.

The Torah says God Created the Universe

1) <u>Jewish</u> teachings about <u>creation</u> come from Genesis 1-2, which says God created <u>everything</u> — see p.3 for more.

2) <u>Ultra-Orthodox</u> Jews, who see the Torah as the <u>literal</u> word of God, tend to <u>accept</u> the account in Genesis. <u>Others</u> may argue the story <u>isn't exact</u> but just a way of <u>understanding</u> how it happened, though they think God created everything. Other parts of the Tenakh <u>support</u> this, e.g. God says "It is I who made the earth" in Isaiah 45:12 NIV.

3) The theologian <u>Maimonides</u> wasn't sure about <u>creation</u> — "the world cannot but be either eternal or created in time. If it is created in time, it undoubtedly has a creator". He came up with forms of the <u>cosmological argument</u> too.

There are Differing Opinions on the Cosmological Argument

1) Some people question its <u>logic</u>. They argue that the argument <u>contradicts</u> itself — it says <u>everything</u> has to have a <u>cause</u>, but then says there must be an <u>event</u> that <u>didn't</u> have a <u>cause</u> — the <u>first cause</u>.

2) There's <u>no evidence</u> that if there is a <u>first cause</u>, it has to be a <u>divine being</u> — a <u>god</u>. Some say that even if a <u>god</u> was the <u>first cause</u>, it doesn't mean they <u>still</u> exist now. It also doesn't give any <u>indication</u> that the god has the <u>characteristics</u> of the <u>Christian</u>, <u>Jewish</u> or <u>Muslim</u> god.

3) Some <u>believers</u> think the <u>Big Bang theory</u> (p.47) <u>supports</u> the argument — God <u>caused</u> the Big Bang.

Blimey, it's enough to make your head spin...

It's a good idea to read these two pages again now to get them in your head — they're pretty complex.

Miracles All religions

Miracles are a form of revelation (p.76-78) — believers may think they prove God exists and reveal his nature.

Many Believe Miracles Prove There is a God

1) Miracles are seemingly inexplicable events, such as people with apparently incurable illnesses being healed.

2) Christianity, Islam and Judaism all involve some belief in miracles, though to differing extents. These include events in their scriptures, though some people believe miracles also happen nowadays. Others argue that the miracles in religious texts should be interpreted symbolically rather than literally.

3) People believe miracles offer proof there is a god because they go against the laws of nature — only God would have the power to do so. They also show God's benevolence, as many miracles are beneficial, e.g. healing someone who is ill. Healing people also shows that God can decide who lives or dies.

Christians Read Stories of Miracles in the New Testament

1) Jesus performed miracles to show he had the power of God, and to show the importance of faith. These included feeding 5000 people with very little food, and walking on water (Matthew 14:13-21 and 22-33).

2) He was known for curing people of their illnesses, e.g. John 4:43-54. Healing miracles are important in Christianity, e.g. the water at the Catholic pilgrimage site Lourdes is thought to cure people (see p.77).

3) Christians believe the birth and resurrection of Jesus were miracles in their own right (see p.4).

Miracles are Important in Judaism

1) Many miraculous events are described in the Torah. A well-known example is God sending down manna (miraculous food) from heaven so the Israelites could eat while they were in the desert — see Exodus 16.

2) Some Progressive Jews say the stories are spiritual messages and aren't literally true. More orthodox Jews may think they did happen. Many Jews prefer to focus more on God, the Torah and creation than miracles.

3) The word 'nes' is used for 'miracle' in Hebrew — it means 'sign' or 'marker', as miracles are signs of God. But the Torah warns Jews not to be influenced by miracles alone — it's more important to focus on God.

> "If a prophet ... announces to you a sign or wonder, and if the sign or wonder ... takes place, and the prophet says, '... follow other gods ...', you must not listen to the words of that prophet ... It is the Lord your God you must follow." Deuteronomy 13:1-4 NIV

Muslims Believe the Qur'an is a Miracle in Itself

1) Muslims believe the Qur'an is a miracle — the direct word of Allah, with a style that's impossible to copy. Qur'an 17:88 says "If mankind ... gathered ... to produce the like of this Qur'an, they could not".

2) Some think the Qur'an contains 'scientific miracles' — it describes facts discovered centuries later, e.g. how human embryos develop (Qur'an 23:13-14). Others disagree, as it's not detailed enough to be sure.

3) Many Muslims think that the prophets performed miracles in order to show they had been sent by God. For example, some believe Muhammad split the moon in two — Qur'an 54:1 says "the moon has split".

Some People Don't Believe in Miracles

1) Some believers prefer to focus on God and living their life in a moral way rather than on miracles.

2) Atheists and humanists don't tend to believe in miracles. They think they can be explained by science, or are fakes or misunderstandings. They might explain someone being cured of a terminal disease by saying they had been misdiagnosed, or the hope of a religious figure healing them had stimulated their recovery.

3) It can be a matter of perspective — a religious person might seek a miraculous explanation for something atheists and humanists would call a coincidence, e.g. something happening soon after you prayed for it.

Don't rely on a miracle to pass your exam — revise well...

... and do exam questions. Miraculously, there's one here — you'll need to answer it in the context of the religion you're studying: Explain two different religious attitudes to beliefs in miracles.   [4]

Revelation

For many religious people, <u>revelation</u> is an <u>important factor</u> in proving God's <u>existence</u>.

Revelation is How God's Presence is Revealed

1) It's <u>difficult</u> to <u>conclusively prove</u> God <u>exists</u>. So Christians, Muslims and Jews look for <u>evidence</u> to reveal God's <u>presence</u>. They believe he is <u>revealed</u> in <u>different</u> ways, including through the <u>scriptures</u>, the <u>world</u> around us and <u>religious experiences</u>.

2) Revelation doesn't just involve knowing God <u>exists</u>, but also what he's <u>like</u> and what he <u>expects</u> of people. Revelations can <u>give rise to</u> or <u>strengthen</u> people's <u>belief</u> in a god. There are <u>two</u> main types of <u>revelation</u>:

Special Revelation

1. <u>Special revelations</u> are revelations to <u>specific</u> people. The scriptures of <u>all three faiths</u> include accounts of these, sometimes about the <u>same people</u> — e.g. <u>God</u> (<u>Allah</u>) appearing to <u>Noah</u> (Nuh) and <u>Abraham</u> (Ibrahim). <u>Jews</u> and <u>Christians</u> believe God made agreements (<u>covenants</u>) with them — he gave them rules for <u>how to live</u>, in return for him <u>caring</u> for them.
2. Special revelations include revelations through <u>prophethood</u> (sometimes written down as <u>scriptures</u>), <u>visions</u> and <u>miracles</u> (see p.75).
3. They're <u>direct</u> and <u>personal</u>, so they can be <u>powerful</u> experiences. However, they're hard to <u>prove</u> because they're <u>personal</u>.
4. Some think they <u>still</u> occur today, while others <u>disagree</u>.

General Revelation

1. <u>General revelations</u> are revelations <u>available</u> to <u>everyone</u>. They're more <u>indirect</u> and therefore have to be <u>interpreted</u>.
2. Many think the <u>world</u> is an <u>example</u> of <u>general revelation</u>. <u>Believers</u> think God <u>created</u> the world, so it <u>proves</u> he exists.
3. Many think our <u>conscience</u> proves God exists, as people all over the world have <u>similar</u> <u>morals</u>, e.g. that <u>killing</u> is wrong. God must have <u>created</u> this within <u>every person</u>.

The Scriptures are Important Revelations

1) Christians, Muslims and Jews believe God's <u>nature</u> and <u>will</u> are revealed in their <u>holy books</u>. Many believe they were either <u>inspired</u> by <u>God</u> or came <u>directly</u> from him. They contain <u>knowledge</u> of <u>God</u> and the <u>faith</u>.

2) Most religious people believe that <u>all</u> or <u>parts</u> of them were <u>special revelations</u>, as they were revealed to <u>specific prophets</u>. In their <u>written</u> form, they also have some <u>features</u> of <u>general revelation</u> — they are <u>available</u> to <u>everyone</u>, all the <u>time</u>, and they need to be <u>interpreted</u> to be <u>understood</u>.

The Bible

The Bible is a <u>collection</u> of books written by <u>various</u> authors. Some Christians think the authors were <u>inspired</u> and <u>guided</u> by God as they <u>wrote</u>, but he didn't <u>directly</u> reveal it to them. The <u>New Testament</u> describes Jesus's <u>life</u> — Jesus is seen as the <u>completion</u> of God's <u>revelation</u> to people. Hebrews 1:1-2 says "God spoke to our ancestors through the prophets at many times and in various ways, but in these last days he has spoken to us by his Son" (NIV). <u>Jesus</u> is seen as the '<u>new covenant</u>' — he <u>died</u> for people's <u>sins</u>, but in return <u>people</u> should <u>worship</u> God.

The Torah

<u>Orthodox</u> Jews believe the <u>five</u> books of the <u>Torah</u> were <u>directly</u> revealed to <u>Moses</u> by God. <u>Progressive</u> Jews tend to believe it contains God's <u>message</u> but the text was <u>written</u> by <u>people</u>.

The Qur'an

Muslims believe <u>Allah</u> revealed the <u>Qur'an directly</u> to Muhammad. It's a <u>fully accurate</u> record of Allah's <u>final</u> revelation to <u>humankind</u>. Muslims believe he gave <u>earlier</u> revelations to prophets such as <u>Musa</u> (Moses) and <u>Isa</u> (Jesus) but the texts have been <u>altered</u>.

3) Many <u>atheists</u> and <u>humanists</u> think the scriptures just depict their authors' <u>ideas</u> about <u>God</u>, and that many of the events in them <u>didn't occur</u>. They may see these ancient texts as largely <u>irrelevant</u> to <u>life today</u>.

Revelations Show God's Nature

For more about the <u>nature</u> of God, see p.1 for <u>Christianity</u> or p.27 for <u>Judaism</u>. For more on <u>Allah</u>, see p.17.

1) <u>Christians</u>, <u>Muslims</u> and <u>Jews</u> have <u>similar</u> beliefs about God's <u>characteristics</u>. Many believe he is <u>just</u>, <u>omniscient</u>, <u>omnipotent</u>, <u>loving</u>, <u>eternal</u>, <u>transcendent</u> and <u>immanent</u>. See p.1, 17, and 27 for definitions.

2) <u>Revelation</u> can give people ideas about <u>what God is like</u>, though people may see him in <u>different ways</u>. For example, many believe they can have a <u>relationship</u> with God, e.g. through <u>prayer</u>, showing he is a <u>personal</u> god. Others see him as <u>distant</u> from people as he <u>rarely acts</u> in the world — so he's <u>impersonal</u>.

3) The scriptures can show God's <u>characteristics</u>, e.g. Qur'an 57:4 says "He is with you wherever you are", while Psalm 139:1 says "Lord … you know me" (NIV). This suggests to believers that God is <u>personal</u>.

4) Believers think God shows his <u>compassion</u> through his <u>intervention</u> in the world — e.g. showing people how to live a <u>better life</u> through the <u>prophets</u> in all three faiths, and through <u>Jesus</u> as Messiah in Christian belief.

Revelation

Some See Nature as Revelation

A beautiful <u>sunset</u> may be seen by some as a <u>numinous</u> experience.

1) Christians, Muslims and Jews believe <u>God</u> created the <u>world</u> — it <u>shows</u> he <u>exists</u>. The natural world can provide <u>numinous</u> (<u>spiritual</u>) experiences, by inspiring <u>awe</u> and a sense of God's <u>presence</u>. <u>Interventions</u> in <u>nature</u>, e.g. <u>miracles</u>, show God's <u>immanence</u>.

2) Nature may show God's <u>transcendence</u> — he <u>created</u> it but isn't <u>present</u> in it — as well as other <u>aspects</u>:

> Many <u>Christians</u> believe <u>characteristics</u> such as God's <u>intelligence</u> are revealed through the <u>complexity</u> of nature. The Catechism of the Catholic Church says "The beauty of creation reflects the infinite beauty of the Creator" (341). Nature is often <u>cruel</u>, which can be hard to explain. Some believe nature became <u>cruel</u> after the <u>Fall</u> — when Adam and Eve <u>sinned</u>. So nature no longer fully shows what God is <u>like</u>.

> Many <u>Jews</u> see the universe's <u>existence</u> as <u>proof</u> enough that God exists — <u>no more proof</u> is needed. The <u>wonders</u> of creation may <u>deepen</u> their <u>relationship</u> with God — Jews may offer <u>blessings</u> to God if they see something <u>beautiful</u> in nature. Jews believe <u>all</u> of nature comes from God, even the <u>negative</u> parts — Isaiah 45:7 says "I bring prosperity and create disaster" (NIV). Jews have a <u>responsibility</u> to <u>look after</u> his <u>creation</u>.

> "The heavens declare the glory of God; the skies proclaim the work of his hands." Psalm 19:1 NIV

> <u>Muslims</u> believe Allah created the universe — all <u>beauty</u> comes from him as a gift, and can move people to <u>faith</u> in its creator. One of the 99 names of Allah is <u>Al-Musawwir</u> — The <u>Shaper</u> of <u>Beauty</u>. The beauty of the <u>world</u> shows the beauty of <u>Allah</u>.

3) <u>Atheists</u> and <u>humanists</u> don't believe that <u>nature</u> reveals <u>God</u>. They argue that even aspects of <u>nature</u> we don't fully understand, e.g. how animals <u>navigate</u> as they <u>migrate</u>, will one day be <u>explained</u> by <u>science</u>.

God can be Revealed Through Religious Experiences

1) Religious experiences are <u>personal experiences</u> of God — they're a form of <u>special revelation</u>.

2) They can take many forms — a <u>vision</u>, a <u>dream</u>, hearing a <u>voice</u>, a feeling of <u>ecstasy</u> or <u>peace</u>, or feelings of being <u>loved</u>, <u>forgiven</u> or <u>guided</u>. They can take place during <u>prayer</u> or <u>worship</u>, or at <u>other times</u>. They can be so <u>powerful</u> they <u>change</u> the <u>life</u> of the person, or they might be more gentle experiences.

3) <u>Other</u> religious <u>believers</u> may take <u>inspiration</u> from someone who's had such an experience. Some people who have had religious experiences become <u>well known</u> — see below and the next page.

Visions are a Dramatic Form of Religious Experience

1) A <u>vision</u> is a religious experience in which a person sees something <u>sacred</u> — such as an <u>angel</u>. <u>Visions</u> usually tell the receiver about <u>God</u> and his <u>will</u>, or about the receiver's <u>own life</u>.

2) Visions are <u>direct</u> and <u>powerful</u> forms of religious experience. They often <u>change</u> how believers <u>live</u> their <u>lives</u> — they can <u>strengthen</u> people's <u>faith</u> or even <u>induce</u> them to believe in something they <u>didn't</u> believe in <u>before</u>. They can convince people that <u>God exists</u> — only <u>he</u> could have made them <u>happen</u>.

There are Many Examples of Visions in Christianity

For Old Testament examples, see the top of p.78.

1) Some <u>visions</u> are reported in the <u>Bible</u>, which gives them <u>authority</u>, as they're part of the <u>scripture</u>.

> - At the <u>transfiguration</u>, the <u>disciples</u> saw a vision of <u>Moses</u> and <u>Elijah</u> with Jesus, who was covered in <u>light</u>. God said "This is my Son ... Listen to him!" (Matthew 17:5 NIV). This and the presence of Moses and Elijah showed <u>Jesus</u> was <u>important</u>.
> - <u>St Paul</u> was originally named <u>Saul</u>. He <u>persecuted</u> Christians. One day he saw a <u>light</u>, and heard <u>Jesus</u> asking <u>why</u> Saul was <u>persecuting</u> him. This <u>transformed</u> Saul's life — he became <u>Christian</u> and spent the rest of his life preaching the <u>gospel</u>.

2) Other visions of <u>Mary</u> or <u>angels</u> appeared to people <u>later</u>. The Churches confirm if they think they're <u>authentic</u>. <u>Belief</u> in this type of vision is more <u>significant</u> in <u>Catholicism</u> than in <u>Protestant</u> Christianity.

> - <u>Joan of Arc</u> was a French peasant. She had <u>visions</u> of the <u>archangel Michael</u>, among others. These encouraged her to lead <u>France</u> against <u>England</u> in the <u>Hundred Years' War</u>. She was <u>captured</u> and <u>killed</u> by English allies. The <u>Catholic Church</u> declared her a <u>saint</u> — Catholics think her visions were <u>genuine</u>.
> - Many Catholics report visions of <u>Mary</u>. One example is <u>Bernadette Soubirous</u>, who claimed she saw Mary several times in 1858 near <u>Lourdes</u> (France). Lourdes is now a popular <u>pilgrimage site</u> — many think people can be <u>healed</u> by visiting it.

Revelation

Judaism was Founded by Men who had Visions of God

1) Many visions are <u>recorded</u> in the <u>Torah</u>, and elsewhere in the <u>Tenakh</u>.

2) Abraham and his wife were <u>old</u> and <u>childless</u>. <u>God's word</u> came to him in a <u>vision</u>, promising him a <u>son</u> and countless <u>descendants</u>. He <u>believed</u> God — and what God promised <u>happened</u>.

> "...the word of the Lord came to Abram in a vision" Genesis 15:1 NIV

3) Jacob had a vision of a <u>ladder</u> with angels on it reaching from <u>Earth</u> to <u>Heaven</u> — see Genesis 28:10-22.

4) God first spoke to Moses from within a <u>burning bush</u> — see Exodus 3. This is an <u>indirect</u> or <u>veiled</u> revelation — another example is God appearing as a <u>pillar of cloud</u> in Deuteronomy 31:15.

5) Moses is the <u>only</u> person to have <u>seen</u> God — he spoke to "Moses face to face, as one speaks to a friend" (Exodus 33:11 NIV). These were <u>direct</u> revelations — a direct experience of God.

6) Many Jews believe in the <u>visions</u> of God in the <u>Tenakh</u>, but some <u>Progressive</u> Jews may see them as <u>metaphorical</u> stories. Visions in <u>more recent</u> times <u>aren't</u> really a key part of <u>Judaism</u>.

The Qur'an Mentions Stories of People who had Visions

1) The <u>Qur'an</u> includes the story of the angel <u>Jibril</u> (Gabriel) appearing to <u>Maryam</u> (Mary), the mother of <u>Isa</u> (Jesus) — see Qur'an 19:16-22. Jibril told her she would bear a <u>son</u>, even though she was a <u>virgin</u>.

2) The angel Jibril appeared to <u>Muhammad</u> while he was <u>meditating</u> in a <u>cave</u> outside <u>Makkah</u>. Muhammad <u>recited</u> the verses Jibril gave to him — these were the <u>first verses</u> of the <u>Qur'an</u> to be <u>revealed</u>.

3) <u>Sufi Muslims</u> are Muslim <u>mystics</u> who seek to be filled with <u>knowledge</u> and <u>love</u> of Allah through <u>direct experience</u> of him, which can include <u>visions</u>. This affects them <u>spiritually</u> at a deep level.

4) Sufis can be <u>Sunni</u> or <u>Shi'a</u>, but many Muslims are <u>sceptical</u> of the Sufis' religious experiences.

5) There are other examples of seemingly <u>miraculous</u> events or <u>visions</u> in Islam. Qur'an 2:118 says "We have shown clearly the signs to a people who are certain [in faith]", showing how Allah reveals himself.

Prayer Can Help Belief in God

You only need to read this if you're studying <u>Christianity</u>. For a reminder of how Christians <u>pray</u>, see p.8 and 11.

1) <u>Prayers</u> are an <u>important</u> part of life for Christians. They believe God <u>hears</u> their prayers and <u>responds</u>. If someone prays for something and it then <u>happens</u>, they may see it as <u>confirmation</u> that God <u>exists</u>, as it can <u>only</u> have been <u>him</u> who heard their prayer and responded.

> "if we ask anything according to his will, he hears us. And if we know that he hears us ... we know that we have what we asked of him." 1 John 5:14-15 NIV

2) Praying on a <u>regular basis</u> can help keep people connected to the <u>faith</u>. Many see prayer as a 'conversation' with God — this <u>personal</u> aspect helps them feel <u>close</u> to God.

Upbringing Can Influence People's Belief

Only learn this if you're studying <u>Christianity</u>.

1) Many <u>Christians</u> bring up their <u>children</u> as Christians too — they may want to <u>pass on</u> their belief in <u>God</u> and their <u>values</u>, or think it's the <u>only way</u> their children will reach <u>heaven</u>.

> "Start children off on the way they should go, and even when they are old they will not turn from it." Proverbs 22:6 NIV

2) Children can be introduced to the faith in <u>several ways</u>, including <u>at church</u> and <u>at home</u> — see p.42.

3) Rituals such as <u>prayer</u> and attending <u>church</u> may help inspire children's <u>respect</u> and <u>dedication</u> to God. Activities at <u>home</u>, e.g. reading <u>Bible stories</u>, may help children believe as they're more <u>fun</u> and <u>accessible</u>.

4) <u>Atheists</u> and <u>humanists</u> may think it's better to let their children <u>decide for themselves</u> when they <u>grow up</u>.

5) If parents are too <u>strict</u> and <u>insistent</u> about their child being <u>Christian</u>, the child may <u>reject</u> the faith.

Branches of the same faith may have different views...

...so make sure you revise different opinions, as you'll often be asked to give multiple beliefs or views in the exam. And try this exam-style question — answer it in the context of the religion you're studying:

Explain two beliefs about visions. Give an example from a source of wisdom and authority in your answer. [5]

Arguments Against the Existence of God

Many People Don't Believe in Religious Experiences

Religious experiences are private, so it's impossible to provide proof of them. Atheists and humanists don't believe in God, so think religious experiences can be explained in other ways. Their arguments include:

1) Some religious experiences may happen because of wish fulfilment — the person wants the experience so much that their subconscious makes it happen. Religious people tend to have visions consistent with their own religious beliefs, and not of figures or ideas from another religion, which casts doubt on their validity.
2) The person involved may be lying about their experience, perhaps because they might profit from being believed.
3) Some religious experiences may result from things which affect the brain, such as mental illness, or physical illness such as brain tumours, or drugs. An example is the 12th century nun Hildegard of Bingen, who saw visions all her life, but some people think she was actually suffering from migraines.
4) Some might misinterpret their experience, or choose to interpret it in a religious way. If you were ill and dreamt you'd be cured the next day, and then you felt better, you might think God helped, or just see it as a coincidence.
5) Religious experiences can bring up contradictions in the ideas people have about God. It's hard to understand why, if God is capable of acting in the world, he doesn't do it more often. Miracles (see p.75) show God's power as they break the laws of nature, but this doesn't explain why he doesn't use his power to prevent suffering.

Some believers may not believe in these experiences either, particularly ones not written in their sacred text. They might prefer to focus on God and living a good life instead of events which may or may not be true.

Evil and Suffering Make People Doubt There is a God

Only read this if you're studying Islam, Judaism or Catholic Christianity.

1) Christians, Jews and Muslims all believe in a God who is omniscient (all-knowing), omnipotent (all-powerful), and benevolent (kind). So they believe he knows what happens in the world, doesn't want people to suffer, and is powerful enough to do something about it.
2) However, there's a lot of suffering in the world, which seems to contradict these ideas. Some people find it hard to see how God could allow it to happen, and therefore doubt he exists.
3) Some may think suffering can't be explained by humans. In the Torah and Bible, Job endures many hardships, but despite this, he decides suffering must be accepted as we can't understand God's plan.
4) In the scriptures, suffering is also often described as punishment for people's sins.
5) However, suffering is widespread and affects everyone, so atheists and humanists might argue that justifying suffering as punishment doesn't make sense. They might also argue that it doesn't seem to add up because animals and plants suffer too, even though they can't be being punished for their sins.
6) Believers might explain it by saying that humans need to be able to choose between good and evil as a test of their character — that's why they have free will. Without bad things happening, good can't exist.
7) Religious people try to relieve the suffering of others, e.g. through charity and prayer.

Catholics believe the concept of original sin can explain suffering (see p.7). God gave people free will — they choose to create suffering or good. St Augustine said suffering was the price people pay for free will. St Irenaeus thought people were created with faults because they had to develop into being children of God — so they needed evil and suffering to exist, else they'd have no concept of what's right. Catholics try to follow God's example of goodness — Psalm 119 asks for his help to do so. Isaiah 45:7 says "I bring prosperity and create disaster" (NIV), which suggests God isn't only responsible for good — he creates suffering as a punishment.

Jews believe suffering is a test from God. A lot of Jewish thought doesn't try explaining evil, and the Holocaust makes it particularly hard to do so. Many Jews struggle to understand why God let it happen, especially as Psalm 103:17-18 says "the Lord's love is with those ... who keep his covenant" (NIV). Many believe evil needs a response, not an explanation — e.g. helping those who are suffering.

Muslims believe suffering can be a test from Allah. Everything is part of Allah's plan and there are good reasons for it, even if we can't see them. Evil gives people the chance to do good and help those in need. If we ourselves are suffering, Muslims believe we must bear it with patience and faith. Qur'an 2:155-156 says: "good tidings to the patient, Who, when disaster strikes them, say, 'Indeed we belong to Allah' ".

Revise thoroughly for the exam — else you'll suffer...

EXAM TIP

In the exam, read each question carefully. You need to know exactly what the questions are asking.

Revision Summary

A whole page of questions — just what you've been waiting for. They'll test whether you remember what you've learnt in the section, and get you used to what you'll be asked to do in the exam. If there's anything you're not completely sure about, go back through the section and have another read of the relevant pages, then give the questions another go.

Answer each of these questions <u>in the context of the religion you've studied</u>.

You can get 3 marks for these, so make three short points in your answer.

1) Outline three justifications for belief in a god.

2) Outline three aspects of the cosmological argument.

3) Outline three elements of special revelation.

4) Outline three ideas about bringing up children as Christians. ← *Only answer this question if you're studying <u>Christianity</u>.*

5) Outline three examples of people who have had religious experiences.

6) Outline three non-religious explanations for religious experiences.

Moving up to 4 marks. Make two points, but this time develop them further to get an extra mark for each.

7) Explain two ways believers respond to the theory of evolution. *To make sure your longer answers are clear, make sure your answer is well-structured.*

8) Explain two religious beliefs about the scriptures as revelation.

9) Explain two religious beliefs about how God's characteristics might be shown through revelation.

10) Explain two religious beliefs about the revelation of God in nature.

11) Explain two reasons why prayer may help people believe in God. ← *Only answer this question if you're studying <u>Christianity</u>.*

5 marks available now. You'll need to give an example from a source of wisdom and authority for top marks.

12) Explain two ways religious people believe creation proves the existence of God. *Only answer this question if you're studying <u>Islam</u>, <u>Judaism</u> or <u>Catholic Christianity</u>.*

13) Explain two ideas about miracles that come from the scriptures.

14) Explain two ways religious people respond to the problem of God allowing evil and suffering.

Finish on a high with this 12 mark question. Before you begin, use the bullet points in the question to make a plan and structure your answer — you'll need to include all the things the bullet points ask for in your answer. Have a quick brainstorm of arguments for and against the statement.

15) 'God doesn't exist.'

Evaluate this statement. Give arguments that support the statement and arguments that disagree with the statement.

You must include:

Have a look at the 'Do Well in Your Exam' section for help with writing essays.

- examples of teachings from the religion you've studied
- non-religious views
- appropriate philosophical arguments ← *Don't be put off by this reference to 'philosophical arguments' — it just means things such as the cosmological argument, or the belief that miracles prove God's existence.*
- a conclusion.

Attitudes to Equality

General, Christianity, Catholic Christianity

Equality is something that many people work towards — for example, in terms of race, sexuality and gender.

Prejudice and Discrimination Prevent Equality

Difference in wealth is another form of inequality — see p.87-89.

1) Prejudice is judging something or someone for no good reason, or without full knowledge of a situation. Discrimination is treating someone unjustly or differently, often because of prejudice.

2) Prejudice comes in different forms. Sexism is the belief one gender is inferior to the other. Racism is prejudice against people of other races. Homophobia is prejudice against people who are homosexual.

3) The Equality Act 2010 says it's illegal to discriminate on the grounds of 'protected characteristics', which include race, gender, age and sexual orientation. The Act aims to ensure everyone is treated equally.

4) Positive discrimination is when someone in a group that often suffers discrimination is given an advantage. This often relates to job applications — it's only legal if they're as well qualified as the other applicants.

Christianity teaches Equality

Jesus said the second most important commandment, after loving God, is "Love your neighbour as yourself" (Mark 12:31 NIV).

1) 'Do to others what you would have them do to you' is a fundamental part of Christian teaching, often called the 'Golden Rule'. Many Christians think everyone was created equal, so try to avoid discrimination.

2) Jesus said "A new command I give you: love one another" (John 13:34 NIV) — i.e. don't mistreat others.

3) The Catechism of the Catholic Church 1935 says "...discrimination ... on the grounds of sex, race, colour, social conditions, language, or religion must be ... eradicated as incompatible with God's design".

> The Good Samaritan parable is an important teaching on prejudice. Two holy men ignore a man who's been beaten and robbed. He's then helped by a Samaritan, a group who were despised at the time. The story shows how prejudices can be wrong.

Christian Attitudes to Gender Equality have Shifted

For more on this, see p.45.

1) Traditionally, Christians believed women's roles were to look after the home and children, while men earnt money and led the family. Some still believe this, but most now think both genders can do either role.

2) Women traditionally had less authority in religion — there were no female church leaders for centuries. There are now female ministers in most Protestant denominations, though not Catholic or Orthodox ones.

Christian Teaching on Racism is Clear

"From one man he made all the nations" Acts 17:26 NIV

1) Christianity teaches that racism is unacceptable, and God made everyone equal — "you are all one in Christ Jesus" Galatians 3:28 NIV. This means many Christians believe it's their duty to fight racism.

2) This can be done by an individual, e.g. by welcoming someone of another ethnicity to the community, or at an institutional level, e.g. a church asking its members to treat everyone equally. The Church of England recommends that people make "neighbours out of strangers" in its report Faithful Cities.

3) Racial equality can be difficult to achieve. The Church of England has been criticised for not having enough ethnic minority people among its clergy — it's now making efforts to increase diversity.

4) Desmond Tutu is an Anglican archbishop who fought against apartheid in South Africa, in which the white minority population oppressed everyone else. After apartheid ended, he led the Truth and Reconciliation Commission, which investigated the crimes of the apartheid era and focused on unity between everyone.

There's a lot of Debate on Homosexuality in the Christian Churches

For more, see p.37 and 39.

Homosexuality is a divisive topic in Christianity. The idea of loving your neighbour seems to contradict the Bible teachings forbidding homosexuality, such as 1 Corinthians 6:9-10. Many Christians focus on loving your neighbour and therefore accept homosexuality. Others focus on the fact it's seen as a sin.

> The Anglican Church is split on the issue. Church of England bishops issued a report in 2017 saying they wouldn't change the Church's definition of marriage as being between one man and one woman (Canon B30), but many members of the Church disagree with this.

> The Catholic Church is in a similar position — its Catechism says homosexual acts are "contrary to the natural law" (2357) but many individual Catholics accept homosexuality.

Now have a read of the Exam Tip on p.82.

Attitudes to Equality

Equality is important in Judaism — the Torah says God made everyone equal.

Different Jewish Traditions Have Different Views on Gender Roles

1) Jews believe that men and women are equal, based on Genesis 1:27, which says "So God created mankind in his own image ... male and female he created them" (NIV).

2) Men and women tend to have different roles in Orthodox Judaism — but they're still seen as equal in God's eyes. Men are obliged to pray 3 times a day, but women aren't (but they should say the Amidah twice daily — see p.31). Only men can read the Torah in synagogue and make up a minyan (the group of at least 10 people needed for some prayers). Traditionally, only men can be rabbis, but this is changing.

3) Women are exempt from such duties as it's expected they'll be looking after the home and children. They have religious duties in the home, such as lighting the Shabbat candles while saying a blessing. Traditionally, 'Jewishness' is passed on via the mother — a child with a non-Jewish mother isn't a Jew.

4) In Liberal, Reform and Masorti Judaism, religious duties can be carried out by women too. All three have male and female rabbis. Liberal, Reform and some Masortis have developed gender-neutral liturgy, e.g. avoiding calling God 'Father' or 'King'. They have equivalent rites of passage for boys and girls (p.32-33).

The Torah Preaches Racial Equality

1) Genesis 3:20 says all of humanity comes from the same source, so Jews see people as equal before God. The Torah makes it clear that people of different ethnicities should be treated the same as each other:

> "When a foreigner resides among you in your land, do not ill-treat them. The foreigner residing among you must be treated as your native-born. Love them as yourself, for you were foreigners in Egypt." Leviticus 19:33-34 NIV

2) Most Jews believe that Jewish people are God's chosen people. This doesn't mean they think they're better than anyone else — just that God gave them extra responsibilities in the covenants (see p.27-28).

3) Jews have often faced anti-Semitism (discrimination against Jews), particularly during the Holocaust, when 6 million Jews were killed. This means many are vocal about racism and make efforts to try to reduce it.

4) Ahavat ha-beriot means loving all of God's creations. It's a mitzvah (commandment) to do so, so it's important. This encourages Jews to accept everyone, regardless of their ethnicity.

5) The Jewish Council for Racial Equality (JCORE) works for racial equality, focusing especially on attitudes to asylum seekers and refugees. It campaigns against negative attitudes to immigrants in the UK.

Views on Homosexuality Also Vary Between Jewish Traditions

1) Orthodox Jews tend not to approve of homosexuality. They're against homophobia, but tend to see being in homosexual relationships as a sin. Sex between men is forbidden in Leviticus 18:22 (so it's assumed sex between women is banned too). Orthodox synagogues don't hold same-sex weddings.

2) Attitudes are beginning to change within the Orthodox community though. Efforts are being made to welcome and support homosexual Orthodox Jews in the community.

3) Progressive Jews accept homosexuality and welcome homosexual people into their communities. They argue that as God created everyone in his image (Genesis 1:27), homosexuality can't be wrong.

4) Both Liberal and Reform Judaism campaigned for the legalisation of same-sex marriage in the UK, and hold same-sex weddings now they're legal. Homosexual people can become Liberal and Reform rabbis.

5) Many Masortis accept homosexuality. They have a shutafut (partnership) ceremony for same-sex marriages or civil partnerships, different from the traditional kiddushin.

Remember, there are usually different opinions...

You'll often be asked to discuss different beliefs in the exam, so make sure you learn both sides of the argument. Make sure you know different opinions within the religion that you're studying.

EXAM TIP

Attitudes to Equality

Islam teaches that Allah <u>created</u> everyone to be <u>equal</u>, even though people are <u>different</u> from each other.

Men and Women have Different Roles within Islam

1) The <u>Qur'an</u> makes it <u>clear</u> that men and women are <u>equal</u> when it comes to their <u>religious obligations</u>, e.g. prayer, fasting, hajj and charity — have a look at Qur'an 33:35 on p.45, which also has more information on <u>gender equality</u>. All that counts is how good a <u>Muslim</u> they are, not their <u>gender</u>:

> "O mankind, indeed We have created you from male and female and made you peoples and tribes that you may know one another. Indeed, the most noble of you in the sight of Allah is the most righteous of you." Qur'an 49:13

2) Women don't <u>have</u> to attend mosque for <u>prayer</u>, but it is <u>permitted</u>. If women do go to the mosque, they must pray in a <u>separate</u> group — behind (or otherwise out of sight of) the men. This is because it's thought it might be <u>distracting</u> for both genders to pray in a mixed group.

3) Women can't lead prayers in <u>mixed groups</u>, but they can lead prayers being said by groups of <u>women</u>.

4) There is a growing movement working for women to have a more <u>prominent role</u> in Islam. Several women have led <u>mixed-gender</u> prayers across the world. Their actions have been <u>condemned</u> by some Muslims as not following the teachings of Islam. There are plans for a <u>mosque</u> run by women in Bradford.

5) Some say it's <u>part of Islam</u> for Muslim women to wear <u>modest clothing</u> — Qur'an 24:31 says "tell the believing women ... to wrap [a portion of] their headcovers over their chests and not expose their adornment". Others argue it doesn't say they have to cover up <u>completely</u> and that their <u>faith</u> and <u>piety</u> are more <u>important</u> than clothing — Qur'an 7:26 says "the clothing of righteousness — that is best".

Islam says People are Created Equal, but not Identical

1) Islam teaches that <u>all people</u> were created by <u>Allah</u>, and were created <u>equal</u> (although <u>not</u> the <u>same</u>). He intended humanity to be created with <u>differences</u>. But this just means we're all <u>individuals</u>.

2) Muslims all over the world are united by the <u>ummah</u> — the <u>community</u> of Islam. The ummah consists of <u>all Muslims</u>, regardless of <u>nationality</u>, <u>tradition</u> (i.e. Sunni or Shi'a) and so on. This helps promote <u>racial</u> and <u>social harmony</u>, as in theory no one's <u>excluded</u> or <u>discriminated</u> against.

> The final sermon of Muhammad is clear that <u>no race</u> is <u>superior</u> to another: "you are all descended from Adam and none is higher than the other except in obedience to Allah. No Arab is superior to a non-Arab. Between Muslims there are no races and no tribes." The only <u>important</u> thing is whether someone's a <u>good Muslim</u> or not.

3) People on <u>hajj</u> all wear <u>simple white clothes</u>, showing everyone's <u>equal</u> — race, gender etc. <u>don't matter</u>.

4) Sahih al-Bukhari 56:681 says everyone should be <u>treated</u> the <u>same</u> way, regardless of <u>who</u> they are.

> <u>Malcolm X</u> was a <u>prominent Muslim figure</u> in the struggle for <u>civil rights</u> for <u>African Americans</u> in the <u>US</u>. He initially advocated <u>black supremacy</u> and <u>separatism</u>, but later supported <u>interethnic dialogue</u>. He inspired many with his campaigning for <u>human rights</u>.

Homosexuality is Controversial in Islam For more on this, see p.40.

1) Many <u>Muslims</u> believe that the Qur'an <u>forbids</u> homosexuality — for example, Qur'an 7:81 says "you approach men with desire, instead of women ... you are a transgressing people" (the quote is addressed to men). This means they're <u>against</u> the <u>legalisation</u> of <u>same-sex marriage</u>.

2) Some Muslims disagree, arguing that as <u>Allah</u> created all people, homosexuality is part of his <u>creation</u>.

3) Muslims often speak against <u>homophobia</u>, as Muslims should be <u>tolerant</u> towards others. Some Muslim organisations state that they are <u>against</u> homosexual acts but believe homosexual people should be <u>respected</u>. Others, such as <u>Imaan</u>, <u>support</u> homosexual Muslims and campaign for their <u>rights</u>.

So, now you know this page off by heart and backwards...

...bear this exam tip in mind. Some questions will ask you about different beliefs, so make sure you know all the sides to the argument — you need to learn different opinions within Islam.

Human Rights

Human rights are <u>moral</u>, <u>legal</u> and <u>political</u> rights that should give people <u>freedom</u> and <u>protection</u> worldwide.

The United Nations Defined Human Rights

The European Court of Human Rights. (I think.)

1) In 1948, the <u>United Nations</u> (UN) published the <u>Universal Declaration of Human Rights</u>. The aim was to lay down minimum <u>rights</u> for <u>every person</u>, in <u>every country</u>.

2) It states that all human beings are born <u>free</u> and <u>equal</u> in dignity and rights. It also lists specific rights, e.g. the right to <u>life</u>, freedom from <u>slavery</u>, freedom from <u>imprisonment</u> or <u>exile</u> without <u>good reason</u>, freedom of <u>opinion</u> and <u>expression</u>, the right to have an <u>education</u> and to seek <u>work</u>.

3) The Universal Declaration of Human Rights <u>stated</u> how things <u>should</u> be, but meant <u>nothing</u> in a court of law. So in 1953, the Council of Europe brought into effect the <u>European Convention on Human Rights</u>, which is a <u>similar</u> list of rights to the UN declaration. It's enforced by the European <u>Court</u> of Human Rights (ECHR). These rights became part of the UK's <u>domestic law</u> in 1998, with the <u>Human Rights Act</u>.

4) Most religious believers agree that all human beings should be treated <u>fairly</u> and with <u>respect</u>. This is based on a belief in <u>human dignity</u> — all human life is <u>valuable</u>, because people are created in the <u>image of God</u> — and a belief in <u>justice</u>, the idea everyone should be treated <u>fairly</u>. Everyone should be <u>free</u> to <u>think</u> and to <u>choose</u> how to act (though hopefully they'll live a good <u>moral</u> life).

5) People applying <u>situation ethics</u> look for the <u>most loving</u> outcome to a situation. They may often <u>support</u> human rights, but in some cases they may feel going <u>against</u> a right gives the best <u>overall</u> outcome.

Many Christians Support Human Rights

1) The <u>Catholic Church</u> highlights the role of the <u>individual</u> as well as the <u>state</u> in <u>protecting</u> human rights. It says human rights aren't just defined by <u>states</u> putting them into <u>law</u>, but "Every member of the community has a duty ... in order that the rights of others can be satisfied and their freedoms respected" (The Common Good and the Catholic Church's Social Teaching: 37).

> "So God created mankind in his own image, in the image of God he created them; male and female he created them." Genesis 1:27 NIV

> "You ... were called to be free. But do not use your freedom to indulge the flesh; rather, serve one another humbly in love." Galatians 5:13 NIV

2) <u>Christians</u> may find their views <u>contradict</u> others' ideas about rights. E.g. many think <u>women</u> should have the right to <u>abortion</u>, but some Christians <u>disagree</u>, believing the <u>foetus</u>'s right to <u>life</u> is more <u>important</u>.

Human Rights are Important for Most Jews

1) Most Jews <u>support</u> human rights — Deuteronomy 16:20 asks Jews to "Follow justice and justice alone" (NIV). <u>Teachings</u> such as the two below ask Jews to <u>protect</u> the rights of <u>specific people</u>:

> "Whoever oppresses the poor shows contempt for their Maker, but whoever is kind to the needy honours God." Proverbs 14:31 NIV

> "When a foreigner resides among you in your land, do not ill-treat them ... Love them as yourself" Leviticus 19:33-34 NIV

2) However, <u>Jewish beliefs</u> can sometimes <u>clash</u> with <u>human rights</u>. For example, many <u>Orthodox Jews</u> think homosexuality is <u>wrong</u>, which may lead to discrimination.

The Qur'an says Justice is Very Important

1) Most Muslims are supportive of human rights. The <u>Qur'an</u> frequently emphasises the <u>importance</u> of <u>justice</u>, saying for example "O you who have believed, be persistently standing firm for Allah, witnesses in justice ... Be just; that is nearer to righteousness" (Qur'an 5:8).

> "Indeed, Allah orders justice and good conduct and giving to relatives and forbids immorality and bad conduct and oppression. He admonishes you that perhaps you will be reminded." Qur'an 16:90

2) Some Muslims argue that <u>Islamic law</u> sometimes <u>undermines</u> Muslim <u>women</u>'s rights, e.g. they don't have <u>equal rights</u> in <u>divorce</u> to men.

Answer in the context of the religion you've studied...

Explain two reasons why many religious people believe human rights are important.   [4]

Freedom of Belief — All religions

The UK is a Diverse, Multi-Faith Society

About half of the population say they have no religious belief.

1) Freedom of religion and belief is a legal right in the UK — it gives the freedom to follow any or no religion.

2) People are protected from being discriminated against because of their beliefs. The beliefs they hold as part of their religion are protected, e.g. religions can choose not to hold same-sex marriages in their places of worship if it doesn't fit with their beliefs. Freedom of belief is sometimes a tricky area though:

- Some people feel there isn't enough recognition of those who don't hold religious beliefs, e.g. in religious studies in schools.
- There can be a fine line between educating people about a faith and influencing them too much. Some may think that e.g. religious charities have too much influence, while the charities would argue they're not trying to convert people, just help them.
- Some people, including religious believers, object to the Church of England being the state church. For example, 26 bishops are peers in the House of Lords, which many see as unfair now that the country is more religiously diverse and many people don't have a religion at all. Others say the UK is a Christian country so it's acceptable — it's part of the culture.
- A religious person saying homosexuality is sinful clashes with homosexual people's right not to be discriminated against and could be seen as hate speech (a crime) — but stopping people from expressing their views undermines their freedom of belief.

3) Most religious believers happily live alongside others in the UK and enjoy the different perspectives it gives them. The Inter Faith Network for the UK promotes mutual understanding and combats prejudice.

4) Living in a multi-faith society can make it harder for some believers to practise their faith — e.g. some Christian festivals are UK bank holidays while other faiths' festivals aren't, making it harder to celebrate.

Many Christians Think People Can Follow Any Faith

1) Though many Christians think Christianity's the true religion, they think people have the right to practise any faith. It's "an inalienable requirement of the dignity of man" (Catechism of the Catholic Church 1747).

2) Some Christians think the only way to reach heaven is by being Christian, so they try to convert people.

3) But generally they support the right to choose — the Bible shows that Jesus didn't make people follow him.

Jews Accept Other Religions

1) Jews are a people as well as a religious group. Jews don't try to convert people, although people can convert if they want after a period of study. Once they've converted, they're seen as Jewish for ever.

2) Freedom of belief is important to Jews as they have often been persecuted, most horrifyingly during the Holocaust, when six million Jews were killed. They're often inspired by the Torah story of Esther, who saved the Jewish people from being killed by Haman. Esther risked her life to beg for mercy. The story shows the importance of allowing everyone to live without persecution, and having faith in the face of it.

The Qur'an Says People are Free to Choose Their Religion

1) The Qur'an says "There shall be no compulsion in [acceptance of] the religion" (Qur'an 2:256) — people are free to choose. Muslims believe that Islam is the only true faith — but some also believe that all righteous people will be favoured by Allah. Most Muslims don't try to convert others to Islam.

- However, Muslims' freedom of belief is often restricted by the common belief that converting to another religion from Islam or becoming an atheist is unacceptable in Islam — it's known as apostasy. Some hadiths say it deserves the death penalty.
- Some Muslims disagree, as the Qur'an leaves judgement up to Allah — Qur'an 3:85 says "whoever desires other than Islam ... he, in the Hereafter, will be among the losers". It can be hard for ex-Muslims — they're often cut off from their family.

2) Muslims call Muslims, Christians and Jews 'people of the book', as they're linked by a shared religious heritage. They all believe in prophets such as Ibrahim (Abraham) and many Muslims believe the Torah and New Testament contain important messages. Qur'an 29:46 says "our God and your God is one".

I can't do GCSEs, exams are against my religion...

...sorry, that won't wash. Try this question — answer in the context of the religion you've studied.

Explain two religious ideas about freedom of belief.   [4]

Social Justice

Social Justice is the Idea that Everyone should be Treated Fairly

1) <u>Social justice</u> is putting into <u>practice</u> the <u>principles</u> of <u>human rights</u>. Working for social justice <u>includes</u>:

> • Trying to ensure different <u>groups</u> of people aren't <u>discriminated</u> against or more <u>disadvantaged</u> than others. This includes discrimination on the grounds of race, gender, religion, social class, poverty, age or disability.
> • Trying to redistribute <u>wealth</u> so everyone can afford to live <u>comfortably</u>. Some members of society are very <u>wealthy</u> while others <u>struggle</u> to meet their <u>basic needs</u> for food, shelter, warmth, etc.

2) Social justice <u>efforts</u> often <u>focus</u> on <u>wealth</u>, as a lack of it can deprive people of other <u>opportunities</u> and rights. <u>Higher</u> taxes for people on <u>high</u> incomes and <u>free healthcare</u> and <u>education</u> are ways to help.

3) Many people try to work for <u>social justice</u>. It's an important part of <u>Christianity</u>, <u>Islam</u> and <u>Judaism</u>. People using <u>situation ethics</u> would often support social justice as the most <u>compassionate</u> thing to do.

Christianity Teaches that People Should Help Those in Need

1) <u>Christians</u> follow Jesus's teaching to "Love your neighbour as yourself" (Mark 12:31 NIV). The <u>parable</u> of the <u>sheep</u> and <u>goats</u> is often used to teach about social justice — see p.14 for more.

> Jesus was <u>known</u> for helping <u>poor people</u> and for <u>healing the sick</u>. In Luke 16:19-31, he teaches that people who <u>don't</u> help others when they're <u>able</u> to will be punished — the story is about a <u>rich man</u> who repeatedly <u>ignores</u> a <u>poor man</u>, and ends up in hell for not helping him. Jesus healed a man with <u>leprosy</u> by <u>touching</u> him, at a time when lepers were <u>outcasts</u> from society. Christians should therefore follow Jesus's <u>example</u> — by helping those who need it, they can express <u>God's love</u>.

2) The <u>Catholic Church</u> emphasises the <u>importance</u> of human <u>dignity</u> in social justice. It says people should be allowed "to obtain what is their due, according to their nature and their vocation" (Catechism 1928) — people should be given <u>opportunities</u> to make the <u>most</u> of their <u>lives</u> and their <u>abilities</u>.

3) Catechism 1928 also says <u>social justice</u> is <u>better</u> for <u>everyone</u> — it's for "the common good".

Islam Encourages Helping Others

1) Muslims should work for <u>social justice</u> as part of their <u>faith</u>. Qur'an 76:8-9 says the <u>righteous</u> "give food in spite of love for it to the needy, the orphan, and the captive, [Saying] ... We wish not from you reward or gratitude". This means people should give <u>help without</u> expecting anything in <u>return</u>.

2) <u>Zakah</u>, charitable giving to <u>redistribute</u> wealth, is <u>central</u> to Islam — it's one of the <u>five pillars</u> (see p.22). The <u>Qur'an</u> says those who "give zakah ... will be the successful" (Qur'an 7:156-157).

3) It promises that those who have <u>wealth</u> to <u>spare</u> and give it away will be <u>rewarded</u>:

> Those who spend their wealth [in Allah's way] ... — they will have their reward with their Lord." Qur'an 2:274

Jewish Teachings say Jews Should be Generous to Others

1) Many Jewish teachings <u>support</u> working for <u>social justice</u>. According to Deuteronomy 15:11, God told Jews "to be open-handed towards your fellow Israelites who are poor and needy in your land" (NIV). Jews should give <u>generously</u> and <u>willingly</u>, "without a grudging heart" (Deuteronomy 15:10 NIV).

2) Jewish ideas of <u>charity</u> (tzedakah) focus on <u>justice</u> — it's not only <u>kind</u> to give to charity, but it's <u>righting</u> a <u>wrong</u>. Amos 5:24 NIV says "let justice roll on like a river, righteousness like a never-failing stream!".

3) The concept of <u>tikkun olam</u> — <u>repairing the world</u> — is linked to this. Jews should be <u>active</u> in <u>improving</u> things that are <u>wrong</u> in the <u>world</u>. This doesn't <u>only</u> mean personally giving to <u>charity</u> and <u>helping others</u>, but also <u>campaigning</u> on a <u>political</u> level to make sure that society is fair and just for <u>everyone</u>.

4) If Jews <u>oppress</u> those who are <u>disadvantaged</u>, God "will certainly hear their cry" (Exodus 22:23 NIV).

Basically, everyone should help people who need it...

There are quite a few different teachings on this page, so as a fun test (or maybe just a test...), write down as many as you can remember without looking at the page. Don't forget to give the source.

Wealth and Poverty

How <u>wealth</u> is <u>used</u>, and how it's <u>distributed</u> among people, is a <u>big issue</u> today.

Wealth Inequality is a Big Problem Today

In the <u>UK</u>, the poorest <u>50%</u> of people own <u>8.7%</u> of wealth, while the richest <u>10%</u> own <u>45%</u>.

1) The <u>gap</u> between the <u>poorest</u> and <u>richest</u> people is <u>huge</u>, and <u>growing</u>. In 2017, <u>Oxfam</u> estimated that the richest <u>8</u> people in the world had <u>more wealth</u> than the poorest <u>half</u> of the world (<u>3.6 billion</u> people).

2) There are two types of poverty — <u>absolute poverty</u> and <u>relative poverty</u>. <u>Absolute</u> poverty is not having <u>enough resources</u> (money, etc.) to meet your <u>basic needs</u>, e.g. <u>food</u> or <u>heating</u>. <u>Relative</u> poverty is defined by <u>where</u> you <u>live</u>, e.g. in the UK, someone who can't afford a <u>TV</u> might be thought of as poor.

3) Poverty has many <u>causes</u>. In the UK, these causes often include <u>low wages</u>, <u>high costs</u> (e.g. renting a house or paying for childcare), a <u>lack of skills</u> so people can't get better-paid jobs, and <u>unemployment</u>.

- <u>Fair pay</u> is an issue. Many in <u>poverty</u> have <u>low-paid</u> jobs, so they work <u>long hours</u> to try to earn enough to live on. In some <u>areas</u>, <u>well-paid</u> jobs <u>aren't</u> available. <u>Part-time</u> work's often low-paid.
- By law, people have to be paid the <u>National Minimum Wage</u>, but many people think it <u>isn't</u> enough. Over-25s must be paid the <u>National Living Wage</u>, which is a bit <u>higher</u> than the minimum wage. However, many say it still isn't <u>enough</u> to <u>live on</u> — it's not a <u>true</u> living wage.
- <u>Businesses</u> are often <u>reluctant</u> to pay people <u>more</u> as it's <u>expensive</u> for them to do so — some try to <u>avoid</u> paying even the minimum wage. Some say <u>increasing</u> wages will mean they <u>can't afford</u> to <u>pay</u> people so they would have to <u>cut</u> the number of jobs, which wouldn't help.

4) <u>Worldwide</u>, poverty is also caused by things such as <u>war</u>, <u>rapid population growth</u>, <u>natural disasters</u> and <u>exploitation</u>. The <u>Fairtrade Foundation</u> works to ensure people in <u>developing countries</u> are paid a <u>fair price</u> for the products they <u>sell</u> and that they have <u>decent working conditions</u>.

High Interest on Loans can be Linked to Poverty

1) People sometimes need <u>extra money</u>, e.g. to pay for something <u>unexpected</u>, or just to afford <u>food</u> until the <u>next payday</u>. One <u>way</u> of covering this is take out a <u>loan</u>. A quick and seemingly easy way to do so is to borrow from a <u>money lender</u>, but <u>money lenders</u> often lend money at <u>rates</u> that go up to <u>thousands</u> of percent of <u>interest</u> (called <u>usury</u>). People might take out <u>small</u> loans, but they soon become so <u>big</u> that they <u>can't repay</u> them.

2) This was a <u>big</u> problem in the UK, so the <u>government</u> introduced some <u>regulations</u> to <u>limit</u> how much people have to <u>repay</u>. Now, people don't have to repay more than <u>twice</u> what they borrowed.

Finding a Solution is Difficult

1) Helping poverty caused by <u>disasters</u> (e.g. <u>war</u>) often involves <u>emergency relief</u> during the <u>disaster</u> and <u>long term</u> help afterwards, e.g. rebuilding houses. It can take <u>years</u> before things get back to <u>normal</u>.

2) In other situations, some people think giving <u>money</u> (e.g. benefits or donations) to people in poverty makes them too <u>reliant</u> on that money — they don't <u>help themselves</u> get out of poverty as they prefer to keep <u>receiving</u> the money. Others argue that this <u>isn't</u> the case, and that people living in poverty need <u>financial help</u>, because <u>not</u> giving it to them means they might not be able to <u>eat</u> or <u>heat</u> their home.

3) Some say it's people's <u>own responsibility</u> to get out of poverty — they should work <u>harder</u> and use money more <u>responsibly</u>. Others say that poverty is a result of <u>many factors</u> and that many do <u>work hard</u> — in 2016, <u>1 in 8</u> people employed in the UK were living <u>in poverty</u> (source Joseph Rowntree Foundation, 2016).

4) They say society should help those who face <u>many issues</u> such as <u>illness</u>, or a <u>lack of skills</u> or <u>opportunities</u>. <u>Charities</u> often try to help people learn <u>new skills</u> on top of giving them <u>money</u> or <u>food</u>.

<u>Virtue ethics</u> says the correct course of action is the one which a <u>virtuous</u> (or <u>good</u>) <u>person</u> would follow. For example, people following virtue ethics would say that people with <u>excess wealth</u> should give to people with <u>less wealth</u>. They might also argue that giving to <u>charity</u> is the <u>right</u> thing to do (see p.88-89), but <u>not</u> to the point where people become <u>dependent</u> on financial aid. They would say that the best course of action is to help out <u>financially</u> in the <u>short term</u>, but to give people the <u>skills</u> to provide for <u>themselves</u> in the <u>long term</u>.

Wealth and Poverty

Christians Believe It's What You Do With Your Money that Counts

1) Christians shouldn't be fixated on wealth — Jesus said "You cannot serve both God and Money" (Matthew 6:24 NIV) and "It is easier for a camel to go through the eye of a needle than for someone who is rich to enter the kingdom of God" (Mark 10:25 NIV). Wealth should be used to help others who are less well off.

2) Many Christians think money should only be earnt in moral ways, not in ways that might harm others, such as working for arms manufacturers or running a business that pays people unfair wages.

3) They also try to avoid using their money in a way that harms others, which includes usury.

> The Church of England has launched an initiative to combat lenders who charge lots of interest. The Church is offering workshops to educate people about money matters, as well as promoting credit unions, which lend money at low rates of interest.

Charity is Important to Christians

1) Giving to charity and helping others is important to many Christians, following the teaching to "Love your neighbour" (Mark 12:31 NIV). It's important to give in a way that helps people to help themselves — the parable of the talents (Matthew 25:14-30) says those who make most of what they have are rewarded.

2) Christians should give to charity as part of their faith. There are many Christian charities — see p.14.

> "If anyone has material possessions and sees a brother or sister in need but has no pity on them, how can the love of God be in that person?" 1 John 3:17 NIV

Checking your donation's gone to a worthy cause is a good idea...

3) It's best to give donations quietly and without boasting about it — Matthew 6:2 tells Christians that "when you give to the needy, do not announce it with trumpets" (NIV).

4) How much you give isn't important — what's important is giving as much as you can. Jesus taught that a poor woman giving a small amount of money she couldn't afford to lose was more important than rich people giving large sums they could easily do without (Mark 12:41-44).

5) Over 7500 churches are involved with the Fairtrade movement. For more on Christian charities, see p.14.

If you're studying Christianity or Catholic Christianity, now head over to the Revision Task on p.89.

Charity is One of the Five Pillars of Islam

1) Charity plays an important role in Islam — zakah (financial aid) is one of the five pillars of Islam, which every Muslim has to follow. Qur'an 2:177 says "righteousness is [in] one who ... gives zakah".

2) With zakah, 2.5% of your yearly wealth should be given as charity, unless your wealth is below a minimum threshold. It's usually given to charities or mosques, or to Muslims who are less well off.

3) Muslims think wealth is given to people by Allah, so they should use it to help others. Being wealthy or poor is Allah's test of people — they should try to help themselves or others, depending on the situation.

> "A man is not a believer who fills his stomach while his neighbour is hungry." Al-Adab al-Mufrad 6:112 (collection of hadith)

4) Sadaqah is another kind of charity. It includes a wide range of charitable acts, from simply smiling at someone to cheer them up, to giving money to help those in need. Sadaqah is seen as a duty, but it involves any amount of effort, time or money — it's up to the individual to decide how much they do.

5) There's a particular emphasis on 'ongoing charity' — actions that will have a long-term effect. It's seen as best to help people become able to support themselves, rather than relying on donations. This means the benefits of sadaqah are long-lasting and help the community — known as sustainable development.

6) There are Islamic charities that help people globally and in the UK, including Muslim Aid and Islamic Aid.

Muslim Aid	Islamic Aid
1. Muslim Aid provides disaster relief and development aid around the world. The charity works in over 70 countries.	1. Islamic Aid is an international organisation dedicated to reducing poverty and deprivation.
2. It provides not only initial emergency aid after a war or natural disaster, but ongoing help. This help includes building new housing, sanitation and schools, and offering interest-free loans to help start-up businesses.	2. It focuses on a long-term approach to helping communities and employs people from the communities it works in.

Wealth and Poverty

Muslims and Jews believe that money should be used for good — anything harmful is seen as wrong.

How Money is Used is Important in Islam

1) Muslims shouldn't use money in ways that harm people — Islamic law says Muslims shouldn't harm others.

2) Islam forbids alcohol, so it's seen as immoral to make money from it. Islam is often focused on sexual modesty, so profiting from sex is forbidden (either directly or indirectly, e.g. sexually suggestive adverts).

3) Qur'an 2:275 says "Allah ... has forbidden interest" and that those who charge it will go to jahannam (hell). In Islam, money doesn't have a value in itself, so it shouldn't be used to make more money. This stops richer people profiting from poorer people, and ensures wealth is spread more fairly.

4) Muslims use Islamic bank accounts and run businesses that don't involve charging interest.

Jews Should Use Their Wealth to Help Others

1) Judaism teaches that there's nothing wrong In being wealthy, so long as you're not obsessed by it, and you give money to others. Wealth is seen as a gift from God. Jews should try to avoid being dependent on others if at all possible — although if they are really in need there's no shame in receiving charity.

2) Unfairness and dishonesty in business are condemned — you're answerable to God for any wrongdoing. All money should be earnt morally, so any job that's harmful in any way is forbidden. Jews particularly frown on work that is damaging to God's creation (e.g. unsustainable tree felling).

3) Jews shouldn't charge interest on loans to other Jews (Leviticus 25:37). This doesn't apply to loans made to non-Jews: "You may charge a foreigner interest, but not a fellow Israelite" (Deuteronomy 23:20 NIV).

4) Jews try to avoid talking about or handling money on Shabbat — the day of rest.

Charity is Important in Judaism

1) This passage from the Torah sums up Jewish teaching on charity:

"If anyone is poor among your fellow Israelites in any of the towns of the land ... do not be hard-hearted or tight-fisted towards them. Rather, be open-handed and freely lend them whatever they need." Deuteronomy 15:7-8 NIV

2) The Jewish scholar Maimonides said the best way to give was to do so in a way that meant the recipient could help themselves. He also said giving anonymously was recommended, so the charity is given for the good of it alone, and not so the giver can be rewarded — they shouldn't expect anything in return.

3) There are two important charitable principles in Judaism — tzedakah and gemilut hasadim:

Tzedakah: tzedakah means charity, but with a sense of justice — it's not just generous to give tzedakah, it's right as it makes society fairer. Everyone, even those in need, is expected to contribute 10% of their wealth. Deuteronomy 14:29 says people should donate some of their produce so "the foreigners, the fatherless and the widows who live in your towns may come and eat" (NIV), showing the importance of helping those in need.
Gemilut hasadim: this means 'acts of loving kindness' — it refers to any compassionate actions towards others.

4) Many Jewish homes have collection boxes (called pushkes) in which money for charity can be placed.

5) Donating clothing and food to people who need them or visiting someone who's sick are considered gemilut hasadim (acts of loving kindness). There are Jewish charities that help people, including Tzedek:

1. Tzedek is a Jewish charity in the UK that seeks to get the Jewish community involved in helping to reduce poverty worldwide.
2. Their focus is on helping local projects, that improve a community's ability to get itself out of poverty.

I hope you feel richer (in knowledge) after these pages...

Have a go at this task, answering about the religion you've been studying.
Write a short summary about religious beliefs on wealth and charity.

Revision Summary

Now here's the fun bit — let's see if you can remember what you've just read in the section.
The questions below will give you an idea of what the exam will be like and how much you'll need to write.
If you're struggling with anything, have another read of the section
and give the questions another go once you're re-read it.

Answer each of these questions <u>in the context of the religion you've studied</u>.

Right, let's get going. These questions are worth 3 marks, so give three short points.

1) Outline three types of prejudice.

2) Outline three examples of human rights.

3) Outline three issues surrounding freedom of belief.

4) Outline three factors that can lead to poverty.

Now onto 4 marks. You need to make two points and develop them to get two marks for each point.

5) Explain two religious beliefs about making money.

6) Explain two ways that believers can work for social justice.

7) Explain two religious beliefs about the status of women in religion.

Make sure your longer answers are clear by structuring your answer well and writing clear points.

5 marks available for these questions. You should include an example from a source of wisdom and authority.

8) Explain two religious ideas about racial equality.

9) Explain two reasons why charity is important to many religious people.

10) Explain two reasons why many religious people support social justice.

11) Explain two different religious attitudes to homosexuality.

And finally... the 12 mark question. Make a plan with arguments for and against the statement
before you start — it'll help you organise things. Don't forget to finish off with a conclusion.

12) 'To make the world fairer, the best thing to do is donate money to charity.'
   Evaluate this statement.
   Give arguments that support the statement and arguments that disagree with the statement.
   You must include:
   • examples of teachings from the religion you've studied
   • a conclusion.

Have a look at the 'Do Well in Your Exam' section for help with writing essays.

Do Well in Your Exam

You've learnt all the <u>facts</u> — now it's time to get those <u>grades</u>.

You'll Sit Two Exams Which are Worth 50% Each

1) For the Edexcel B course, you must study <u>two</u> Areas of Study (from a choice of three). You'll have studied each Area of Study in the context of <u>one religion</u>, with a <u>different religion</u> for each one. You'll sit an exam paper on <u>each</u> of your two Areas of Study — these will be Papers 1, 2 or 3, depending on what you've studied. You'll be asked about '<u>beliefs</u>' and '<u>living the religious life</u>' for the religion you've covered in that Area of Study. You'll also be asked about the other topics within your Areas of Study:

- <u>Paper 1</u> covers <u>Marriage and the Family</u> and <u>Matters of Life and Death</u>.
- <u>Paper 2</u> covers <u>Crime and Punishment</u> and <u>Peace and Conflict</u>.
- <u>Paper 3</u> covers <u>Philosophy of Religion</u> and <u>Equality</u>.

> This information is for the <u>full course</u>. For the <u>short course</u> you'll sit <u>two shorter exams</u>, with <u>two questions per paper</u>.

2) Both papers are <u>1 hour and 45 minutes</u> long, and they're each worth <u>50%</u> of your <u>overall mark</u>. Each exam has <u>4 questions</u> — aim to spend roughly <u>25 minutes</u> on each question. Each question is broken down into <u>4 parts</u>: a), b), c) and d).

The Basics — Read the Questions

1) <u>Read</u> the questions <u>carefully</u>. Remember to answer <u>all the parts</u> of the questions.

2) Be aware of how much <u>time</u> you're using. Leave plenty of time for the long-answer questions. The more <u>marks</u> a question's worth, the <u>longer</u> you should be spending on it — for these exams, allow around <u>1 minute per mark</u>. Try to leave yourself 5 minutes at the end to <u>check your work</u>.

3) Some questions will have extra marks available for <u>Spelling, Punctuation and Grammar</u> (SPaG) — <u>6 marks</u> in total for <u>each paper</u>. The exam paper will tell you which questions offer SPaG marks — so make your writing for these the <u>best</u> it can be (see p.93-95 for more).

4) Don't use any fancy colours — write <u>only</u> in <u>black</u> ink.

There are Two Types of Part a) Questions

1) Part a) questions are worth <u>3 marks</u>. They're pretty <u>straightforward</u> — <u>3 short points</u> will earn you full marks. You'll be asked to either '<u>State</u>' or '<u>Outline</u>'.

2) **'STATE' QUESTIONS** — these will only ask you to write down <u>three religious traditions</u> in the UK.

> State three religious traditions in the UK. You should not include Christianity in your answer.

> Judaism
> Islam
> Buddhism

This answer would get you <u>three marks</u> — you <u>don't</u> need to write in <u>sentences</u>. You could also put Sikhism or Hinduism too.

3) **'OUTLINE' QUESTIONS** — these questions could ask you about different things, e.g. religious <u>beliefs</u> on a topic, <u>teachings</u> or <u>ways</u> that believers do something. Keep your answers <u>short</u> — 3 points for 3 marks.

> Outline three Muslim beliefs about contraception.

> Some Muslims believe that contraception is allowed in the hadith.
> Both partners should agree to use contraception.
> Others think preventing conception is against Allah's will.

Don't be tempted to write lots — this answer would be enough to get you <u>three marks</u>.

'Twas the night before the exam...

...and some people were up late, studying RS. Make sure you get a good night's rest before your exam — you won't be able to do your best if you're half asleep.

Do Well in Your Exam

There are some <u>subtle differences</u> between the question types, so make sure you're clear what's what.

Part b) Questions Might Ask you to Describe Differences

<u>Part b)</u> questions are worth <u>four marks</u>. Questions <u>1 b)</u> and <u>3 b)</u> could ask you to talk about two differences between either <u>forms of worship</u> or <u>beliefs about life after death</u>.

1. If you're studying <u>Christianity</u>, you'll be asked to compare it to another religion you've covered.
2. If you're studying <u>Catholic Christianity</u>, you need to compare it to other branches of the main religious tradition in the UK, which means other Christian denominations.
3. If you're studying <u>any other religion</u>, you'll be asked to compare it with the main religious tradition in the UK — Christianity.

Describe two differences in beliefs about life after death between Judaism and the main religious tradition in the UK.

The <u>first</u> sentence presents a <u>fact</u> about Judaism, then the <u>second</u> explains how Christianity is <u>different</u>.

Many Jews believe that people can move on from Gehinnom. Christians believe that once you're sent to hell, you don't leave.
Some Progressive Jews don't believe in life after death, and prefer to focus on this life. But most Christians believe that people are judged by God, then sent to heaven or hell.

Part b) Questions Might Ask you to Explain Things

1) Most <u>part b)</u> questions will ask you to explain <u>two</u> things — e.g. religious <u>teachings</u> or <u>attitudes</u>, <u>reasons why</u> something is important in a religion, or <u>ways</u> that religious people respond to something.

2) Make <u>two points</u>, but you'll have to <u>develop</u> them in order to get the <u>full 4 marks</u>.

Explain two Jewish beliefs about forgiveness.

Jews believe that God is prepared to forgive sins, and so they should accept his forgiveness and follow his example by forgiving others.
They also believe that seeking forgiveness from others is very important. God can only forgive a sin against God, not a sin committed against another person.

The <u>first</u> half of the sentence here <u>introduces</u> a point, and the <u>second</u> half <u>develops</u> it further.

For Part c) Questions You Must Include Sources of Wisdom

1) Part c) questions are worth <u>five marks</u>. They will ask you to <u>explain</u> two things, such as <u>beliefs</u>, <u>teachings</u>, <u>ways</u> that believers respond, or <u>reasons why</u> something is important.

2) You need to give two points and <u>develop</u> them, but for full marks you must <u>refer</u> to a <u>sacred text</u> or religious <u>teaching</u>. This could be by including a <u>quotation</u>, or by <u>paraphrasing</u> (explaining what's said in your own words). You'll need to say which text or teaching the information <u>comes from</u>.

Explain two Muslim teachings on jihad. You should include an example from a source of wisdom and authority.

There's only <u>one mark</u> available for including a source, so <u>one quote or reference</u> will do.

You could also write something like 'The Qur'an gives Muslims permission to defend themselves if they're being fought'.

Greater jihad is the struggle to live life according to Allah's teachings. It's a personal struggle, and individuals must work to be the best Muslims they can be. Lesser jihad can involve defending Islam. This could be in a peaceful way, or by fighting a threat to Islam in self-defence. The Qur'an says: "Permission [to fight] has been given to those who are being fought".

Don't let exam nerves get the better of you...

A large chunk of how well you do in the exam will come down to, well... how good you are at exams. Make sure you spend enough time practising doing exam-style questions under timed conditions. It'll pay off in the end.

Do Well in Your Exam and SPaG

And now... the part d) question. Pay close attention to what you write — you can get <u>marks</u> for <u>SPaG</u>.

For Part d) Questions You Need Both Sides of the Argument

1) You'll need to write a <u>longer answer</u> for the <u>part d)</u> question. It's worth 12 or 15 marks, depending on whether it tests SPaG (see below). You'll be given a <u>statement</u> and a <u>list</u> of bullet points — these tell you what to put in your answer.

2) You need to give arguments <u>for</u> and <u>against</u> the statement, so read it carefully, then make a rough list of all the <u>views</u> on each side that you can think of.

3) <u>Plan</u> out your answer <u>before</u> you start writing — it needs to be <u>clear</u> and <u>organised</u> for the examiner.

> 'Animal experimentation should be allowed if it benefits humanity.'
> Evaluate this statement. Give arguments for and against
> the statement. You must include:
> • examples from Christian teachings
> • different Christian opinions
> • appropriate ethical arguments
> • a conclusion.

The bullet points <u>vary</u> depending on the <u>question</u>. For some topics, you might be asked about <u>non-religious opinions</u> or <u>philosophical ideas</u>. You'll <u>always</u> have to include <u>religious teachings</u> and a <u>conclusion</u>.

Some Christians share this point of view. They believe that animal testing is acceptable if it is for valid reasons, such as producing life-saving medicines. But many Christians see themselves as stewards of the Earth, and believe they must care for animals — the Bible says that righteous people look after their animals. They think that the animals must be treated humanely, and no unnecessary pain caused.

> This answer starts by giving some <u>views</u> along with some Christian <u>teachings</u>.

This view is reflected in the Catechism of the Catholic Church. It says that animal testing is allowed if it brings about scientific or medical advances, but the animals shouldn't be allowed to suffer.

Some Christians might look at animal testing from a utilitarian point of view, and look for the best balance of outcomes overall. If a few animals suffer, but lots of people could be helped, they might decide it's acceptable.

> This paragraph explains how <u>ethical arguments</u> could be used.

However, not all Christian denominations tolerate animal experimentation. The Society of Friends (Quakers) are against causing any kind of suffering to animals. They would think it's wrong to inflict pain on animals just to further our knowledge of science and medicine.

> This paragraph discusses arguments <u>against</u> the statement.

I think that, although allowing animals to suffer is wrong, if the experiments benefit humanity then they should be allowed. But only essential advances should be considered beneficial — testing out non-essentials such as cosmetics isn't a good enough reason.

> Finish with a <u>conclusion</u> — say what <u>you</u> think, and <u>back it up</u> with ideas you've discussed.

Some Part d) Questions Have 3 Extra Marks for SPaG

1) <u>Part d)</u> of questions <u>1</u> and <u>3</u> has <u>3 extra marks</u> for spelling, punctuation, grammar and specialist terminology. So that's <u>6</u> marks per <u>exam</u>, and <u>12</u> marks in <u>total</u>.

2) The examiner will look at your spelling, punctuation and grammar in <u>general</u>, but they'll also look at how many <u>technical terms</u> you use and how <u>accurately</u> you use them.

3) Leave <u>5 minutes</u> at the end of the exam to <u>check your work</u>. That <u>isn't</u> long, so there <u>won't</u> be time to check <u>everything</u> thoroughly. Look for the <u>most obvious</u> mistakes.

4) <u>Start</u> by checking questions 1 d) and 3 d) since they're the <u>only ones</u> that award SPaG marks. <u>Only</u> check the rest of your answers if you've got <u>time</u>.

My favourite kind of SPaG...

Thou shalt use correct punctuation...

Between spelling, punctuation and grammar, there's a lot of stuff to check. This is why it's really important to practise before the exam. That way you'll start to do it automatically, and make fewer errors in the first place.

Spelling, Punctuation and Grammar

Making a mistake in your exam is <u>not</u> the end of the world. Just correct it and you won't lose any marks.

Make Your Corrections Neatly

1) If the mistake is just <u>one word</u> or a <u>short phrase</u>, cross it out <u>neatly</u> and write the correction <u>above</u> it.

> A stable family can give a child a sense of identity and a feeling of security, teaching
> him or her how to behave in different social situations and how to give and ~~recieve~~ ^{receive} love.

2) If you've <u>forgotten</u> to start a <u>new paragraph</u>, use a <u>double strike</u>
(like this '//') to show where the new paragraph should <u>begin</u>:

> The Third Pillar of Islam commands that Muslims give 2.5% of their wealth to charity. The money is often collected
> and distributed by the mosque. **//** How money is earned is also important in Islam. Muslims shouldn't make
> money from anything seen as immoral, such as alcohol. They also shouldn't earn money from charging interest.

Use an Asterisk to Add Extra Information

1) If you've <u>missed something out</u>, think about whether you have space to write the missing bit
<u>above</u> the line you've already written. If you <u>can</u>, use a ' ∧ ' to show <u>exactly where</u> it should go.

> Jews greet each other by saying 'shalom', which means 'peace'. Generally, they believe that war ^{is a}∧bad thing,
> but may be necessary in some circumstances, for example in self-defence or to help neighbouring countries.

2) If the bit you've missed out <u>won't</u> fit above the line, use an <u>asterisk</u>
(like this '*') to show the examiner <u>where</u> the missing bit should go.

3) Write the <u>missing words</u> at the <u>end</u> of your answer with another asterisk next to them.

> Christianity teaches that animals should be treated kindly.* Some Christians
> believe that animal testing is wrong because they think it is unhelpful.
> *and shouldn't be made to suffer unnecessarily.

Cross Out Anything You Don't Want to be Marked

1) If you've written something that you <u>don't</u> want the examiner to mark, <u>cross it out neatly</u>.

2) Cross out any <u>notes</u>. But — if you don't <u>finish</u> your answer <u>in time</u>, don't cross out
your <u>plan</u> — the examiner might look at it to see what you were <u>going to write</u>.

3) Don't <u>scribble things out</u> without thinking — it'll make your answers look <u>messy</u>.

Spell Technical Words Correctly

1) There are a lot of <u>technical words</u> in RS. You need to be able to <u>spell</u> them <u>correctly</u>.

2) Here are some examples to start you off. The <u>coloured letters</u> are the tricky bits to watch out for.

reconciliation	euthanasia	deterrence
omniscient	pacifism	justice
procreation	sanctity	contraception
revelation	environment	transcendent

> Make sure you know the specific technical words for your topics. For example, if you're studying views on marriage, you would need to know words like 'kiddushin' (part of a Jewish wedding ceremony) and 'nikah' (a Muslim wedding ceremony). There's a list of technical terms in the glossary on p.96-98.

Do Well in Your Exam and SPaG

Spelling, Punctuation and Grammar

This page is full of tips for good <u>punctuation</u> and <u>grammar</u> to help you keep silly mistakes at bay.

You Need to Punctuate Properly...

1) Always use a <u>capital letter</u> at the start of a <u>sentence</u>.
   Use capital letters for <u>names</u> of <u>particular people</u>, <u>places</u> and <u>things</u>. For example:

   <u>M</u>any <u>J</u>ews live in <u>I</u>srael, where the official language is <u>H</u>ebrew.

   All sentences start with capital letters. The name of a group of religious believers. A country. The name of a language.

2) <u>Full stops</u> go at the end of <u>sentences</u>, e.g. 'Muslims worship Allah<u>.</u>'
   <u>Question marks</u> go at the end of <u>questions</u>, e.g. 'What is divorce<u>?</u>'

3) Use <u>commas</u> when you use <u>more than one adjective</u> to describe something or to separate items in a <u>list</u>:

   > Christians believe in a <u>benevolent</u>, <u>compassionate</u> God. They believe <u>the Father</u>, <u>the Son</u> and <u>the Holy Spirit</u> make up the Trinity.

4) <u>Commas</u> can also <u>join two points</u> into one sentence with a joining word (such as '<u>and</u>', '<u>or</u>', '<u>so</u>' or '<u>but</u>'):

   > Salah ideally takes place in a mosque, <u>but</u> it can be done anywhere.

   > The Earth is seen as being a product of the love of Allah, <u>so</u> we should treat it with love.

5) <u>Commas</u> can also be used to separate <u>extra information</u> in a sentence:

   > The Big Bang theory, <u>the idea that the universe began in an explosion of matter and energy</u>, was first put forward by a priest.

   When you use commas like this, the sentence should still make sense when the extra bit is taken out.

...and Use Grammar Correctly

1) <u>Don't change tenses</u> in your writing by mistake:

   > Muslims only <u>allow</u> animal testing if there <u>is</u> a good reason for it.

   This sentence is correct because <u>both</u> verbs are in the <u>present tense</u>. Writing '<u>was</u>' instead of '<u>is</u>' would be wrong.

Past, present... they all made Brian tense.

2) <u>Don't</u> use <u>double negatives</u>. You should only use a negative <u>once</u> in a sentence:

   > Creatures with fins and scales are kosher, but Jews keeping kosher shouldn't eat <u>any</u> other seafood.

   Don't put 'no' here.

3) Write longer answers in <u>paragraphs</u>. A paragraph is a <u>group of sentences</u> which talk about the <u>same thing</u> or <u>follow on</u> from each other. You need to start a <u>new paragraph</u> when you start making a <u>new point</u>. You show a <u>new paragraph</u> by starting a <u>new line</u> and leaving a <u>gap</u> (an <u>indent</u>) before you start writing:

   This gap shows a new paragraph.

   > Weapons of Mass Destruction (WMDs) are weapons that can destroy large areas of land or lots of people at once. They harm anyone in their path, both soldiers and civilians.
   >   Nuclear weapons are one type of WMD. All Christian denominations are against the indiscriminate killing they cause, but some people think that possessing them keeps the peace.

   When <u>planning</u> long answers, remember that you should write a <u>new paragraph</u> for each main point.

Now you're fully SPaG-ed and ready to go...

Having good SPaG is a great way to get marks in the RS exams, and it might even make a difference to your grade.
That's why it's really important that you learn all the stuff on this page — and all the other pages too.

Glossary

The purple definitions are relevant to Christianity and Catholic Christianity. The red ones are terms in Judaism. The green ones are terms in Islam. The blue ones are general terms.

abortion	Removing a foetus from the womb before it is able to survive, ending the pregnancy.
adultery	A married person having sex with someone who isn't their husband or wife.
Advent	The period of time that begins four Sundays before Christmas.
al-Adab al-Mufrad	A collection of hadith.
al-Akhirah	The concept of life after death. This is a key Islamic belief.
al-Qadr	Predestination — the idea that Allah has already decided everything that will happen.
the ascension	When Jesus rose up to heaven to be with God again.
atheism	A complete denial of the existence of a god.
atonement	Making amends for wrongdoing — often refers to people repairing their relationship with God.
bar/bat mitzvah	The coming of age ceremony — bar mitzvah for boys, bat mitzvah for girls.
barzakh	Where souls wait for Yawm ad-Din (the Day of Judgement).
benevolent	Being kind and loving.
brit milah	The circumcision of baby boys when they're 8 days old.
capital punishment	The death penalty as punishment for a crime.
catechism	A series of statements laying down the official teachings of the Roman Catholic Church.
celibacy	Not taking part in any sexual activities.
cohabitation	Living together in a sexual relationship without being married.
confession	Admitting sins to God.
confirmation	The act of 'confirming' your faith, often at an age when you can decide for yourself.
conscience	An inner feeling of what's right and what's wrong.
contraception	Also known as birth control, it stops a woman from conceiving.
corporal punishment	Punishing a criminal through physical pain.
covenant	A formal agreement between two or more people.
creed	Statement of religious beliefs.
disciples	Followers of Jesus. This can refer to just his followers in the Bible or to all Christians.
discrimination	Treating different people, or groups of people, differently (usually unfairly).
dominion	The belief that people have power over God's creation and can use it as they like.
the Eucharist	When Christians remember the Last Supper with bread and wine.
euthanasia	Ending someone's life to relieve their suffering, especially from an incurable, painful illness.
evangelism	Spreading the Christian message in order to convert people.
fasting	Not eating and/or drinking for a set time.
free will	The ability to choose how to behave. All three religions believe humans have free will.
Gan Eden	Garden of Eden or paradise — where good people spend the afterlife.
Gehinnom	The place where souls go before Gan Eden. The truly wicked never move on from there.
gemilut hasadim	Kind and compassionate actions towards others.
Gethsemane	The garden where Jesus prayed before his arrest.
Golgotha	The 'place of the skull' where Jesus was crucified.
grace	God showing favour to those who haven't earned it.
hadith	Islamic scripture containing a collection of things the Prophet Muhammad said and did.
hajj	The pilgrimage to Makkah.
holy orders	Ordination to a deacon, priest or bishop.
holy war	A war where people believe that God is 'on their side'.

Glossary

homophobia	Prejudice against people who are homosexual.
human dignity	The idea that all human life is valuable and everyone has the right to be treated with respect.
human rights	The moral, legal and political rights that every human being on Earth is entitled to.
humanism	The belief that God doesn't exist, and humans should live good lives based on their knowledge.
humanity	The entire human race.
immanent	God/Allah is present in the human world.
incarnation	The act by which Christians believe God became human, in the form of Jesus.
jahannam	The place where people who have done bad deeds will be sent in the afterlife.
jannah	The afterlife paradise — described as "gardens of pleasure" in the Qur'an.
jihad	The struggle to be a good Muslim (greater jihad) and to make the world better (lesser jihad).
just war	A war that meets certain conditions to be classed as necessary.
justice	The idea of each person getting what they deserve, and maintaining what's right.
kashrut	The food laws written in the Torah.
ketubah	The marriage contract, which sets out the couple's rights and responsibilities.
khalifah	The belief that Muslims must look after the Earth as vice-regents or trustees.
kiddushin	Betrothal — the first part of the marriage ceremony.
kosher	Food that is permitted under kashrut.
Last Judgement	The Day of Judgement when all of humanity's actions will be judged by God/Allah.
Lent	The period spent remembering Christ's 40 days of fasting in the desert.
liturgical	Worship that follows a set pattern that's been written out by the Church.
Maimonides	A Jewish scholar — he wrote the 13 principles of faith and compiled a lot of mitzvot.
Messiah	A leader who will bring peace to Earth. Christians believe that Jesus is the Messiah.
miracle	An event believed to be the work of God, that can't be explained by the laws of science.
Mishnah	The part of the Talmud that explains how the mitzvot in the Torah should be applied.
Mishneh Torah	The list of mitzvot from the Torah compiled by Maimonides.
mitzvot	Jewish laws — there are 613 mitzvot in total.
mourning	A period of deep sorrow for someone who has died.
Muwatta Malik	A collection of hadith.
nuclear family	A family made up of a mother, a father and their children living together.
omnibenevolent	Being all-good.
omnipotent	Having unlimited powers — all-powerful.
omniscient	Knowing everything — in the past, present and future.
oral Torah	Jewish teachings passed down orally and recorded in the Talmud.
original sin	The flawed nature that humans have been born with since Adam and Eve first sinned.
pacifism	The idea that war and physical violence are wrong under any circumstances.
parable	A story about daily life which has a message about spiritual truth.
pikuach nefesh	The principle of saving a life, even if it means breaking mitzvot.
pilgrimage	A journey to a place of religious significance.
Pirkei Avot	Part of the Talmud.
polygamy	Marriage to multiple people.
positive discrimination	When someone who may often be discriminated against is given an advantage.
prejudice	Judging something or someone with no good reason, or without full knowledge of a situation.
procreation	Having children.
promiscuity	Having many sexual partners.

Glossary

prophet	A person on Earth who communicated God/Allah's will.
Purgatory	A place where Catholics believe sins are paid for before going to heaven.
racism	Discrimination against people of other races — often based on unfair stereotypes.
reconciliation	Returning to harmony and friendship after conflict.
reformation	The idea that punishment should aim to change criminals so that they won't reoffend.
reincarnation	The rebirth of a soul in a new body after death.
resurrection	Being brought back to life after death.
retribution	Punishing a criminal by making them 'pay' for what they've done.
revelation	An experience that reveals God's presence.
the Rosary	A string of beads used by Catholics when praying.
sacrament	A ceremony, or outward sign, of the direct communication of God's saving grace.
Sahih al-Bukhari	A collection of hadith.
Sahih Muslim	A collection of hadith.
salah	The action of praying five times a day.
salvation	The soul being saved from death and sin so it can reach heaven.
sanctity of life	The belief that all life belongs to God/Allah, so it is holy.
sawm	The Muslim obligation to fast during daylight hours through the month of Ramadan.
Second Coming	The belief that Jesus will return to Earth.
Sermon on the Mount	A summary of Jesus's teachings on how to live a Christian life — Matthew 5-7.
sexism	Discrimination based on someone's gender (male or female).
Shabbat	Also called the Sabbath, it is the Jewish day of rest (Saturday).
shahadah	A Pillar of Islam — the Muslim declaration of faith.
shari'ah	The Islamic religious law.
Shekhinah	God's presence in a particular place on Earth.
shirk	Believing there are other gods or that anything is equal to Allah — it's considered the worst sin.
sin	An act that breaks a religious law, i.e. when God's teaching is disobeyed.
situation ethics	An ethical principle where decisions are made based on what is best in individual cases.
social justice	The idea of fairness in society and putting the principles of human rights into practice.
Stations of the Cross	Pictures in church of Jesus's suffering, used by Catholics as a focus for contemplation.
stewardship	Taking care of the Earth as God's creation, so it can be passed on to the next generation.
Sunan Abi Dawud	A collection of hadith.
Tawhid	Belief that Allah is the one and only God.
tikkun olam	The belief that Jews should 'mend the world', e.g. by caring for the environment and the poor.
transcendent	A characteristic of God/Allah — he is beyond this world.
transubstantiation	Transformation of the Eucharistic bread and wine into the flesh and blood of Christ.
the Trinity	The belief that God exists in three 'persons' — the Father, the Son and the Holy Spirit.
tzedakah	The practice of giving 10% of your wealth to charity.
usury	Charging high rates of interest on a loan.
utilitarianism	The idea that the correct course of action has the best balance of good and bad outcomes.
virtue ethics	Deciding what course of action to follow by looking at what a virtuous (good) person would do.
vision	A religious experience where a person sees something sacred.
wudu	The ritual washing of exposed body parts before prayer.
Yawm ad-Din	The day when everyone will be judged by Allah based on their actions.
zakah	A Pillar of Islam — all Muslims must donate 2.5% of their wealth to charity.

Index

A

abortion 51-53
Abraham (Ibrahim) 17, 19, 24, 27, 32, 78
Adam (and Eve) 3, 7, 17, 77
addiction 57, 58
Advent 12
afterlife 4-6, 20, 29, 54, 56, 67
Allah 16-20, 76
al-Qadr (predestination) 16, 20
Amidah 31
Amr-bil-Maroof 21
angels 16, 19
animal experimentation 50
anointing the sick 10
anti-Semitism 68, 82
apostasy 85
Ark (Aron Hakodesh) 30, 31
articles of faith 16-20
ascension 5
Ashura 24
atheism 65, 73, 79
atonement 4, 5, 34

B

baptism 9, 10, 42
bar / bat mitzvah 33, 42
benevolent 1, 3, 7, 17, 27, 75, 79
Bible 1, 76
Big Bang theory 3, 47, 74
brit milah 32, 42

C

CAFOD 14, 49
capital punishment 62
charismatic worship 8
charity 13, 14, 21, 22, 28, 57, 58, 71, 86, 88, 89
Christian Aid 14, 49, 71
Christmas 12
cohabitation 37, 39-41
commandments 5, 28, 81
community service 60, 61
compassion 17, 51, 52, 76
compensation 61, 62
confirmation 9, 10, 42
conflict 14, 64-71
contraception 38
corporal punishment 60, 61
cosmological argument 74
Council of Nicaea 2
courts 60, 61
covenant 27, 76
  with Abraham 27, 32
  with Moses 28
creation 3, 17, 27, 47, 49, 73, 74, 77

crime 56-62
crucifixion 4, 5, 12

D

David (Dawud) 17-19, 29
death penalty 62
denominations 1
design argument 73
disciples 4
discrimination 44, 45, 81, 85
divorce 39-41, 43
dominion 3, 49, 50

E

Easter 12
ecumenism 13
environment 48, 49
eternal 1, 3, 27, 74, 76
Eucharist 4, 8-10
euthanasia 51-53
evangelism 13
evil 7, 56, 79
evolution 3, 47, 73
Exodus, the 28, 32, 35

F

fair pay 87
fair trial 60, 61
families 42, 43
fasting 12, 22, 24, 33, 34
Five Pillars 21-23
forgiveness 1, 5, 10, 22, 23, 34, 59, 60, 62, 70
freedom of belief 85
free will 7, 20, 28, 56, 79
funeral rites 10, 33

G

Gan Eden 29, 54
Gehinnom 29, 54
gemilut hasadim 28, 89
gender equality 44, 45, 81-83
Gethsemane 4
global warming 48
God, the nature of 1, 3, 17, 27, 76
Golgotha 4
grace 5, 6, 9, 10, 54

H

hadith 19
hajj 21, 23, 83
halal 42, 50
hate crime 57, 58
heaven 5, 6, 20, 29, 54
hell 6, 20, 29, 54
holy orders 10
Holy Spirit 2, 3, 5, 10

holy war 65-68
homosexuality 37, 39-41, 81-83, 85
humanism 53, 62, 65, 69, 79
human rights 60, 61, 71, 84, 86

I

Id ul-Adha 23, 24
Id ul-Fitr 24
Id ul-Ghadeer 24
imams 16
immanent 1, 2, 17, 27, 76, 77
incarnation 2, 4
Injil 19
interest (on loans) 87-89
Isma'il (Ishmael) 17, 18, 24
Israel 27, 29, 49, 61, 62, 68, 69, 71

J

jahannam 20, 54
jannah 20, 54
Jerusalem 4, 11, 12
Jesus (Isa) 1-6, 9-14, 17-19, 39, 45, 56, 59, 60, 62, 65, 66, 75, 76, 81, 88
Jibril (Gabriel) 18, 19, 78
jihad 21, 23, 67, 69
Job 7, 51, 79
judgement 6, 16, 20, 29, 49, 53, 54, 56, 58, 70
justice 14, 16, 56, 70, 84, 86
just war 65-69

K

Ka'aba 17, 18, 23
ketubah 33
Ketuvim 26
khalifah 49, 50, 70, 71
khums 21
kiddushin 33, 41
King, Dr Martin Luther 57, 66
kosher 32, 50

L

Last Supper 4, 9
law 56-58
Laylat al-Qadr 22
Lent 12
Liberal Judaism 26
Litany 8
liturgy 8
Lord's Prayer 8, 11, 59
Lourdes 11, 77

M

Maimonides 28, 29, 37, 41, 54, 68, 74, 89
Makkah (Mecca) 18, 22, 23

Index

marriage 33, 39-41
  polygamous 40, 41
  same-sex 39-41, 81-83, 85
Masorti Judaism 26, 41, 82
Mass 8, 10
matrimony 10
mercy 17, 20, 27, 56, 59, 70
Messiah 4, 29, 65, 68
milchemet mitzvah / reshut 68
minyan 30, 82
miracles 75-77, 79
missionaries 13
mitzvot 26, 28, 31-34, 56, 82
Moses (Musa) 17-19, 28, 78
mourning 10, 33
Muhammad 16-22, 45, 70, 76, 78, 83
murder 57, 58, 62

N

Nahi Anil Munkar 21
natural resources 48
nature 48, 77
Ner Tamid 30
Nevi'im 26
Nicene Creed 2, 4, 8
Noahide Laws 50, 58
Nonconformists 1
nuclear weapons 69

O

omnipotent 1, 3, 7, 17, 27, 76, 79
omniscient 1, 27, 76, 79
original sin 5, 7, 9, 56, 79
Orthodox Church 1, 8, 9, 45, 81
Orthodox Judaism 26, 28-33, 37, 38, 41-43, 45, 76, 82

P

pacifism 64-68, 71
Palm Sunday 12
parents 42-44
passive resistance 66, 67
Pax Christi 14, 71
peace 14, 64-68, 70, 71
persecution 14, 24, 82
personal god 1, 2, 76
Pesach 35
pikuach nefesh 28, 32, 50, 52, 61, 68
pilgrimages 11, 21, 23, 77
Pope 1
poverty 14, 57, 58, 87-89
prayer 8, 11, 21, 22, 30, 31, 34, 78
prejudice 81
prison 60, 61
Progressive Judaism 26, 28-33, 37, 38, 41-43, 45, 76, 82

Promised Land 27, 29, 68
prophets 16-19, 76
punishment 56, 59-62
Purgatory 6, 54

Q

Qur'an 16-19, 22, 47, 75, 76

R

rabbi 30
racial equality 81-83
rak'ah 21, 22
Ramadan 21, 22, 24
reconciliation 5, 10, 14, 59, 70
redemption 5
Reform Judaism 26
religious experiences 77, 79
repentance 5, 34, 56, 59, 60
restorative justice 57, 59
resurrection 4-6, 12, 16, 20, 29, 54
revelation 75-79
rites of passage 10, 13, 32, 33, 42, 43
Rosary 11
Rosh Hashanah 34

S

sacraments 1, 9, 10
sadaqah 88
Sahifah 19
salah 21, 22
salvation 5, 13
sanctity of life 28, 51, 57, 60, 62, 64, 69
Satan 51, 56
sawm 21, 22, 24
Second Coming 6
self-defence 23, 64, 65, 67-69
Sermon on the Mount 4, 65, 71
Shabbat (Sabbath) 31, 32
shahadah 17, 21
shari'ah 40, 56, 58, 61, 62
Shavuot 35
sheep and goats (parable) 1, 6, 14, 56, 70, 86
Shekhinah 27
Shema 31
Sheol 29
Shi'a Islam 16, 19-22, 24
shirk 17, 21, 59
simchat bat 32, 42
sins 5, 7, 9, 56, 79
situation ethics 38, 39, 53, 60, 62, 65, 84, 86
social justice 86
Son of God 2-4
soul 5, 6, 20, 29, 51-54
Stations of the Cross 11
stereotypes 44

stewardship 3, 48-50
Street Pastors 13, 57
suffering 4, 5, 7, 50-53, 56, 79
Sufi Islam 78
Sukkot 35
sunnah 19
Sunni Islam 16, 20-22, 24
synagogue 30, 31, 82

T

Tabarra 21
Talmud 26
Tawalla 21
Tawhid 16, 17
Tenakh 26
Ten Commandments 1, 5, 28, 57, 62
Ten Obligatory Acts 21-23
terrorism 23, 64, 66-68
theft 57, 58
tikkun olam 28, 49, 86
Torah (Tawrat) 19, 26, 28, 30, 31, 76
torture 60, 61
transcendent 1, 2, 17, 27, 76, 77
transubstantiation 9
trial by jury 60, 61
Trinity 2, 3
Tutu, Desmond 81
tzedakah 28, 34, 58, 71, 86, 89

U

ummah 42, 83
upbringing 42, 57, 58, 78
'Usul ad-Din 16-18, 20
utilitarian ethics 50, 62, 69

V

vale of soul-making 7
vegetarianism 50
violence 60, 61, 64-69
virtue ethics 87
visions 77-79

W

war 14, 64-71
wealth 86-89
weapons of mass destruction 67, 69
Word, the 3, 4
worship 8-11, 21, 22, 30, 31, 43, 44
wudu 22

Y

Yawm ad-Din 20, 54
Yom Kippur 34, 59

Z

Zabur 19
zakah 21, 22, 24, 58, 71, 86, 88